Garment and Textile

Dictionary

TE DL

George L. Conway

Delmar Publishers

an International Thomson Publishing company I(T)P®

Albany • Bonn • Boston • Cincinnati • Detroit • London • Madrid
Melbourne • Mexico City • New York • Pacific Grove • Paris • San Francisco
Singapore • Tokyo • Toronto • Washington

NOTICE TO THE READER

Publisher does not warrant or guarantee any of the products described herein or perform any independent analysis in connection with any of the product information contained herein. Publisher does not assume, and expressly disclaims, any obligation to obtain and include information other than that provided to it by the manufacturer.

The reader is expressly warned to consider and adopt all safety precautions that might be indicated by the activities herein and to avoid all potential hazards. By following the instructions contained herein, the reader willingly assumes all risks in connection with such instructions.

The Publisher makes no representation or warranties of any kind, including but not limited to, the warranties of fitness for particular purpose or merchantability, nor are any such representations implied with respect to the material set forth herein, and the publisher takes no responsibility with respect to such material. The publisher shall not be liable for any special, consequential, or exemplary damages resulting, in whole or part, from the readers' use of, or reliance upon, this material.

Cover Design: Douglas J. Hyldelund

Delmar Staff

Acquisitions Editor: Christopher Anzalone
Editorial Assistant: Judy A. Roberts
Developmental Editor: Jeffrey D. Litton

Project Editor: Eugenia L. Orlandi
Production Manager: Linda J. Helfrich
Art and Design Coordinator: Douglas J. Hyldelund

Printed in the United States of America
4 5 6 7 8 9 10 XXX 02 01 00

For more information, contact Delmar, 3 Columbia Circle, PO Box 15015, Albany, NY 12212-0515; or find us on the World Wide Web at http://www.delmar.com

International Division List

Japan:
Thomson Learning
Palaceside Building 5F
1-1-1 Hitotsubashi, Chiyoda-ku
Tokyo 100 0003 Japan
Tel: 813 5218 6544
Fax: 813 5218 6551

Australia/New Zealand
Nelson/Thomson Learning
102 Dodds Street
South Melbourne, Victoria 3205
Australia
Tel: 61 39 685 4111
Fax: 61 39 685 4199

UK/Europe/Middle East:
Thomson Learning
Berkshire House
168-173 High Holborn
London
WC1V 7AA United Kingdom
Tel: 44 171 497 1422
Fax: 44 171 497 1426

Latin America:
Thomson Learning
Seneca, 53
Colonia Polanco
11560 Mexico D.F. Mexico
Tel: 525-281-2906
Fax: 525-281-2656

Canada:
Nelson/Thomson Learning
1120 Birchmount Road
Scarborough, Ontario
Canada M1K 5G4
Tel: 416-752-9100
Fax: 416-752-8102

Asia:
Thomson Learning
60 Albert Street, #15-01
Albert Complex
Singapore 189969
Tel: 65 336 6411
Fax: 65 336 7411

Library of Congress Cataloging-in-Publication Data:
Conway, George L.
    Garment and textile dictionary / George L. Conway
        p.   cm.
    Includes bibliographical references.
    ISBN 0-8273-7986-2
    1. Clothing trade—Dictionaries. 2. Clothing and dress—Dictionaries. 3. Textile industry—Dictionaries. 4. Textile Fabrics—Dictionaries. I. Title.
TT494.C66   1997   96-13600
677'003—dc20   CIP

Dedication

⟫•◦•⟪

This dictionary is dedicated to:

My Assistant
My Best Friend
My Biggest Fan
My Bridge Partner
My Business Partner
My Button Dyer
My Confidante
My Cook
My Driver
My Gofer
My Housekeeper
My Lover
My Secretary
My Sounding Board
My Spouse
My Tennis Partner

and finally, the Mother of
my six terrific children.

Mary Dorothy Wilhelm Conway
She died of cancer on February 21, 1995,
before this book could be completed.
She will be sorely missed.

George L. Conway
Mother's Day, May 14, 1995

Contents

Garment and Textile Dictionary

ABO (Association of Buying Offices)   An organization of New York buying office executives which helps to standardize and unify buying services.

abraded yarn   A two-ply combination yarn, of which one ply is abraded and the other is filament viscose rayon.

abrasion (uh-*bray*-zhun)   Rubbing or scraping off of the surface of a fabric. The word is only important to the consumer when a phrase such as "abrasion resistance is used." Some permanent press finishes lessen abrasion resistance so that, for instance, the knees and cuffs of slacks wear out more quickly than they otherwise would. Draperies that are opened and closed frequently should be made of abrasion resistant fabrics.

absorbent finish   Chemical treatment of fabrics to improve their absorptive qualities.

absorption   The attraction and retention of gases or liquids within the pores of a fiber; the retention of moisture between fibers within yarns and between fibers or yarns within fabrics.

accessories   Items such as shoes, scarves, stockings, jewelry, hats, and purses that coordinate and enhance the appearance of a fashion garment.

accordion pleats (uh-*kor*-dee-un pleetz)   Very narrow, straight pleats; similar to knife pleats but face in any direction desired for effect. They fan out from the garment in uniform creased folds.

accordion shades (uh-*kor*-dee-un shaydz)   Shades made of accordion pleats sharply creased at regular intervals horizontally across their width. Accordion shades take up relatively little room when drawn up to uncover the window.

accoutrements (uh-*koo*-truh-mehnts)   Accessories.

A

Acele (uh-*seel*)   Trademark of DuPont for acetate fiber. *See* acetate and sections on fibers and care.

acetate (*ass*-uh-tayt)   A manufactured vegetable and chemical fiber or yarn formed by a compound of cellulose and acetic acid that has been extruded and hardened. Solution and spun-dyed acetates are colorfast against sunlight, perspiration, and air pollution whereas others may not be. Acetate is often used for luxurious fabrics because it resembles silk. It is mixed occasionally with other fibers to give additional sheen or to lower the cost. Acetone (part of most nail polish removers and some perfumes) destroys acetate. *See* triacetate and cellulose, fibers and care.

acetate dye   *See* disperse dye.

acetate process   Method of making man-made fibers derived from cellulose.

acid dye   A type of dye used on wool and other animal fibers. When used on cotton or linen, a mordant is required. It has poor color resistance to washing. A special method of application is required for acrylic fibers of Orlon 42. Dynel modacrylic fibers may be colored in light shades.

Acrilan (*ak*-rill-on)   Trademark of Monsanto Textiles Co. for acrylic fiber.

acrylic (uh-*krill*-ik)   The generic name of fibers made from acrylic resin (at least eighty-five percent acrylonitrile units), which comes from coal, air, water, petroleum, and limestone. Acrylic is lighter in weight than other fibers for the warmth it gives and is extremely popular for blankets or as a substitute for wool.

acrylic resin   Thermoplastic in nature, of synthetic type. These resins are polymerized from acrylic and methacrylic acid.

acrylonitrile (*ak*-rih-lahn-uh-tril)   A chemical compound from which acrylic fiber is made. This compound results from the reaction of ethylene oxide and hydrocyanic acid. It is used to treat cotton to make it permanently resistant to mildew and to give it a greater affinity for dyes.

adaptations   Designs that have all the major features of a certain original, but are not exact copies.

adsorption   The retention of gases, liquids, or solids on the surface areas of fibers, yarns, or fabrics.

afghan   A knitted or crocheted blanket or throw. An afghan is usually made in sections which are subsequently joined together, although it may be made in one piece. Traditionally, afghans were made from wool, but in recent years, with the increasing availability of acrylic knitting yarns they are more likely to be made of acrylic. Patterns range from ones with intricate designs inspired by fishermens' sweaters to the simplest of plain knitting or crochet stitches. Afghan stitch in crochet forms a simple, raised design.

Agilon (*ah*-ji-lon)   Trademark of Derring Milliken Inc. for textured nylon. Agilon is often used in hosiery and was one of the first stretch yarns used to make panty hose.

aigrette (*ay*-gret)   Feathers from the egret, a heron. This bird has been protected for some years and true aigrette feathers are no longer available. The word is used occasionally to mean any spray of feathers or jewels. *See* feathers.

airbrushing   The blowing of color onto a fabric with a mechanized airbrush.

air-bulked yarn   A textured yarn made by subjecting the filaments to air jets, which blow loops on the surface of the yarn and in the yarn bundle.

ajour (*ah*-zhur)   An openwork design used in lace or embroidery with the pattern scattered on the ground.

alençon (ah-*len*-sun or al-*en*-sohn)   Lace with a solid design, usually floral and outlined by cord. This lace is made on a sheer net fabric and it may have one scalloped edge.

a-line   A dress or skirt whose silhouette resembles the letter A.

alizarin dye (uh-*liz*-uh-rin dy)   A vegetable dye originally obtained from the madder root, now produced synthetically. It is best used on wool but can be used on cotton, particularly in madder prints.

alligator (*al*-uh-gay-ter)   A common name in leather for the animal's hide.

allover (awl-*oh*-ver)   A word used to describe the arrangement of lace designs; distinguishes patterns or laces of this type from others where the designs might be arranged in strips, along an edge, or set off by large plain areas. It is wide lace in which the design covers the entire width of one or more yards.

aloe lace (*al*-oh layss)   Usually a bobbin or tatted lace made from aloe plant fibers, a group of plants that includes the agave. *See* bobbin lace and tatting.

A

alpaca (al-*pak*-uh)   Domesticated member of the llama family, a species of "South American camel." The animal has long hair that is considered a wool. Alpaca fabric is one of the luxury fabrics. Soft, silky, and fairly lightweight, it resembles mohair. Today, the term alpaca is also used for fabrics made from a blend including some wools that have a similar appearance to true alpaca. *See* llama.

angora (or mohair) (ang-*gor*-uh [ahr *moh*-hayr])   One of those terms about which there is some difference of opinion. Strictly speaking, angora is the wool of the Angora goat whose long, soft coat is called "mohair" when made into fabric or yarn. It is usually blended with other fibers. The angora rabbit's soft, silky hair is also made into fabrics. The Wool Labeling Law requires that a garment be referred to as "angora rabbit hair" rather than "angora" or "angora wool."

anidex (*ann*-ih-dex)   A generic name for an elastomeric fiber in which the fiber-forming substance is any long chain synthetic polymer composed of at least fifty percent by weight of one or more esters of amonohydric alcohol and acrylic acid. It gives permanent stretch and recovery to fabrics and resists gas, oxygen, sunlight, chlorine bleaches, and oils. *See* fibers.

aniline dye (*an*-uhl-een dy)   A term generally applied to any synthetic, organic dye. Any dye that is derived from aniline.

Anim (*ann*-im)   Trademark of Rohm and Haas Company for anidex fiber.

antibacterial finishes   *See* germ resistant.

antique lace (ann-*teek* layss)   A heavy lace on a square knotted net with designs darned onto the net. Machine-made antique lace is often used for curtains. *See* darn, under embroidery.

antique oriental rug   A hand-tied oriental rug at least 100 years old.

antique satin (ann-*teek sat*-uhn)   A satin-weave fabric made to resemble silk satin of an earlier century. It is used for home-furnishing fabrics, primarily draperies and can be used on either side. The face is a classic lustrous satin and the reverse has a slubbed look similar to shantung. *See* shantung.

antique taffeta (ann-*teek taf*-eh-tah)   Originally, a pure silk fabric with a nubby texture, but today is comprised of polyester warps and silk fillings. It is often woven of douppion silk to resemble the beautiful fabrics of the eighteenth century. It may be yarn-dyed with two colors to give it an iridescent effect. *See* shantung.

A

antistatic   The build up of static electricity is a problem with many synthetic fibers. This causes typical static electricity situations: shocks when touching metal while wearing something that has built-up static electricity, clinging of clothing, and crackling when removing clothing. Antistatic finishes are used on fabrics of this type to cut down on or eliminate the problems, one of which, not widely recognized, is static electricity's affinity to attract dirt. At home, the use of a fabric softener in every four or five washings cuts down on, if not entirely eliminates, most of the effects of static electricity.

antistatic finish   A chemical treatment applied to noncellulosic synthetic fibers in order to eliminate static electricity.

Antron (*ann*-tron)   Trademark of DuPont for a type of nylon. *See* nylon.

apparel (uh-*payr*-uhl)   Clothing.

apparel contractor   A business that supplies sewing services to the apparel industry.

apparel jobber   In garment manufacturing, a business that handles all aspects of garment making (designing, planning, cutting, selling, and shipping apparel) except for the actual sewing.

apparel manufacturer   A business that handles all the steps required to produce a garment.

Appenzell (ap-pen-*zel*)   A type of embroidery named for the section of Switzerland where it originated.

application printing (ap-lih-*kay*-shun *print*-ing)   Another term for direct or roller printing. *See* printing.

appliqué (ap-lih-*kay*)   A decoration. Appliqué refers to a piece of fabric cut out and added to another fabric (*appliqué* is French for *applied*) by sewing, embroidering, gluing, or fusing. Appliqués are especially popular on children's clothes and often represent scenes or objects from nature such as animals or pieces of fruit. They move in and out of adult fashions and home furnishings.

aramid (*ayr*-ah-mid)   Generic name for a noncellulosic man-made fiber. A class of aromatic polyamide fiber that differs from nylon's polyamide fiber.

ardil (*ahr*-dill)   A fiber derived from protein in peanuts and made in England. A type of azlon.

A

area rug   A small, usually decorative rug, often placed on a carpet as an accent in a room. *See* rugs and carpets.

argentan lace (ahr-*jen*-ten layss)   A lace similar to alençon, but the designs usually are not outlined with cord and are often larger and bolder.

argyle knit (*ahr*-gyl nit)   A knitting pattern in which diamonds are crossed by narrow stripes; popular at various times for socks and sweaters and said to be of Scottish origin.

argyle plaid (*ahr*-gyl plad)   A plaid pattern of diamonds, often with thin stripes running over the diamond patterns in the same direction as the sides of the diamonds. Originally, argyle designs appeared only in knits, but today they are also found woven and printed.

Arnel (ahr-*nell*)   Trademark of Celanese Corp. for triacetate fiber. *See* triacetate. *See also* sections on fibers and care.

arrowhead (*air*-o-hed)   Used to reinforce and accent points of potential wear on clothing, such as the tops of pleats. Arrowheads are made with satin stitch and are triangular in shape.

art linen   A plain-weave, medium-weight linen or blended fabric in ecru, white, bleached, or natural color. It is used for embroidery, dresses, uniforms, table linens, and other types of embroidered items.

artificial silk (art-ih-*fish*-ul silk)   One of the early names for rayon.

asbestos (ass-*bess*-tus)   A mineral fiber that is nonmetallic. Its greatest virtue is that it is nonflammable. It is used in combination with other fibers for theater curtains and in industrial clothing where flameproofing is essential. Asbestos is often used to make ironing board covers and potholders.

ascot (*ass*-kaht)   A neck scarf looped under the chin. It is worn with its ends tucked into a tailored shirt left open at the neck.

aspirin dots   Popular circular designs, usually positioned in a regular pattern on the fabric, although the placing may also appear random. Dots may be woven, knitted, or printed. Sizes usually determine the name of the dots. Aspirin dots are the size of an aspirin tablet and are also called polka dots.

astrakhan (*ass*-truh-kan)   Originally the word for the wool from karakul lambs. The term is also used today to describe fabric woven or knitted to look like this wool. It is curly and fairly heavy. *See* karakul.

A

Astroturf   Trademark of Monsanto Company for its nylon product designed to imitate grass.

atelier (*ah*-tell-yeah)   A studio or workroom where high-fashion garments are made.

Aubusson (oh-boo-*sohn*)   Originally, Aubusson referred to tapestries made in Aubusson, France, that were used as wall hangings. Later, the word was applied to patterned rugs with little or slight rib and no pile.

Aubusson carpet   A term used for carpets made with a round wire and uncut looped pile to distinguish them from cut pile carpets.

Austrian shade (*aws*-tree-uhn shayd)   A shade made of fabric which is shirred across the width of the shade. When drawn up, Austrian shades hang in graceful loops of fabric. *See* shirring.

autoclave   A vessel similar to a pressure cooker in which a chemical solution is heated under pressure.

avant-garde (ah-vahnt-*gahrd*)   New or experimental ideas in fashion designs, styles, or use of materials.

Avlin (*av*-lin)   Trademark of FMC Corporation for polyester. *See* polyester.

Avril (*av*-ril)   Trademark of FMC Corporation for high wet modulus rayon.

awning stripes   Stripes seen on awnings designed to protect windows from sun. Awning stripes are sometimes used on fabric for apparel, are usually brightly colored, and are at least $1^1/_2''$ wide. Awning stripe patterns may also have a narrow stripe about $^1/_4''$ wide on each side of the main stripe.

axminster (*aks*-min-ster)   Machine-made rug with oriental designs or velvet (cut pile) construction on an Axminster loom. This makes complicated designs possible. The process is designed to resemble hand-knotted rugs. They are often referred to as sheen-type rugs.

azlon (*az*-lon)   A generic name for manufactured fibers made from regenerated naturally occurring proteins, such as casein, zein, soybean, and peanut. It gives a soft feeling when blended with other fibers.

azoic dye (uh-*zoh*-ik dy)   *See* naphthol dye.

Defect	Explanation	Severity
Askewed or Bias	Condition where filling yarns are not square with warp yarns on woven fabrics or where courses are not square with wale lines on knits.	Major or Minor (depending on severity)

GARMENT

AND

TEXTILES

babushka (bab-*oosh*-kuh)   A triangular scarf worn around the head and tied at the chin.

backed cloth   A double cloth that has two sets of fillings and one set of warps, or two sets of warps and one set of fillings. *See* double weave.

backed fabric   A fabric with an extra warp or filling—or both—to make it heavier, thicker, and provide additional warmth.

backing   Carpet yarns are tufted into a backing that is made from fibers such as olefin or jute. The backing is usually latex-coated; good backings have a second layer of latex, forming what is called a double backing. *See* jute, olefin, and latex.

bagheera (bahg-*eer*-uh)   Name for an uncut pile velvet clothing fabric that is crease resistant because the surface is not smooth. *See* pile, velvet.

baize (bayz)   Loosely woven fabric, originally made from cotton or wool, but now made from other fibers. Traditionally used for school bags and as covers for the doors leading to English servants' quarters, baize also has industrial uses. Baize is usually dyed green, but comes in other colors as well.

baku straw (bah-*koo* straw)   *See* straw.

balance of cloth   The proportion of warp yarns to filling yarns.

balance of count   The number of warps and fillings (to the inch) are nearly the same.

balanced plaid   A plaid in which the arrangement of stripes is the same on the cross and on the length of the grain. Also called even plaid.

B

balanced stripes   A pattern of stripes in which the same colors and widths are used on both sides of the center. A blue stripe on a white ground with a narrow red stripe on each side is an example of a balanced stripe. A blue stripe on a white ground with a narrow red stripe on the right side and a narrow yellow stripe on the left side is an example of an unbalanced stripe.

balanced yarns   Yarns in which the twist hangs in a loop without kinking, doubling, or twisting upon itself.

balibuntal straw (*bal*-ih-*bun*-tuhl straw)   *See* straw.

ball fringe   A trimming of round fluffy balls (pompoms) attached by threads to a band of fabric. It is often used on curtains and upholstery.

ballet slipper   A lightweight, low-cut, soft shoe with a round or slightly squared toe, flat sole, and no heel. Adapted from the slippers worn by ballet dancers.

balmacaan (bal-muh-*kahn*)   Swagger-style coat with slash pockets, no belt, raglan sleeves, and a military collar. Fabrics used are gabardine, tweed, and cashmere (in solid colors for dress). The balmacaan was named for an estate near Inverness.

Baluchistan rug (buh-*loo*-chee-stahn)   A hand-tied oriental rug from Baluchistan, commonly called Baluchi.

band collar   A narrow strip of fabric (usually no more than one inch deep) which stands upright from the neckline.

bandanna (ban-*dan*-uh)   An evenly woven fabric, usually about 24" square, and hemmed on all sides that is used for a handkerchief, neckerchief, or head scarf. Traditionally, bandannas were printed in stylized geometric patterns on bright blue or red fabric with black and white contrasts. A bandanna print imitates this look and often is made of individual bandanna squares. The traditional red and blue colors are not always used today.

bandeau (ban-*doh*)   A narrow, lightweight, brassiere-like band or tube top worn by women.

banding   A narrow, flat fabric which may be woven, knitted, or braided. It is used to trim an edge or folded over to bind an edge.

bandolier (*ban*-duh-leer)   A belt worn over the shoulder and diagonally across the breast.

bangkok straw (*bang*-kock straw)   *See* straw.

Banlon (*ban*-lon)   Trademark of Bancroft Licensing for a texturizing process that uses heat settings to add bulk and a small amount of stretch to the filament yarns of thermoplastic fibers. *See* heat setting, thermoplastic, and filament.

barathea (bayr-uh-*thee*-uh)   A silk, rayon and cotton, or rayon and wool closely woven mixed fabric with a pebbly texture. The broken rib pattern in a finely woven design resembles a brick wall. The fabric is used for dresses, neckties, trimmings, and lightweight suits.

bargello (flame stitch or Hungarian stitch) (bar-*jeh*-loh)   A type of needlepoint design in a zigzag pattern that creates repetitive geometric designs, such as diamonds, and peaks and valleys (flames). Unlike traditional needlepoint in which the stitches slant as the canvas mesh is filled, bargello is composed of stitches which run parallel to the threads of the needlepoint canvas. Bargello stitches usually cover two or more meshes with each stitch and the work goes very quickly. A bargello-like print is sometimes used in fabric for apparel. *See* needlepoint.

bark crepe (bark crayp)   Another fabric designed to resemble bark, but the effect is more exaggerated than barkcloth. Usually one fiber is used for the warp and another for the filling to help create the textured look of bark. *See* barkcloth.

barkcloth   Originally, the term referred to a fabric found throughout the South Pacific and is made from the inner bark of certain trees. The bark is beaten into a paper-like fabric, then dyed or otherwise colored. Tapa cloth is one of the best known types of true barkcloth. Barkcloth is a term that also refers to a fabric, often cotton or rayon, with a somewhat crepe-like feel that is designed to resemble true barkcloth. This fabric is used extensively for draperies, slipcovers, and other home furnishings. *See* crepe and tapa cloth.

barre (bah-*ray*)   A fabric, either knit or woven, in which stripes run in crosswise directions. Barre also refers to flaws in fabric that appear as unwanted crosswise stripes of texture or color.

basic dye   A type of dye that colors wool and silk without a mordant. It can be used on cotton with a mordant.

basic finishes   Regular processes (mechanical or chemical) applied in some form to a fabric after it has been constructed.

B

basket weave   One of the most important patterns in weaving. Basket weave is made with two or more filling threads passing over and under an equal number of warp threads on alternate rows.

bast fiber   Fiber between the pithy center of the stem and the skin. Flax, jute, hemp, and ramie are bast fibers.

bateau (or boat) neck (bah-*toh* nek)   A high, wide neckline with a straight horizontal line.

bath mat   A floor covering often made of tufted chenille.

bath rug   Usually a comparatively small rug with cotton, rayon, or nylon suitable for a bathroom.

batik (bah-*teek*)   A form of resist dyeing of Indonesian origin. Wax is pile-spread on fabric before dyeing. The unwaxed areas take the color whereas the wax-covered fabric retains its original color. Often several waxings and dyeings are needed to achieve a final pattern. The wax usually cracks during the dyeing process, giving a characteristic veined effect to the design. Batik is extensively copied by machine printing today. *See* resist dyeing, under dyeing.

batiste (bah-*teest*)   A fabric named for Jean Baptiste, a French linen weaver. (1) In cotton, a sheer, fine muslin, woven of combed yarns and given a mercerized finish. It is used for blouses, summer shirts, dresses, lingerie, infants' dresses, bonnets, and handkerchiefs. (2) A rayon, polyester, or cotton-blend fabric with the same characteristics. (3) A smooth, fine wool fabric that is lighter than challis, and similar to fine nun's veiling. It is used for dresses and negligees. (4) A sheer silk fabric either plain or figured, similar to silk mull. It is often called "batiste de soie" and is made into summer dresses.

Battenberg lace (*bat*-en-berg layss)   A lace similar to Renaissance lace with a pattern formed by tape or braid joined by bars. *See* Renaissance lace.

battening   Pushing each filling (or pick) against the previous filling.

batting (*bat*-ing)   Batting is usually stocked in linens and domestics departments although it is used today primarily for crafts. Batting is a filling material used to stuff pillows, toys, and quilts. At one time, batting was made of cotton; today, usually polyester fiberfill. Batting may be sold in bulk form or in true batting form as a long flat sheet. Only the sheets should be called batting, but the term has come to be used for this type of stuffing in all forms.

B

bayadere (bye-ar-*dare*)   Stripes that run in the crosswise direction of a fabric. This term is usually used to describe only very brightly colored stripes. *See* barre.

beaded velvet (*beed*-id *vel*-vit)   Also called cut velvet. *See* velvet.

beading (*beed*-ing)   (1) The beads sewn onto fabric to form a pattern or completely cover the fabric's surface. (2) A type of lace made by the bobbin lace method. (3) An openwork lace or embroidery that has holes designed for the insertion of decorative ribbon. *See* bobbin lace, lace, and embroidery.

beaver   A glossy, coat-weight fabric made with a long nap that resembles beaver fur. *See* furs.

bed head   A synonym for headboard, a bed head is a board or frame at the pillow end of a bed and stands perpendicular to the floor. Headboards may be made of wood, slipcovered, or upholstered to match a bedspread or other decorative areas of a room.

bed linen   Any cotton, linen, or nylon sheeting for use on a bed.

bed pad   A mattress cover. A quilted, fairly thick pad placed on top of a bed mattress and beneath a bottom sheet to protect the mattress and make the bed more comfortable. A mattress cover often has elastic at all corners to hold it on the bed. It should completely cover the top of the mattress.

Bedford cloth (*bed*-ford kloth)   A strong woven fabric with lengthwise ribs used extensively for upholstery and riding breeches. It may be made from any fiber.

Bedford cord   Lengthwise heavy ribbed durable cloth made of cotton, wool, silk, rayon, or combination fibers, for outer garments or sports clothes. The corded effect is secured by two successive warp threads woven in plain-weave order. Heavier cords are created with wadding, a heavy, bulky yarn with very little twist, covered by filling threads.

bedspread   Usually a decorative covering that covers the blankets and pillows on a bed during the day. Bedspreads are available in many styles from simple throws arranged casually over the bed to tailored box spreads.

beetling (*beet*-ling)   A finish primarily applied to linen or cotton whereby the cloth is beaten with large wooden blocks in order to produce a hard, flat surface with a sheen. It gives a linen-like appearance to cotton.

B

Belgian lace (*bel*-jin layss)   Any lace made in Belgium. Originally the term meant a bobbin lace worked on a machine-made net. *See* bobbin lace.

bell sleeve   A set-in sleeve that is narrow at the shoulder and widens at the bottom edge; it may be any length.

bellboy cap   A small, round, stiff brimless hat worn at the front of the head.

belting (*belt*-ing)   A heavy cotton, rayon, silk, or mixed fabric with large fillingwise ribs. It may be knit. Any heavyweight, fairly stiff fabric used to support the top of a skirt, a pair of pants, or line a belt to give additional support. Beltings come in various widths.

Bemberg (*bem*-burg)   Trademark of Beauknit for cuprammonium rayon. *See* rayon.

Benares (beh-*nahr*-eez)   Lightweight fabric from India, usually woven with metallic threads.

bengaline (*beng*-uh-leen)   A ribbed fabric similar to faille, but heavier, with a coarser rib in the filling direction. It may be silk, wool, acetate, or rayon warp, with wool or cotton filling. The fabric was first made in Bengal, India, and is used for dresses, coats, trimmings, and draperies.

beret (buh-*ray*)   A rimless cap with a tight headband and full, flat top made of soft material.

bias (*by*-us)   A fabric cut diagonally across the warp and filling yarns. A true bias is cut on a 45° angle from the lower left to the upper right of a cloth. This part of a woven fabric has the greatest amount of stretch.

bias plaid   A plaid design that actually forms a diamond pattern with the intersection of its lines. Argyle plaid is an example of a bias plaid.

bias tape   A strip of fabric cut on the diagonal between the lengthwise and crosswise grain of the fabric. Because bias tape has considerable stretch, it is used to bind edges (such as curved areas) where a certain degree of stretch is necessary for a smooth finish. Bias tape can also be used for purely decorative trimming. It is available precut and comes packaged in a wide range of colors.

bib   The part of an apron-like garment or overalls that extends above the waist.

B

bicomponent fiber   A fiber in which two filaments of the same generic class but different composition have been extruded simultaneously. This results in a continuous-filament man-made fiber composed of two related components, each having a different degree of shrinkage. Stretch results from crimping of the filament.

biconstituent fiber   (by-kuhn-*stich*-oo-uhnt *fy*-ber) A fiber made by mixing two different man-made generic fiber materials together in their syrupy stage before forcing the mixture through a spinneret.

billiard cloth (*bill*-yard kloth)   The cloth used on billiard tables, and always dyed green. This is traditionally a very fine twilled fabric made from quality wool. Today, billiard cloth may be made from other fibers.

Binch lace (beench layss)   A lace comprised of hand-made lace motifs appliqued to a machine-made net background. The name comes from Binche, a town in Belgium, where the lace is said to have originated.

binding (*bynd*-ing)   Any narrow fabric used to enclose or bind edges, usually raw edges. It can also be used for purely decorative purposes. *See* bias tape.

birds-eye (*berdz*-eye)   Fabric with a woven-in dobby design. The pattern has a center dot and resembles the eye of a bird. It is used in cotton diapers, piqué, and wool sharkskin. *See* piqué.

bishop sleeve   A set-in sleeve that has fullness at the wrist and is gathered or pleated into a cuff or band.

blanket   Any loose covering, especially those used on beds for warmth. Most blankets were formerly made of wool, but today many are made of acrylic and other man-made fibers. Blanket cloth is a heavy-weight fabric, often vividly patterned in plaid designs, and usually used for coats. It often has a napped surface. Blanket is also a technical term referring to an experimental piece of fabric that shows a designer how the final cloth will look. Blankets of this kind often have several designs and colorings woven or knitted on one piece.

blanket plaid   A vividly colored plaid design, usually on napped fabrics, similar to those used for blankets.

blanketing   A heavily napped fabric of wool, cotton, or man-made fibers in blends or mixtures, woven sixty or eighty inches or more in size. In plain or twill weave.

B

blazer   A casual sport-type jacket, typically with a notched collar and patch pockets, with metal, pearl, or leather-like buttons on the front closing and cuffs. Suede or flannel are popular fabrics.

blazer cloth (*blayz*-er kloth)   Fabric traditionally used for loosely fitting tailored jackets worn by men and women. The fabric was formerly made of wool with a satin weave; today it is made from any fiber. Blazers may be striped, plaid, or solid colored, and are especially popular with students when in school colors.

blazer stripe (*blayz*-er stryp)   A type of stripe originally used on jackets, ultimately called blazers, because of the bright blazing colors used in the stripes. Blazer stripes are usually $1^{1}/_{2}$" wide, and are vividly colored.

bleach   A chemical that removes color from an item. Fabrics are often bleached after manufacture and before dyeing to ensure the dyed colors are "true." Household bleach is used to disinfect clothing and remove soil from whites and colorfast colors. Chlorine bleaches are the most common household bleaches, but are too strong for some colors and fabrics.

bleaching   A basic finishing process to whiten fabrics. Different chemicals are used for different fabrics. Sun, air, and moisture are good bleaches for some materials, although bleaching by this method is slower.

bleed   An elegant term for running, or the way in which nonfast dyes merge into each other and "run" into the water when immersed. The term bleed, when applied to fabrics, is often used in a positive sense (bleeding Madras) where the bleeding process is considered desirable. When the bleeding is undesirable, it is more likely to be referred to as running.

blend   A combination of different fibers in the same yarn, producing a fabric that has the best qualities of each fiber. The development of blends of polyester and cotton, producing fabrics that require a minimum of ironing, has been one of the most significant developments in fabrics during the past twenty-five years. In reality, the term "blend" refers only to fabrics made from yarns that have been spun to combine the two fibers in one yarn. The term "mixture" should be used to describe fabrics in which, for instance, the warp thread is polyester and the filling thread is cotton. *See* mixture and biconstituent fiber.

B

blended yarn   A strand of fibers produced from two or more constituent fibers that have been thoroughly mixed (blended) before spinning.

blending (*blehnd*-ing)   Blending describes the process of combining different fibers. Occasionally, blending is done for reasons of economy (when an expensive fiber is blended with a cheaper one) rather than as an attempt to mix two desirable qualities. Traditionally, blending is a process used in the production of natural fiber yarns. Fibers from several lots of a single natural fiber are mixed together to provide a yarn of greater uniformity than would result from the use of any single lot. *See* blend.

blinds (blyndz)   The term blinds is a synonym for shades.

blister   A bump on a fabric. Blisters are often used to give additional depth to a design. Flowers, for example, may be blistered to make them stand out from the rest of a fabric. Blister crepe is a fabric produced chemically by shrinking some of the yarns and leaving others unshrunk in a crepe pattern after the fabric is manufactured. In practice, many crepe fabrics with well-defined patterns are referred to as blister crepes whether or not they are actually made in this way. *See* crepe.

block printing   A hand-printing process in which a design is carved on a block of wood or linoleum. Dye is placed on the surface and the block is placed on the fabric, thereby transferring the dye. Every color requires a different block, making this type of printing tedious and expensive. It is now almost entirely limited to the craft field. *See* printing.

blouson (*blue*-sohn)   A garment gathered at the waist by elastic or a drawstring producing a fullness of fabric that falls over the gathering.

Blue "C" (bloo see)   Trademark used by Montsanto to identify some of their fibers. It must be used with the fiber's name as in "Blue 'C' nylon."

bluing (*bloo*-ing)   A liquid, bead, or flake-type mild blue dye traditionally added to white clothes in the final rinse water after washing to make them look whiter. The blue tint has no real whitening or cleansing action but offsets the yellow cast some white fabrics tend to acquire with age. It is used mostly on cotton or linen. With changes in laundry techniques, bluing of clothes as a separate step in washing has almost disappeared. A form of bluing is, however, added to some washing detergents. Bluing is occasionally used in a similar way and for a similar purpose in fabric finishing. *See* optical brighteners and optical dyes.

boa (*boh*-uh)   A long scarf worn at the neck, usually made of fur or feathers.

board   A flat piece of cardboard or plastic foam around which fabric, sold by the yard, is wrapped.

board ends (bohrd endz)   The ends of the board around which fabric is wrapped. Board ends are often marked with fiber content and care instructions.

boarding   A process similar to heat setting, used in the manufacture of hosiery that is not full-fashioned, such as seamless stockings and panty hose. Because of nylon's thermoplastic nature (it changes shape under heat), these stockings are knitted with the same number of stitches in the leg. Shaping for ankle and calf is created by placing the hosiery on forms in the desired shape and submitting the hosiery to high temperatures. With the development of stretch yarns for hosiery, this step has become unnecessary because the stocking easily conforms to the shape of the leg. It is still used, however, to improve the appearance of the finished product made of stretch yarns. *See* full-fashioned and heat setting.

boardy fabric   A fabric that is too stiff because of excessive amounts or improper application of chemical finishing materials.

boater   A straw hat with a stiff, flat crown and brim.

bobbin (*bob*-in)   A spool, usually hollow, that holds thread on a sewing machine or yarn on a loom.

bobbin lace (*bob*-in layss)   Lace made by using a pillow to hold the pins around which thread is arranged. Bobbins are used to hold and feed the thread. Bobbin lace is also called bobbinette lace and pillow lace.

bobbinette lace (*bob*-in-et layss)   Also called bobbin lace and pillow lace.

bodice (*bahd*-is)   The upper portion of a girl's or woman's dress.

body shirt   A close-fitting blouse or shirt with a sewn or snapped crotch.

bolster (*bohl*-ster)   A long, narrow pillow, either round or rectangular in shape, that is the width of the bed. It is used for decoration and support.

B

bolt   A rather loose term referring to a quantity of fabric. Most fabric sold in fabric and department stores is folded in half lengthwise, then wrapped around a flat piece of cardboard or plastic. The fabric and board together are called a bolt. A bolt usually has between fifteen and twenty yards of fabric, but may have slightly more or less. The term is also used to mean "a great deal of fabric," as in "I used bolts of fabric to decorate the living room."

bombazine (bom-buh-*zeen*)   A black twilled fabric used for mourning clothes in the past.

bonded-face fabric   The side of a bonded fabric used as the face (right side) of the cloth in a garment or other end use.

bonding   A process of joining two or more layers of cloth with a layer of adhesive, or pressing fibers into thin webs or mats held together by adhesive, plastic, or self-bonding that melts when heat is applied. Nonwoven fabrics are made in this way. The term occasionally is used as a synonym for laminating, but this is technically incorrect.

boot topper   A footless sock that extends from the ankle to the knee; generally worn under boots or as a cover over them.

border   Any type of distinct edging, such as a decorative edging on a fabric or pillow.

border design   A printed, woven, or knitted design that runs along the selvage edge of a fabric. Border designs often are made so they taper from small to large across the width of the fabric. To utilize the design properly, border fabrics must be used with the length of the goods running horizontally around the body, in contrast to the usual practice.

Botany (*bot*-uh-nee)   A name for Australian wool from Botany Bay, a section of Australia. Because this wool has a reputation for high quality, the term is also used in trade and store names.

bouclé (boo-*klay*)   A fabric woven with bouclé yarns that have a looped appearance on the surface. The fabric has a textured, nubby surface that is usually dull unless shiny yarns are used. In some bouclés, only one side of the fabric is nubby; in others, both are rough. Sometimes the bouclé yarn is used as a warp rather than as a filling, a look that moves in and out of fashion. Bouclé fabrics may be woven or knitted by hand or machine.

B

bouclé yarn   A rough, fairly thick, quite slubby linen yarn that is characterized by tight loops projecting from the body of the yarn at fairly regular intervals. It is a novelty yarn often plied with yarns of other fibers for textural interest. Bouclé yarn is very popular in the knitting trade because there are many varieties and weights.

bourdon lace (*boor*-dohn layss)   Lace made by machine usually in a scroll design. The design usually is outlined with a heavy thread.

bow tie   A thinnish necktie shaped into a bow; worn by both men and women.

box coat   A single- or double-breasted straight-hanging coat with notch or peak lapels. It generally has a regulation sleeve. Occasionally it is half-belted in back.

box pleats   Box pleats are made by folding fabric so that the edges of two pleats face in opposite directions on the right side of the fabric.

box spread   A shaped and fitted bedspread that has a tailored appearance. The corners are square, giving the spread its name.

box-edged pillow   A pillow that has three dimensions rather than two-sided, as are most bed pillows. The pillow fabric covering is shaped like a round or rectangular box, and has a fabric band (boxing) that covers the edges of the pillow and joins the top and bottom sides.

boxing   A term describing the straight strip of fabric that covers the sides of a three-dimensional round or square pillow. The boxing is joined to the rest of the cover with seams and occasionally includes a decorative trimming such as welting.

braid (brayd)   A term used to describe narrow trimmings that contain woven multicolored designs. Various types of braid (peasant braid) are popular during certain fashion periods.

braid rug (brayd rug)   A braid rug is made by joining strips of braid together with stitches. Braid rugs may be either rectangular, oval or round. *See* rugs and carpets.

braiding (*brayd*-ing)   Also known as plaiting. A method of making fabric by interlacing three or more yarns of cotton, wool, or other materials.

brassiere or bra   An undergarment that covers the bust and may extend to the waistline.

B

breaker   A machine containing a tooth cylinder used to remove all loose dirt, sand, and so forth, and to separate the whole fleece into small sections.

breaking load   The minimum force required to rupture a fiber, expressed in grams or pounds.

Breton (*bret*-uhn)   A woman's hat with a brim rolled up evenly all around.

Breton lace (*bret*-uhn layss)   Lace made on open net, usually embroidered with heavy, often brightly colored, yarns. Breton is the area in France where the lace is said to have originated.

brief   A short panty. *See* panty.

briefcase purse   A large, flat, rectangular purse with two strap handles and a zipper or hardware closing. It often has additional open or zippered pockets.

bright yarns   High luster yarns made with rayon or acetate fibers.

brins   The two adjacent silk filaments extruded by the silkworm.

broadcloth (*brawd*-kloth)   Although the term broadcloth originally meant any fabric made on a loom of a certain width, it now means a fine, tightly woven fabric with a faint rib. Originally, it was made of mercerized cotton, but today the term is used to describe several dissimilar fabrics made with different fibers, weaves, and finishes. (1) Originally, a silk shirting fabric so named because it was woven in widths exceeding the usual twenty-nine inches. (2) A plain-weave, tightly woven, high-count cotton fabric, with fillingwise rib finer than poplin. Best grades are made of combed pima or Egyptian cotton, usually with high thread counts (136x60 or 144x76). The fabrics are usually mercerized, sanforized, and given a soft lustrous finish, and are used for women's blouses, tailored summer dresses, and men's shirts. (3) A closely woven, medium-weight wool cloth with a smooth nap, velvety feel, and lustrous appearance. Wool broadcloth can be made with a two-up-and-two-down twill weave or plain weave. In setting up a loom to make the fabric, the loom is threaded wide to allow for a large amount of shrinkage during the filling process. The fabric takes its name from this wide threading. High-quality wool broadcloth is fine enough for garments that are closely molded to the figure or draped. Its high-luster finish makes it an elegant cloth. Wool broadcloth is ten to sixteen ounces per yard and is now being made in chiffon weights. (4) A fabric made from silk or man-made filament fiber yarns and woven in a plain weave with a fine crosswise rib obtained by using a heavier filling than warp yarn.

broadloom (*brawd*-loom)   A carpet term referring to any carpeting woven on a loom which is nine, twelve, fifteen feet, or wider. The term is frequently used incorrectly in advertising to imply a high quality product.

brocade (broh-*kayd*)   A drapery or upholstery fabric in a rich Jacquard weave with an allover interwoven design of raised figures or flowers. The name is derived from the French word meaning "to ornament." The brocade pattern is emphasized with contrasting surfaces or colors and often has gold, silver, or other metallic threads running through it. The background may be either satin or twill weave. In clothing fabrics, brocade refers to a heavy, luxurious fabric made on a Jacquard loom. Patterns often include flowers and leaves. Although true brocades are woven, today the term is also used for knits with a similar luxurious look. In carpeting, a brocade rug is one in which different yarns of the same color create a subtle pattern. Brocade is used for formal dresses, blouses, evening wraps, handbags, neckties, lounge wear, vests, and robes.

brocaded satin   A satin fabric with raised designs in Jacquard weave.

brocatel or brocatelle (broh-kuh-*tel*)   A fabric similar to brocade made on a Jacquard loom. It is a drapery and upholstery fabric made in double-cloth construction with a silk- or rayon-fibered face. Best grades have a linen back. The design stands in relief from the background, giving it a padded effect, similar to Italian tooled leather, in which the background is pressed and the figures are embossed. Both the background and the figure are tightly woven, generally with a warp effect in the figure and a filling effect in the background.

broderie anglaise (brohd-ur-*ee* on-*glayz*)   Another name for eyelet embroidery. *See* embroidery and eyelet.

broken check   A check pattern in which the checks are irregular rather than perfect squares.

broker   One who represents a buyer or seller, but who does not have direct physical control of the merchandise.

brushed rayon   A rayon fabric that has been heavily napped. This type of fabric is highly flammable and must be treated to make it fire resistant.

B

brushing   Removing short, loose fibers from a cloth by means of cylinder rolls covered with bristles. Brushing is also a finishing process in which the fabric is swept by bristles to raise the nap. Blankets are often brushed, and recently, brushed denim has been popular. Hand-knitted yarns, when made into garments, can be brushed for a soft, fluffy effect.

Brussels (*bruss*-selz)   *See* curtains, lace, and rugs and carpets.

Brussels curtains (*bruss*-selz *kur*-tenz)   Net curtains with an embroidered design done either by hand or machine over the net. The net may be one or two layers.

Brussels lace (*bruss*-selz layss)   Brussels lace may be either a bobbin lace or a needlepoint lace. It is usually worked on a machine-made ground and sometimes the designs are appliqued. Because of the importance of Brussels, Belgium in the history of lace-making (many patterns developed there), several different laces are called Brussels lace. *See* bobbin lace and needlepoint lace.

bubble umbrella   An umbrella that completely covers the head and shoulders with a clear, vinyl, dome-shaped canopy.

buckram (*buck*-rum)   A stiff, open-weave fabric made from coarse yarns and used primarily for stiffening in interfacings and hat shaping. Originally, buckram was sized with starch that was not permanent, but today most buckrams have a permanent stiff finish.

buckskin (*buhk*-skin)   A fairly inexpensive leather from deer and elk skins. Also, a fabric made in a form of satin weave with a napped finish. Originally wool, the term buckskin is now applied to various synthetic fabrics with smooth surfaces, with or without the napped finish. *See* leather.

bugle beads   Tube-shaped beads, originally made of glass, but often man-made today. They are used for jewelry and sewn to dresses as decoration.

builder   An ingredient in a detergent that reduces hardness in wash water, provides the proper alkalinity, and helps keep soil from being redeposited on clothing.

built soap   Has a builder, such as phosphate, added.

bulking   A yarn finishing process in which the yarn is made thicker or "bulkier" by heat setting crimp into the filaments or by looping

B

individual fibers with an air jet. Bulking gives yarn and fabrics a less shiny, fluffier appearance. Bulking is often used in making sweater yarns. *See* crimp and heat setting.

bulky yarn   A yarn that has been textured to give it bulk without increasing weight.

bullion (*bool*-yun)   A twisted, shiny, cord-like fringe used primarily in upholstery.

bunting   A loosely woven fabric used primarily for flags and draping. Bunting used in public places must be flameproof. Bunting is also a term used to describe a simple rectangular square of material in which a baby is wrapped for warmth.

burlap (*burr*-lap)   A coarse, rough, heavy, stiff fabric in plain weave, often called gunny sacking and made from jute, hemp, or cotton. It is used for draperies, upholstery, wall coverings, commercial items (sacks), and occasionally fashion items. It is also used as interlining in men's suits. This is a poorer fabric than hair canvas for the purpose. Burlap dyes well but may have a disagreeable odor unless treated.

burling   Removal of irregularities (such as knots or slubs) with a small pick.

burn-out printing   Burn-out printing refers to a process whereby a fabric made of two fibers with different characteristics is printed with a chemical that eats away (burns out) one of the fibers and not the other. This method is used to make some sculptured velvets (the pile of the velvet is eaten away) and to make fabrics with some sheer and some nonsheer areas. In making the sculptured velvets, the pile of the velvet reacts to the chemical; in making the sheer fabrics, the yarn is spun from two fibers, one of which is sensitive to the chemical and one which is not.

busheling   The tailoring of men's garments done after the item has been purchased and fitted to the customer. Also referred to as the repairing of a piece of clothing in a garment factory after it has been completed and inspected.

butcher rayon   A coarse rayon, or rayon and acetate blend, medium-weight fabric woven in a plain weave and originally intended as a substitute for butcher linen; used for butchers' aprons.

butcher's linen (*butch*-erz *lin*-uhn)   Strong, heavy, plain weave fabric, originally of linen (and originally worn by butchers), now made of any fiber.

B

buttonhole twist (*but*-n-hohl twist)   A thick, twisted silk cord. Buttonhole twist is lustrous and is used for topstitching (decorative, straight stitching, usually along seams or garment edges). It is also used for sewing buttons on a garment as well as for making buttonholes. It may be used for embroidery.

Defect	Explanation	Severity
Back Fabric Seam	Backing fabric is often used to cushion fabric being printed. If there is a joining seam in the backing fabric, an impression will result on printed fabric.	Major
Bad Odor	Any of a host of objectionable odors often noted in fabrics unfinished or finished. Usually caused by some chemical action that has not been properly controlled, such as in application, washing, scouring, or fulling.	Minor
Bad Place	A convenient term for defects that sometimes defy description. Usually used to describe localized places where the weave has been severely disrupted.	Usually Major
Balky Selvage	A broad term that implies the yarn may be of an incorrect yarn count and/or ply, unevenly twisted, crowded selvage ends, ends in the reed, poor harness timing, harness skips, or poor temple setting.	Usually Major
Barre	Occurs in circular knit. A condition generally characterized by a somewhat patterned unevenness-of-appearance in the course or width direction of a fabric. Some causes are uneven yarn, uneven tension, and yarns with different dye affinities. Fabric appears to have horizontal streaks.	Usually Major
Barre Marks, Barry	The former is the French term. It is observed in fabrics that have bars or stripes detrimental to the finished cloth. It runs in the warp direction in some instances, but is usually found in the filling direction when one or more picks are seemingly different in color from the adjoining picks. Usually caused by slight variations in the number of picks to the inch in the texture of the material.	Usually Major

Defect	Explanation	Severity
Bias Filling (also Skew)	Observed in the finishing of the cloth, it comes as the result of the filling not running at absolute right angles to the warp yarns. Tenter framing of the goods is where this error or defect occurs. In knits, the courses are off square to the wales. Another name for the blemish is bowed filling.	Major or Minor (depending on degree of warp)
Birds-eye	Caused by unintentional tucking from malfunctioning needle. Usually two small distorted stitches, side by side, contrary to the design of the fabric.	Major or Minor (depending on severity)
Bleeding	A running of one or more colors in a cloth; bleeding naturally spoils the material. Faulty dye-stuff is the cause of this, and bleeding is most pronounced when the colors in the fabric are run through the wet-finishing treatments in the plant.	Major
Bowing	Usually caused by finishing. Woven filling yarns lie in an arc across fabric width; in knits the course lines lie in an arc across width of goods. Establish standards of acceptance: critical on stripes or patterns; not as critical on solid color fabrics.	Major or Minor
Box Mark	A fine but disturbing line in the filling direction of cloth caused by a small number of picks not woven correctly. Usually results from rough spots or splinters on the outside of the shuttle. Improper timing of the shuttle boxes will also produce this effect.	Major
Broken Color	This occurs when the pattern becomes "broken" because of some error or irregularity on the part of an operator. The pattern, if "broken," will not show in the fabric according to the planned design.	Major

Defect	Explanation	Severity
Broken End	Caused by tender yarn, rough spots or splinters on the shuttle surface, or improper timing of the shedding action in the loom. May also be noticed where a warp yarn has ruptured and been repaired. Often characterized by the broken end being woven into the fabric.	Minor
Broken Pick	A filling yarn that has become broken in its flight through the shed of the loom. Shuttles, shuttle boxes, and weak yarn are the main causes of broken picks.	Major
Bruise, Temple Bruise	A condition where the yarn, while being woven, or the fabric, after being woven, has been scuffed so as to disorient the fibers and result in a fuzzy appearance.	Major
Burl Mark	When a slub or extra piece of yarn is woven into the fabric, it is often removed by a "burling tool." This usually leaves an open place in the fabric.	Major
Burrs	1. These are rather minute seed particles found when processing cotton in picking, carding, combing, and spinning the fibers into yarn. Very often they carry through into the finished goods.	Minor
	2. In woolens, burrs may consist of vegetable matter such as motes, shives, granules, or other particles that were embedded in the grease wool and not removed in the scouring of the stock. Often noted in cheviot, homespun, tweed, and shetland fabrics for suitings and coatings. Burrs in woolen fabrics may be removed by carbonizing, where the vegetable matter is dissolved out of the animal matter.	Major
Buttonhole Selvage	A selvage defect caused by excessive tension buildup in the shuttle just before filling change. This tension tends to restrict the selvage yarns from proper shedding and interlacing, resulting in a defect that resembles a buttonhole.	Major

cable cord   The result of twisting singles together in various directions of twist, such as S/Z/S or Z/S/Z. *See* S twist and Z twist.

cable stitch fabric   A knit fabric. The pattern looks like a plaited rope or cable running lengthwise down the fabric; used mostly for sweaters.

café curtains (ka-*fay kur*-tenz)   Curtains that are hung in tiers so that one row covers the top half of a window and the second row, the bottom. They are hung on a wood or metal pole placed across the top and center of the window. Café curtains often are finished with scalloped edges through which the pole slides. There are also café curtain rings available for hanging them. These curtains are usually hung in two tiers, but may be hung in any number of tiers with about three inches of overlap.

calender printing (*kal*-en-der *print*-ing)   A synonym for cylinder, direct, and roller printing. *See* roller printing.

calendering (*kal*-en-der-ing)   A finishing process for fabrics that produces a shiny, smooth surface. The cloth is passed through hollow, heated cylinder rolls by running it through a friction or glazing calender, as in chintz.

calfskin   A common name in leather for the hide of a calf with the fur removed. It is used for shoes, belts, and purses.

calico (*kal*-ih-ko)   A smooth-surfaced, plain weave cloth. Today, the term is almost always applied to fabric with bright, sharply contrasting, usually small-print designs. Calico is usually woven, although calico prints may appear on knits. Calico is a traditionally popular fabric for patchwork. It is also used for dresses, sportswear, and aprons.

cambric (*kaym*-brik)   A closely woven, plain weave, white fabric that is finished with a slightly glossy surface. The fabric is traditionally made from cotton or linen, but can be made from any fiber. It was formerly used in underwear and handkerchiefs, but today its major uses are to reinforce book bindings and to upholster the underside of chairs and sofas. Very low count, heavily sized glazed cambric is used for costuming.

cambric finish (*kaym*-brik *fin*-ish) A glossy finish applied to fabrics.

camel's hair True camel's hair, a luxury fiber, is considered a wool, and comes from the soft lustrous underhair of the Bactrian, a two-humped, pack-carrying species of camel. The fabric is light tan to brownish black in color. Today, camel's hair is almost always blended with other fibers, sometimes sheep's wool, sometime man-made acrylic fibers. Camel's hair is also a term used to describe a rather yellowish tan color.

camisole (*kam*-ih-sohl) (1) A neckline that falls straight across the top of the bustline and has straight shoulder straps. (2) A top, either under-garment or blouse, with the typical camisole style.

candlewick (*kan*-duhl-wik) A thick, soft yarn used to form tufts by pulling it through a base fabric and then cutting it. The term also describes the fabric made by this method, a traditionally popular bedspread fabric. *See* tufted fabric.

Canton crepe (*kan*-tun krayp) A thick fabric, heavier than crepe de Chine, with a slightly ribbed crepe filling. It was originally made of silk in Canton, China. Now it may be made of rayon or acetate, and is used for business and afternoon dresses.

Canton flannel A heavy, warm cotton material with a twilled surface and a long soft nap on the back, produced by napping the heavy soft-twist yarn. It is named for Canton, China, where it was first made. The fabric is strong and absorbent and is used for interlinings and sleeping garments.

Cantrece (kan-*treess*) DuPont trademark for a biconstituent nylon yarn that is crimped through a heat treatment and results in a stretchable yarn. Often used for "one size fits all" hosiery.

canvas A heavy, strong, usually plain weave fabric that historically was made of flax, hemp, or cotton. Today, it is usually made of cotton, but some fabrics made of man-made fibers or blends are also called canvas. Canvas is, roughly speaking, heavier than duck or sailcloth although the three names are often used interchangeably.

C

The unbleached fabric is used for coat fronts, lapels, and linings of men's suits. Hair canvas for interlinings is made of goat's hair and wool. *See* duck and sailcloth.

cap sleeve   A short extension of fabric shaped to fit the shoulder; it may be cut and stitched on separately or cut in one piece with the garment.

cape   An overgarment without sleeves that hangs from the shoulders; it may or may not have slit openings for the arms.

capelet (*kayp*-let)   A small cape which covers the shoulders.

Caprolan (*kap*-roh-lan)   Trademark of Allied Chemical for nylon.

carbonizing   A chemical treatment of wool to burn out vegetable matter.

card sliver   A rope like strand of fibers about three-quarters of an inch to one inch in diameter; the form in which fibers emerge from the carding machine.

cardigan   A style of sweater that buttons up the front.

carding (*kard*-ing)   Carding is a process in the conversion of cotton, wool, some silks, and man-made staple fibers into yarn. It separates, opens, and cleans the fibers, and puts them in a filmy sheet called a sliver. *See* combing.

carpet (*kar*-pit)   Originally a term used as a synonym for rug, today the word carpet usually refers to a heavy fabric floor covering that covers the entire floor and is most often fastened to it in a somewhat permanent fashion. This soft floor covering can be made of a variety of different fibers. It is sold by the yard and cut to any size. *See* rugs and carpets.

carpet rayon   A specially constructed fiber and yarn for carpets that has greater tensile strength and is coarser than rayon for clothing.

carpet wool   Very coarse wool from Turkey, Siberia, China, and South America, primarily used in carpets; not suited for clothing.

carrier   An agent that swells fibers to improve the diffusion rate of disperse dyes into the fiber. Widely used in the dyeing of conventional polyester.

cartridge pleats (*kar*-trij pleetz)   Unpressed, very narrow pleats. They are usually used more as a decoration than to control fullness.

C

casein (*kay*-see-in)   A protein compound found especially in milk. Synthetic fibers can be derived from this protein.

casement cloth (*kays*-ment kloth)   A general term for fabrics, usually sheer, that are used for casement windows, curtains, draperies, or shades, although in practice the term is usually limited to open weave curtain fabrics.

cashmere (*kash*-meer)   Cashmere is the fleece (fine down, undercoat hair) of the cashmere (or Kashmir) goat of Tibet, Mongolia, China, Iran, India, and Iraq, and is noted for its softness. Cashmere is one of the luxury fibers and today is usually blended with sheep's wool or man-made fiber to lower the cost of the finished fabric and to improve its wearing ability. It is used for men's and women's sweaters, scarves, and coats.

catalyst (*kat*-ah-list)   A substance or agent that initiates a chemical reaction, and makes possible for it to proceed under milder conditions than otherwise possible.

Caucasian rug   Hand-tied oriental rug from Caucasia and Transcaucasia on the Black and Caspian seas. Names include Kabistan, Shirvan, Kazak, and Karaja.

cavalry twill   (*kav*-uhl-ree twill) A sturdy twill-weave fabric with a pronounced diagonal cord. It is used for sportswear, uniforms, and riding habits. *See* elastique.

Celanese (*sel*-ah-neez)   Celanese Corporation is a fiber producer.

cellular cloth (*sel*-you-lar kloth)   A fabric woven so that it traps air, reproducing the effects of layers of clothing or blankets. A cellular blanket should be used with another, noncellular covering on top of it to hold in the warm air produced by the body.

cellulose (*sel*-you-lohs)   The naturally occurring polymer (giant molecule) that forms the solid framework of plants. Cellulose from wood pulp is the base for rayon and acetate, both of which are man-made fibers. Cotton is more than ninety percent cellulose before it is cleaned (scoured). *See* cotton, rayon, and acetate.

cellulosic fibers (*sel*-you-loh-sik *fy*-bers)   Fibers made from cellulose.

chain warp   A warp that joins or binds together the upper and lower surfaces of a rug.

chainette fringe (*chayn*-et frinj)   A yarn fringe designed to resemble chain. It is used as a trimming for window shades.

chalk stripe   A narrow white stripe, usually on a dark-colored ground fabric. *See* pinstripes.

challis (*shal*-ee)   One of the softest fabrics made, it is named for the Anglo-Indian term shalee, meaning soft. It is a fine, light-weight, plain-weave fabric, usually made of wool, cotton, or man-made fibers. Challis was traditionally printed with vivid floral patterns on dark grounds or with paisley designs, but now is produced in darker tones of allover prints and solid colors, in the finest quality fabrics. It is normally used for neckties, dresses, blouses, scarves, bed jackets, and infants' sacques.

chambray (*sham*-bray)   (1) A plain-woven fabric with an almost square count (80x76), a colored warp, and a white filling, that gives a mottled, colored surface. The fabric is named for Cambrai, France, where it was first made for sunbonnets. Although chambray is traditionally woven, the look itself is so popular it is imitated in knitting. It is similar in appearance to denim but much lighter in weight. It is used for women's and children's summer dresses and men's shirts. (2) A cotton print cloth made of yarn-dyed yarns that can also be woven in patterns and woven in stripes. (3) A similar but carded-yarn fabric used for work clothes and children's play clothes. *See* denim.

Chambre Syndicale de la Couture Pariesienne (*chahm*-bruh sahn-dee-*kahl* duh lah koo-*ture* pah-*ree*-zee-ehn)   A French organization that regulates management and labor relations in the couture (high-fashion) industry. It also sets dates for couture shows and operates a dressmaking school.

chamois (*sham*-wa [correct pronunciation] *sham*-ee [customary pronunciation])   Soft, pliable leather from the skin of the chamois goat, although other animal skins may be substituted. It is used for gloves and as a cloth for washing autos. Chamois cloth is woven to imitate the leather, usually has a slightly napped surface, and is usually yellow, as is the goat skin. It is also used in clothing.

Chanel (shuh-*nel*)   Gabrielle (Coco) Chanel (1883-1971) was a French fashion designer whose influence has lasted beyond her lifetime. A Chanel tweed is a colorful tweed woven from bulky yarns that are usually thick and thin with many slubs. The term "Chanel tweed" is used loosely for any large-patterned tweed of this kind, and comes from the tweeds used by this designer for suits. A Chanel chain is a metal linked chain sewn into the bottom edge of suit jackets to help them keep their shape.

Chanel purse (shuh-*nehl* purss)   A quilted bag with two chain handles; originally designed by Coco Chanel.

changeable fabric (*chayn*-juh-buhl *fab*-rik)   Fabric woven with yarns of one color in the warp and another color in the filling so that the fabric seems to change color as the light strikes it. Other names for this type of fabric are iridescent and shot.

chantilly (*shan*-til-ee [incorrect pronunciation, but the only one used])   One of the most popular of bridal laces, often used for the trimming on bridal veils. It is made by the bobbin method and has designs outlined by thick cords. It is a delicate lace with vine or tree branch motifs; similar to Alençon lace. *See* bobbin lace.

Chardonnet, Count Hilaire de (*Shahr*-duhn-nay, kownt hill-*yeah* duh)   Maker of the first synthetic fiber by dissolving nitrocellulose in alcohol and ether.

check   A check is any small, regular pattern of squares woven or knitted into, or printed on, a fabric. *See* types of checks following.

broken check   A check pattern in which the checks are irregular instead of perfect squares.

district check   The name given to several quite different woven check patterns that originated in Scotland. The term applies to designs ranging from glen checks to shepherd checks

gingham check (*ging*-uhm chek)   Regular check in which the design is woven so that, in a red and white checked gingham, for example, there are squares of solid red, squares of solid white, and squares of white warp and red filling, as well as squares with red warp and white filling. Gingham checks are also printed on woven and knitted fabrics, and are knitted into some fabrics by means of a Jacquard attachment.

glen check   Glen check patterns usually consist of checks in varying colors with overlines or overchecks of other colors. Glen checks and glen plaids are the same.

gun club check   A double check design in which a large check is superimposed on a smaller one. The name is rarely used in the United States but the design is a popular one.

houndstooth check   A broken check, but regular in pattern. This check is extremely popular. It shows up periodically on everything from woolens to shower curtains.

overcheck   A design in which one check is woven or printed over another of a different size. Glen checks are overchecks.

pin check   A checked pattern in which the squares are extremely small.

shepherd check   A pattern of small, regular checks, usually brown and white or black and white. It is called a shepherd check because (as one theory states) the wool could be taken from white and black sheep and woven without further dyeing.

Tattersall check (*tat*-er-sol chek)   Tattersall checks are an overcheck pattern in two colors, usually on a white or other colored ground. An example is a pattern of brown lines going in one direction, crossed by green lines in the opposite direction, thereby forming the checks on a yellow background. These checks were named for Richard Tattersall who used the pattern on horse blankets. *See* overcheck.

cheesecloth   A sheer, very low count, slackly twisted, loosely woven, plain weave, carded cotton fabric originally used in making cheese. Today, cheesecloth is popular as a polishing cloth because of its softness and economy. The yarn width is called tobacco cloth. From time to time, cheesecloth becomes fashionable for curtains. It is also used for costumes.

chemical finishing processes   Treatments with alkalies, acids, bleaches, starch, resins, and the like.

chenille (shuh-*neel*)   A fabric of silk, wool, cotton, or man-made fibers, woven from fuzzy caterpillar-like (chenille) yarns or tufts. Usually the filling is the chenille yarn and the warp a regular textile yarn. A pile yarn originally made by weaving a pile fabric and subsequently cutting it into strips. Chenille is popular in rugs, bedspreads, and bathroom accessories. It is used for draperies and bedspreads. *See* pile.

chenille blanket   A loosely woven fabric (often cotton warps and large woolen fillings) cut into narrow strips that are pressed in V-shapes.

chenille rug   A floor covering made with chenille (caterpillar) yarn used as a filling. It may be carved. *See* chenille blanket.

chenille yarn   A soft, lofty yarn, somewhat rough in texture. *See* chenille rug.

Chesterfield (*chess*-tur-feeld)   An overcoat adapted from the style worn by Lord Chesterfield. It has a very long skirt, is single- or double-breasted, and may or may not have a velvet collar.

Cheviot (*shev*-ee-ut)   A woolen or worsted, rough-textured fabric in twill weave, originally made of wool from sheep of the Cheviot Hills along the English-Scottish border. It has a slightly rough, napped surface, and is popular at various times, primarily for men's and women's coats.

chevron (*shev*-run)   A design that forms horizontal rows of joined Vs. Also called flame stitch. In effect, chevron fabrics are almost identical to bargello or Florentine embroidery. *See* embroidery.

chiffon (shif-*ahn*)   An extremely sheer, airy, gossamer, lightweight, drapeable, plain-weave crepe fabric, originally made of silk, but now also made from wool, rayon, nylon, and other man-made fibers. It is an open weave with slightly twisted yarns and either soft or stiff finish. Chiffon is usually available in a wide color range from soft pastels to bright bold colors. It is often used for dresses of colored layers (for a rainbow effect), scarves, and handkerchiefs.

chiffon velvet   A lightweight, soft, usually silk fabric with a dense pile.

China silk (*chy*-nuh silk)   A lightweight. soft, plain-weave silk fabric used for lingerie, dress linings, and soft suits. Traditionally, an inexpensive, lightweight, lining fabric. China silk has almost disappeared today and has been replaced with lining fabrics of man-made fibers.

chinchilla (chin-*chil*-uh)   Heavy twill-weave coating that may be all wool or mixed with cotton. Chinchilla cloth has a short, more or less curly surface design (little nubs or tufts of nap), that makes the characteristic surface mock chinchilla fur. It is used primarily as a fabric for coats and jackets.

chinchilla fur (chin-*chil*-uh fur)   A soft bluish-white fur with dark tips. One of the most expensive furs.

chine (*shee*-nay)   This French word, meaning speckled, is used for fabrics in which the warp threads are printed before weaving whereas the filling threads are left plain, giving a shadowy effect to the finished fabric. *See* warp printing.

Chinese rug   A hand-tied oriental rug made in China, often characterized by dragons and flowers in circles.

chino (*chee*-no)   A twill-weave cotton originally used for slacks, sport shirts, and summer military uniforms. It is made of two-ply cotton combed yarns, vat-dyed, and is mercerized and Sanforized. Today, the name is given to any medium-weight, sturdy fabric with a slight sheen. Khaki green and military tan are common chino colors, but the fabric is also made in other colors.

Chinoiserie (sheen-*wah*-zer-ee)   French term denoting designs with Oriental or Chinese design influence.

chintz (chintz)   Any closely woven, plain-weave, glazed cotton and blends of polyester/cotton fabric, often printed in bright designs and gay colors, which are most often floral. It is used for draperies, slipcovers, bedspreads, upholstery, and now mens' and boys' shirts, and ladies' and girls' dresses.

chip straw   Most straw today is used for baskets and handbags of various kinds. Chip straw is used almost exclusively for baskets. It is a by-product of the lumber industry and is made from chips and other pieces of wood, including shavings.

chlorinated wool (*klor*-uh-nayt-id wool)   Woolens chemically treated to decrease shrinkage and to increase affinity for dyes.

chlorine   A quick liquid type of bleach.

chlorine retentive (*klor*-een ree-*ten*-tive)   Term used to describe fibers and fabrics that yellow and lose strength when chlorine bleach is applied to them. Spandex is a chlorine retentive fiber. Chlorine also renders some finishes ineffective.

chrysalis (*kris*-uh-liss)   The dormant silk larva in the cocoon.

chubby   A short, boxy jacket, often made of long-haired fur.

chukka (*chuh*-kuh)   An ankle-high suede or leather boot with a buckle or lace closing and a thick sole. It is generally considered a sport boot.

cinch belt   A stretch elastic belt that fits snugly at the waist; also a wide belt that laces up the front.

circular   A term used to describe both weaving and knitting machines and their finished products. A circular loom or knitting machine produces a tubular fabric, often slit as one of the manufacturing steps, to make it more like flat fabrics.

circular knit   Knitting in tubular form. Shaping is done by tightening or stretching stitches.

cire (*seer*-ay)   An extremely shiny, glossy surface given to fabrics as part of the finishing process. Cire fabrics have a much higher shine than glazed fabrics and are usually somewhat slippery.

C

cisele velvet (*sis*-eh-lay *vel*-vit)   A satin-weave fabric with a pattern of velvet on a sheer ground. It is occasionally imitated by the burn-out method of printing. *See* Jacquard and burn-out printing.

classic   A term applied, quite loosely, to any traditional print, pattern, design, weave, or style considered excellent over a period of years.

clipped-spot design   Ornamental woven effect in which extra filling yarn is shot through at regular intervals in weaving a cloth. The extra filling yarns are floated and later cut between designs. One design consists of several clipped parallel filling yarns.

clips of knitted fabric   New wool; never used or worn in any way.

cloche (klohsh)   A high crowned, close-fitting hat with a very small brim or no brim.

clock   A small decorative design, usually knitted or flocked in a vertical line on the outer ankle of stockings and socks.

clog   A backless shoe with a large slip-on toe portion and thick wood or cork platform.

cloque (*kloh*-kay) Term used to describe a fabric with a raised effect Jacquard, usually knitted from two colors, and often used interchangeably with matelasse and blister. Cotton cloque is frequently popular for summer dress and jacket or coat costumes. *See* blister, matelasse.

cloth   Another term for fabric or material. Implicit in the word cloth and not in the fabric or material is the use of fibers to produce the resulting product.

cluny lace (*kloo*-nee layss)   A heavy lace, often made of thick cotton or man-made fibers using the bobbin method. It is the traditional lace for doilies and place mats, but is also used in apparel. *See* bobbin lace.

clutch   Any purse that does not have handles.

coating   A term used to describe a fabric suitable for outerwear, such as coats, as in coating fabric. Also, something applied to a finished fiber or fabric, such as a rubber coating to make a fabric impervious to water. Coating suggests a thicker layer of the substance than does the word finish. A rubber-coated fabric is probably more resistant to water than one that has been treated with a water-resistant finish.

cocoon   A covering of silk filaments extruded by the silkworm.

cohesiveness   The ability of fibers to adhere to one another in yarn-manufacturing processes.

coin dots   Popular circular designs, usually positioned in a regular pattern on the fabric although the placing may appear random. Sizes usually determine the name of the dots. Coin dots are approximately the size of a nickel or a quarter.

cold water detergent   An agent that cleans and germ-proofs in cold water.

Coloray (*kul*-er-ray)   Trademark of Courtaulds for rayon.

colorfast (*kul*-er-fast)   A term that implies the color in a fabric will not wash out or fade when exposed to sunlight or other atmospheric elements. There are no standards for the use of this term, so it may be relatively meaningless to the consumer.

combination yarn   A ply yarn composed of two or more single yarns of the same or different fibers or twists.

combing (*kohm*-ing)   A process in the manufacture of cotton and manmade yarns in which the fibers are combed to make the fibers parallel in the sliver, and to remove short lengths of fiber, leaving only longer ones. Combed fibers are finer than ones that are not combed. A similar process, called hackling, is used on flax in the course of manufacturing linen. Carding, another similar process, is a first step in refining yarns; combing produces even finer yarns.

comforter (*kum*-fer-ter)   A quilted bed covering filled with down feathers. Also called eiderdown. *See* eiderdown.

completely washable fabric   A fabric washable by machine in water hot enough to clean the fabric efficiently (160 degrees in the tub).

conditioning   A finishing process of sizing a fabric after dyeing to give it a hand.

coney (*koh*-nee)   An inexpensive rabbit fur often dyed to resemble other furs or for fashion impact. Also called lapin.

conjugate-spun fiber (*kahn*-joo-git-spun *fy*-ber)   Distinct polymer compositions in a specific configuration, for example, side-by-side, sheath-core.

construction   The way a cloth is fabricated. Construction includes weaving, knitting, felting, knotting, bonding, braiding, laminating, and so on.

contemporary style   A present style in home furnishings that emphasizes the mobile and functional in furniture.

continuous filament (kon-*tin*-you-us *fil*-ah-mint)   A term emphasizing the long, uncut nature of a filament of fiber, always man-made except in the case of silk. Nylon made in continuous filament form for carpeting wears better than other fiber forms.

contract carpeting   Floor covering in considerable yardage contracted for by motels, bowling alleys, schools, and institutions.

convertible collar   A roll collar (one that rises and then falls at the neck) that can be worn open or closed.

copolymer   A polymer composed of two or more different monomers.

coq (kohk)   A term used to describe feathers, usually fairly short ones, used in trimming.

cord (kord)   A heavy, round string consisting of several strands of thread or yarn twisted or braided together. The result of twisting together ply yarns in a third twisting operation. *See* cording.

cord gimp   Cord gimp combines cord (a round decorative edging) with gimp (an edging that often has small scallops of fine cord along its edges). *See* cording and gimp.

corded fabric (*kord*-id *fab*-rik)   The term corded fabric (often shortened to cord) refers to fabrics with a lengthwise rib, often woven in stripes. Any fabric with a lengthwise rib.

cording   A round decorative edging. The term is also used to describe white cord that can be covered with bias strips of fabric to form welting or piping. *See* welting.

cordovan (*kor*-de-van)   A common name in leather for the hide of an animal with the fur removed.

corduroy (*kor*-duh-roy)   A ribbed, high-luster, cut-pile fabric with extra filling threads that form lengthwise ribs or wales. The rib has been sheared or woven to produce a smooth, velvet-like nap. The thread count varies from 46 x 116 to 70 x 250. Traditionally made of cotton, corduroy can be made of many different fibers, such as rayon and polyester blends. It is used for dresses, coats, sports jackets, sports shirts, bathrobes, slacks, and draperies.

core yarn   A yarn in which a base or foundation yarn is completely wrapped by a second yarn.

cornice (*kor*-niss)   A decorative heading for window draperies, often covered with fabric to match. It has corners and usually juts out into the room. A cornice is often made of wood.

coronizing (*kor*-oh-niz-ing)   A finish for fiberglas that heat-sets the fibers, crimps the yarn, wets the weave, and produces abrasion resistance, color retention, water repellency, and launderability.

C

corselet (*kors*-uhl-et)   A type of girdle with a boned front that extends from above the bust to below the buttocks. Bras may hook onto a girdle.

corset (*kor*-sit)   A heavily boned foundation garment for the torso.

cortex (*kor*-teks)   Cortical cells in the wool fiber consisting of bundles of fibrils.

cotton   A white or yellowish white vegetable fiber from a plant related to the hollyhock, and grown in the United States, Russia, China, India, and other countries. Cotton is the name of the fiber and also the fabric made from the fiber. Different types of cotton plants produce cotton of higher or lower quality, usually associated with staple length and fineness of the fiber. Certain names for these plants are occasionally seen in advertising—Sea Island, Egyptian, and Pima—to indicate quality of the fiber.

cotton gin   The machine that revolutionized cotton production by enabling the removal of seeds from cotton by machine instead of by hand.

cotton knits   Cotton knits are made by the same methods as other knits, although they often are of finer gauge than wool and man-made fiber knits. They are the traditional underwear fabric, but recently have become popular for shirts, dresses, and sportswear. Many cotton knits today include some man-made fiber to reduce shrinkage and give the knit greater stability.

cotton linters   Cotton fibers that are too short for yarn or fabric manufacturing.

count of cloth   Number of picks and ends to the square inch.

count of yarn   Size of yarn as distinguished by its weight and fineness. This term is applied to cotton, wool, and spun yarns.

courses   A series of successive loops or horizontal ridges (components of the loops) lying crosswise in weft knitting.

couture (koo-*tour*)   The business of designing, making, and selling high-fashion, custom-made clothing.

couturier or couturiere (koo-tour-ee-*aye*) or (koo-tour-ee-*ayher*) A dressmaker or designer.

coverlet (*kuhv*-er-let)   Any piece of fabric—such as an afghan or bed-spread—that does not fit closely to the item it is covering, but instead is arranged on or over it casually. *See* afghan or spread.

covert cloth (*koh*-vert kloth)   A medium-heavy cotton or wool fabric in a closely woven warp-face twill weave. It originally had a flecked appearance because one of the ply yarns was white and the other one colored; now it is generally made in solid color (in wool or mixtures). Wool covert may be used for suits, coats, topcoats, sportswear, riding clothing, raincoats, and uniforms. It is very durable and is made in cotton fabrics for work clothes.

cowboy belt   A tooled leather belt that generally has a metal buckle.

cowhide   A common name in leather for the hide of an animal with the fur removed.

cowl neck   A neckline of softly draped fabric.

crabbing   One of the final finishing processes in the manufacture of woolens, similar to heat setting. This finish gives woolens their final appearance. *See* finishing.

crash   A coarse linen, cotton, or rayon fabric with uneven yarns woven in plain weave. It is used in binding books and, occasionally, for dresses, suits, table linens, and draperies.

crease resistant   A term meaning that a fabric has been treated to wrinkle less than it would normally. Fabrics are usually made crease resistant as part of the finishing process. *See* finishing.

crease retention   A fabric's ability to retain or hold folds that have been pressed into the fabric.

crepe (krayp) A lightweight fabric of silk, rayon, cotton, wool, man-made, or blended fibers, and characterized by a crinkled surface. This surface is obtained through the use of crepe yarns (yarns that have such a high twist that the yarn kinks), and by chemical treatment with caustic soda, embossing, or weaving (usually with thicker warp yarns and thinner filling yarns). Although crepe is traditionally woven, crepe yarns are now used to produce knit crepes. *See* finishing.

crepe-backed satin (krayp-bakt *sat*-uhn)   A two-faced fabric that can be used on either side. One is satin whereas the reverse, made of twisted yarns, is crepe.

crepe de Chine (*krayp* duh sheen)   Traditionally, a very sheer, pebbly, washable silk with the fabric degummed to produce crinkle. Today, it is a sheer, flat crepe in silk or man-made fibers. It is used for lingerie, dresses, and blouses.

crepe georgette (krayp jor-*jet*)   A sheer fabric, similar to chiffon, made with a crepe yarn that gives the fabric a crepe appearance. *See* chiffon and crepe.

creping   A chemical or embossing process that, when applied as a finish, gives cloth a crinkled surface.

Creslan (*kres*-lan)   Trademark of American Cyanamid for acrylic fiber.

cretonne (kreh-*tahn*)   A plain-weave, carded cotton fabric, usually printed with large designs. Cretonne is unglazed, and is used for draperies, slipcovers, and other home furnishings.

crew hat   A fabric hat with a crown of four pieces stitched together, a button on top, and a stitched brim.

crew neck   A round, ribbed neckline that rises slightly below the base of the neck.

crewel (*kroo*-uhl)   A type of embroidery which utilizes almost every embroidery stitch and is worked with a fairly thick wool yarn called crewel yarn. The designs are often quite large and often extremely stylized.

crimp (krimp)   The waviness of a fiber, usually visible only under magnification, that affects the final performance. Wool has a natural crimp. Man-made yarns are often crimped during yarn processing. Crimp is desirable because it increases resiliency, absorbancy, and resistance to abrasion. It also adds bulk and warmth to the final fabric.

crimped yarn   A textured yarn made from man-made fibers that have been crimped to resemble wool.

crinkle crepe (*krink*-uhl krayp)   A fabric with an uneven surface, created by use of caustic soda that causes it to shrink unevenly. Plisse is an example of a crinkle crepe fabric. Crinkle crepe and plisse usually have a larger pattern to surface irregularities than crepe. *See* plisse and seersucker.

C

crinoline (*krin*-uh-lin)   Although crinoline is used as a term for a stiff, bouffant petticoat, designed to support a very full skirt, strictly speaking, it refers to the fabric from which these petticoats are made—a stiff, open fabric heavily sized in the finishing process. Originally, crinoline was made of linen and horsehair but today, any fiber such as nylon may be used.

crisp fabric   A comparative, descriptive term used as the opposite of soft fabrics. Organdy is a typical crisp fabric. Crisp fabrics stand away from the figure and have more body than soft fabrics.

crochet (kroh-*shay*)   A method of making fabric in which one yarn and one needle are used to form loops into which other loops are inserted. True crochet is a handcraft. Machine-made crochets are usually knitted on raschel machines.

crochet knit   Machine-knitted tie fabric made to resemble hand knitting.

crocheted lace (kroh-*shayd* layss)   Lace made with a single yarn. A crochet hook is used to form loops that are joined to other loops to form the design. It is used for bedspreads and table covers.

crock   Technical term that describes the way in which dye on the surface of a fabric rubs off onto other fabrics or skin. In some fabrics, such as colored suede leathers, crocking is unavoidable.

crock meter   A standard device for testing a fabric's fastness to crocking.

crocodile   A common name in leather for the hide of the animal.

cross stitch   One of the most common embroidery stitches.

cross-dyeing (krawss *dy*-ing)   A method of coloring fabrics made from more than one kind of fiber, for example, a wool and cotton blend. Each fiber in a fabric designed for cross-dyeing takes a specific dye in a different color or in variations of a color. A fabric that is cross-dyed is more than one color. Cross-dyeing is often used to create heather effects (soft, misty colorings), but strongly patterned fabrics can also be achieved, depending on the fibers used in the fabric.

crystal pleating   Narrow, shallow pleats that resemble small ripples; often used for sheer, dressy fabrics.

cuff   The turned-back fold at the bottom of a sleeve or a trouser leg.

culotte (koo-*lot*)   A skirt that is divided and seamed into two sections, one for each leg.

cultivated silk   Fibers from a silkworm that have had scientific care.

cummerbund (*kum*-muhr-bund)   A wide fabric belt that fastens in the back, and is worn with a tuxedo evening suit.

Cupioni (koo-pee-*oh*-nee)   Trademark of Beaunit for a slubbed cuprammonium rayon fiber. *See* rayon.

cuprammonium rayon (kyou-pre-*moh*-nee-um *ray*-on)   Rayon made by a process that allows very fine filament fibers to be formed by dissolving cellulose in ammoniacal copper oxide, extruding the solution, and hardening. The fineness of its filaments is its best-known characteristic.

curing (*kyoor*-ing)   The application of heat to a fabric or garment to impart properties, such as dimensional stability, crease resistance, water repellency, and durable press.

curled yarn   A textured yarn made by a heated blade that curls the filaments.

curtains and draperies (*kur*-tenz and *dray*-per-eez)   Curtains are a window covering, usually unlined, that hang within the framework of the window, ending at the windowsill. They are decorative and functional at the same time. Draperies are almost always lined, and are usually made of fairly heavy fabrics that are often quite luxurious, such as satin or velvet. They normally hang to the floor, but in very formal rooms, may even lie on the floor. Curtains and draperies can be made of almost any fabric, and fabrics made of glass fiber are extremely popular. "Drapes" is an abbreviation for draperies, commonly used instead of the longer word. Following are specific types of curtains and draperies.

Brussels curtains (*bruhs*-selz *kur*-tenz)   Curtains made of net with an embroidered design, either by hand or machine, over the net. The net may be one layer or two.

café curtains (ka-*fay kur*-tenz)   Curtains that are hung in tiers, so that one row covers the top half of a window, a second row the bottom. They are hung on a wood or metal pole placed across the top and center of the window. Café curtains are often finished with scalloped edges through which the pole slides, or there are café curtain rings available for hanging them. These curtains are usually hung only in two tiers, but may be hung in any number.

glass fibers (glass *fy*-berz)   Curtains made of glass fiber yarns. Sheer glass fiber curtains are often used behind draperies, but glass fiber curtains are also available in heavier, opaque fabric constructions. Glass fiber curtains should be washed carefully by hand and hung to dry while they are still wet. *See* fiberglas.

tie-backs (ty-baks)   A full length (either to the windowsill or to the floor) curtain or drapery looped back at the side of the window with a band of trimming or self-fabric. The curtain or drapery is closed at the top of the window, and almost entirely open at the point of the tie-back. The look is popular in informal houses in fabrics such as organdy and batiste, and in formal houses in luxurious fabrics.

cushion (*kuhsh*-uhn)   *See* pillow. *See also* padding (for rugs and carpets).

cut   Number of needles per inch on the circular bed of a weft-knitting machine.

cut pile   Many fabrics are formed with loops on the surface. When these are cut, they form a cut pile. Some velvets and many pile rugs are made in this manner. *See* pile.

cut velvet or beaded velvet   One method of making cloth using double cloth construction in which two layers of fabric are woven with long threads joining them. After the double fabric is woven, the center threads that join them are cut, thereby producing two pieces of velvet.

cut-and-sewn   A description of how certain knit garments are made. A cut-and-sewn knit garment is made by cutting the garment pieces from a piece of knit fabric and then stitching the pieces together. The other method of making knit garments is full-fashioned. *See* full-fashioned.

cylinder printing (*sil*-en-der *print*-ing)   A synonym for roller printing, perhaps the most important method of printing used today. The design is etched onto a roller through which the fabric is passed. For each color in the design a different roller is used. High speed is obtained in cylinder printing. *See* calender and roller printing.

Defect	Explanation	Severity
Chafe Mark	An abrasion or chafe mark where the surface of the cloth has been damaged by some friction. Causes include improper setting or action of the sand roller, temples, reed, or harnesses on the loom; poor fabric handling also gives a chafe mark. This effects the dyeability, and often results in warp streaks or filling bands.	Minor
Chopped Filling	An unevenness in the filling direction characterized by a distinct or measured pattern resulting from the eccentric behavior of a drafting roll.	Major
Clip Marks	Enlarged pinholes, tears, and "shift marks" that run along the selvage areas of the cloth. Caused by improper framing of the piece goods or a defect in the clips or pins of the tenter frame as it brings the cut of cloth to the proper width.	Major
Cloudy Goods	Material that is off-shade because of uneven dyeing and faulty finishing of the goods.	Major
Coarse Ends	Ends whose diameter is noticeably greater than that normal to the fabric. This results from poor dressing of the warp yarn on the loom beam, slippages, poor creeling or winding, or from trouble in the spinning frame, such as belt slippages, improper tensions, loose spindle banding, and so forth.	Usually Minor, but can be Major
Cockled Fabric	In knits, crinkled, shriveled, or ridgy fabric that will not lie flat on the cutting table. May be caused by irregular twist in the yarns, uneven tension during knitting, or varying degrees of reaction by the yarns in the fabric to the finishing processes.	Major

Defect	Explanation	Severity
Cockled Yarn	A yarn in which some fibers appear wild or tightly curled and disoriented. This results from some fibers being too long for draft roll settings. The succeeding roll grips the fiber before the preceding roll releases it, causing the fiber to snap and curl. Cockled yarn often appears as tiny slubs in the fabric.	Usually Minor, but can be Major
Cockling	An uneven shrinking that causes the cloth to become blistered or "corduroyed." Cockling may also arise because of the unevenness of the stock used, especially cotton, wool, reworked wool, reused wool, and sometimes rayon. The blend, if the material is of this structure, has very likely been poorly prepared. Faulty designing can also cause cockling because of the improper dispersement in the length of the floats in the pattern.	Major
Color Fly	Fibers of a different color appearing in a yarn or fabric as contamination.	Minor (but can be Major)
Color Misdraw	In wovens, the drawing of colored yarns through the loom harness contrary to the color pattern and/or weave design. In warp knits, the drawing of colored yarns through the guide bars contrary to the pattern design.	Major
Color Out	In printing, when the color paste runs low in the reservoir, resulting in blank skips in the print pattern.	Major
Color Smear	In printing, when the color is smeared, distorting the pattern.	Major
Compactor Crease	In knits, hard set creases resulting from the introduction of wrinkled fabric into the shrinking control and stabilization process.	Major
Corrugation	A washboard effect resulting from a malfunctioning sanforizer blanket	Major

Defect	Explanation	Severity
Cover	A term used to describe the face of a fabric in relation to the amount of warp of filling-show, prominence of design, or other desired characteristic achieved by varying the influence of one or the other of the two yarn systems.	Major
Crack	An open streak that runs parallel to the filling, and may run for the entire width of the cloth. Often caused by the beating in action for the filling pick functioning when no pick has been inserted through the shed of the loom.	Major
Crease Mark and Crease Streak	Differs from crease streak in that the streak will probably appear for the entire roll. Crease mark appears where creases are caused by fabric folds in the finishing process. On napped fabric, final pressing may not be able to restore fabric to original condition. Often, discoloration is a problem.	Major
Crease Streak	Occurs in tubular knits. Results from creased fabric passing through squeeze rollers in dyeing process.	Major or Minor depending on product
Creases	Caused by an uneven tension and tautness when the goods pass through the wet and dry finishing departments of the mill. Often caused by carelessness on the part of some worker. Creases must be combatted in the finishing so that the fabric will have eye appeal. They are very difficult to remove altogether.	Major
Crocking	Caused by dyestuff coming off the material in the form of powder or granules. The excess coloring matter rubs, flakes, or chips off because of improper penetration or fixation of the dyestuff.	Major or Minor depending on how high on Chromatic Scale

Defect	Explanation	Severity
Crowsfoot	Small, indistinct, or mottled markings on printed, dyed, or other finished goods; often caused by carelessness on the part of some operator.	Minor
Cut Selvage or Listing	One that has been cut in the shearing of the goods or damaged by the weaver, and allowed to go for some distance in the cloth without being remedied. Cut selvage ends should be fixed at once.	Minor

Dacron (*day*-kron)   Trademark of DuPont for polyester fiber.

damask (*dam*-usk)   A glossy, heavy, firm-textured Jacquard weave fabric, similar to brocade, but lighter, with flat and reversible patterns. It is made of silk, linen, cotton, rayon or a combination of fibers in double or single damask. It is used for tablecloths, napkins, home furnishings, draperies and upholsteries, and occasionally clothing, such as afternoon and evening dresses.

darn   A form of embroidery normally used to repair worn spots in fabric, the darn is occasionally used for the sake of novelty. A darn is formed by making a series of long stitches in one direction covering the area to be darned. Another thread is woven over and under these long stitches to form the finished darn.

decating   A process for setting the luster on wool, silk, spun silk, and rayons.

décolletté (day-cohl-uh-*tay*) An extremely low-cut neckline.

decorative fabrics (*dek*-uh-rah-tiv *fab*-riks)   A term used to describe fabrics for upholstery, slipcovers, curtains, and draperies. These fabrics are usually of heavier weights than the fashion fabrics used in clothing. Also called decorator fabrics and home furnishing fabrics.

decorator fabrics (*dek*-er-ay-tor *fab*-riks)   Another name for decorative fabrics and home furnishing fabrics.

defoliation (dee-foh-lee-*ay*-shun)   Chemical treatment of cotton plants to make them shed their leaves.

degumming   A process for removing natural gum from silk by boiling it in a soap solution.

delamination (dee-*lam*-uh-nay-shun)   The separation of the layers of fabric in bonded goods.

delavé (*day*-lah-vay)   French word for "washed out" that applies to jeans. When jeans became popular all over the world, the bleached jeans became popular, too. American buyers importing jeans from France into America picked up the word delavé and used it in preference to the word bleached. *See* jeans.

delinting   Mechanically removing short fuzzy fibers from cotton seeds.

D

delustered fibers   Those fibers permanently dulled by incorporating mineral oil or microscopic solids in the spinning solution. When delustered, fibers are said to be pigmented, for example, pigment taffeta.

delustering (dee-*lust*-er-ing)   A process that dulls the characteristic shine of man-made fibers. Particles of a chemical are added to the fiber mixture before it is spun. This results in fibers with softer, muted color tones.

denier (*den*-year)   A technical term referring to a unit of yarn number equal to the weight in grams of 9000 meters of the yarn. It is used for silk and man-made yarns in hosiery as a description of sheerness.The lower the denier number, the more sheer the stocking, panty hose, or garment. For instance, 40 denier hose are much finer and more sheer than 60 denier hose.

denim   A cotton twill weave fabric made of single hard-twisted yarns. The staple type has colored warp and white or undyed filling thread. When the fabric (and the look) became popular, the name denim was given to many other types of fabric, including cross-dyed fabrics and brushed fabrics, both knit and woven, that resemble true denim. Most jeans are made of denim and the most popular and traditional denim color is blue. Sports denim is softer and lighter in weight. It is now available in many colors, and in plaids and stripes. Woven-in stripes and plaids are popular for draperies, upholstery, and bedspreads.

derby (or bowler)   A man's hat (occasionally adapted for women) with a round crown and a small, rolled-up brim.

design   The choice and arrangement of shapes or forms and color to produce a decorative effect.

details   The various elements that give a garment its form or shape, including shoulder, sleeve, and waist treatments, pant and skirt length and width, trimmings, and so forth.

detergent (dih-tur-*jent*) An agent or solvent used for cleansing fabrics. The term was originally applied to soap, soap savers, and softeners. At present, the term connotes washing products called synthetic detergents, that are organic chemicals.

developed dye A type of dye in which one color may be changed by use of a developer. The intensity of the color and the fastness of the dyestuff may also be changed by this treatment.

D

diamanté (dee-ah-*mahn*-tay) Another word for rhinestone. *See* rhinestone.

dimensional stability The degree to which a fiber, yarn, or fabric retains its shape and size after having been subjected to wear and maintenance.

dimity (*dim*-uh-tee) Literally, double thread; a fine checked or ribbed lightweight, moderately sheer fabric with ribs spaced at regular intervals, either in crosswise stripes or in crossbars. It is made by bunching and weaving two or more threads together and often has fine woven stripes or other patterns such as small flowers. This fabric was traditionally made of cotton but now is often made of man-made fibers. It is used primarily for dresses and curtains. Dimity is used for children's summer dresses, blouses, bedspreads, and curtains.

dip dyeing A process of piece dyeing hosiery or other knitted goods after construction.

direct designing A trial-and-error method in the use of yarns of different fibers and blends to create a visual design. It is done directly on a hand-loom with no point-paper pattern.

direct dye A type of dye with an affinity for most fibers. It has poor resistance to washing.

direct printing (duh-*rekt print*-ing) Application of color by passing the cloth over a series of rollers engraved with the designs. Developed direct dyes have good resistance to washing. *See* roller, calender, and cylinder printing.

discharge printing (*dis*-charj *print*-ing) A method of obtaining light designs on a very dark ground. The fabric is piece dyed first, then the color is discharged or bleached in spots, leaving white designs in a pattern. An additional step is often the roller printing of these design areas with patterns and colors. *See* dyeing.

D

dish towels One of the few textile products still made of linen. Although occasionally they are made of cotton or even paper. Dish towels are used for hand-drying dishes after washing. Many linen dish towels are made in Ireland and printed with colorful pictures. Dish towels can also be made of terry cloth and huck toweling. *See* terry cloth and huck.

disperse dyes Dispersions of colors or pigments in water, and originally known as acetate dyes. At present, these dyes are also used to color the newer synthetic fibers.

dobby (*dahb*-ee) A dobby fabric is one with small geometric figures incorporated into the weave, and is made with a dobby attachment on the loom. Less elaborate than a Jacquard attachment, which also produces geometric designs, the dobby is used to produce geometric designs such as those found in piqué fabrics. *See* piqué.

doeskin (*doh*-skin) Today, usually the skin of a white sheep, although originally it was the skin of a deer, hare, or rabbit. Also used for any fabric made of wool or man-made fibers with a soft, often napped, finish. *See* leather.

dolman sleeve (*dohl*-muhn sleev) A sleeve that is very wide at the armhole and gradually narrows to fit tightly at the wrist; it is often cut in one piece with the rest of the garment. An extremely full-cut dolman sleeve is sometimes called a batwing.

domestic rugs Floor coverings manufactured in the United States.

domestic wools From the eastern and middle-western states.

domestics (doh-*mes*-tiks) A classification of textile merchandise, used by retail stores, that includes towels, table covers, and all bed coverings. Domestics are also items made in the United States. *See* linens and domestics.

Donegal tweed (*dohn*-eh-gahl tweed) Originally a thick woolen homespun fabric woven by hand by Irish peasants in County Donegal, Ireland. Today, the term is used to refer to any tweed in plain weave characterized by thick, colorful slubs woven into the fabric. *See* tweed.

dope dyeing (dohp *dy*-ing) The process of coloring a man-made fiber before it is solidified or spun while at the syrupy or melted stage. Also called solution dyeing and spun dyeing.

dots   A popular circular design, usually positioned in a regular pattern on the fabric, although the placing may appear random. Dots may be woven, knitted, or printed. Sizes usually determine the name of the dots. Aspirin dots, for example, are the size of an aspirin tablet and are also called polka dots. Coin dots are approximately the size of a nickel or quarter. Swiss dots are ones that look like those on dotted Swiss, whereas pin dots are extremely small.

D

dotted Swiss   Swiss is a fine, sheer fabric of almost any fiber whose name has been almost forgotten except in the form of dotted Swiss. Dotted Swiss is this fabric with very small dots on it, often woven in. The dots, however, may be flocked, clipped spot, swivel dots, or even printed, colored, or white. Dotted Swiss is used for children's party dresses, women's summer dresses, lingerie, and curtains. Some knitted fabrics, made with a thread on the surface that forms a dot, are also called dotted Swiss, although they are not the traditional Swiss fabric.

double backing   Formed when a second layer of latex is coated to a backing into which carpet yarns are tufted. *See* backing.

double cloth   A double cloth fabric is made of two fabrics woven one above the other and joined at the center with threads. A true double cloth can be split into two distinct layers of fabric by cutting the threads between the layers. Velvet is often made as a double cloth and then cut to form the pile.

double damask (*duh*-buhl *dam*-usk)   A rich traditional tablecloth, made in a heavier weight than ordinary damask.

double face   A double cloth which can be used on either side. Also used to describe any fabric with two right sides.

double knit (*duh*-buhl nit)   1. Fabric knitted on circular machines with two sets of cylindrically disposed needles, each set placed and operating at a right angle to the other. 2. A fabric made on a weft knitting machine. Both sides are usually identical with a characteristic fine vertical wale unless the fabric has a pattern.

double weave   Two cloths are woven at the same time, face to face. Two sets of warps and two sets of fillings are used. One set of warps binds the two cloths together. The two cloths may or may not be cut apart. *See* backed cloth.

double yarn and twist yarn   A two-ply yarn made from single yarns of different colors. A mottled effect is produced.

double-breasted   A garment that overlaps in front with two rows of buttons to close it.

double-faced satin (*duh*-buhl-fayst sat-uhn) A satin fabric that has the satin appearance on both sides, unlike ordinary satin that has a definite right and wrong side.

D

doupion (*doo*-pee-ahn)   Silk that comes from the fiber formed by two silk worms who spun their cocoons together in an interlocking manner. The yarn is uneven, irregular, and larger than regular filaments. It is used to make shantung and doupioni. Also called douppioni, dupion, and dupioni.

down   The softest, shortest feathers of birds are called down. Types of down include eiderdown, originally only from ducks, but now used to refer to any very soft feathers. The term also describes a feather-filled bed covering and goose down.

drapeable fabric (*drayp*-uh-buhl *fab*-rik)   A descriptive term for fabrics that are soft and flowing, tend to cling somewhat to the body, and can be arranged in soft gathers. Drapeable fabrics are made from a variety of yarns and in a variety of ways, including knitting and weaving. They must be fairly lightweight to drape properly.

draperies   Curtains that are almost always lined, and usually made of fairly heavy, often quite luxurious, fabrics such as satin or velvet. Draperies normally hang to the floor, but in very formal rooms, they may lie on the floor. Draperies can be made of almost any fabric. Fabrics made of glass fiber are extremely popular for window coverings as curtains or draperies. Drapes is an abbreviation for draperies, commonly used instead of the longer word.

drawing   The process by which slivers of natural fibers are pulled out or extended after carding or combing. It is attenuating a sliver until it becomes narrower and narrower. Drawing is synonymous with drafting.

drawstring   Any material such as cord or ribbon, inserted into a casing or hem, and pulled to form a smaller opening with gathers.

drill   A heavy, strong, durable twilled fabric of cotton or man-made fibers, similar to denim, that has a diagonal 2x1 weave running up to the left selvage. When strength of fabric is essential, drill is suitable for slacks, uniforms, overalls, and work shirts. *See* twill.

drip-dry   A method of drying a fabric without wringing or squeezing. The term drip-dry was used at one time as a synonym for durable press. After a garment has been cleansed and rinsed, it is hung directly on a hanger. Every care is taken not to wrinkle it so that it will drip and dry with no wrinkles, thus reducing ironing to only a touch-up.

driving glove   A short leather, or knit and leather, glove that has extra stitching and ventilating holes; originally designed for driving, it has now been adapted to accessorize a total sportswear look.

drop   A term that generally refers to the length between the chest and waist measurements on men's jackets. Traditional suit jackets typically have a six-inch drop, whereas designer suit jackets have a seven-inch drop.

drop waist   A dress waist seam that falls below the waistline.

drop-stitch knit   Open design made by removing certain needles at intervals.

drugget (*drug*-it)   A coarse, felted floor covering made from mixtures of such fibers as cotton, jute, wool, and cow's hair. Drugget is usually napped on one side and is a traditionally inexpensive floor covering used in institutions, sun porches, and summer cottages.

dry cleaning   A method of removing soil from certain fabrics done with organic solvents instead of water.

dry decating   A process of setting the luster of a wool fabric.

dry spinning   A derivative to be spun is dissolved in a solvent that can be evaporated, leaving the desired filament to be hardened by drying in warm air.

drying   One of the finishing processes in the manufacture of fabrics. A great deal of water is used in the course of making fabrics, and drying is important to remove the water. Fabrics dried at too high a temperature for too long a time become harsh, so drying is carefully watched. *See* finishing.

duchesse satin (du-*shess sat*-uhn)   One of the heaviest and richest look-ing satins. It is important for such formal clothing as wedding gowns.

duck   Originally, a fabric lighter in weight than canvas. Today, the terms are synonymous. A durable plain-weave, closely woven cotton, gen-erally made of ply yarns, in a variety of weights and thread counts. It is used for uniforms, belts, awnings, tents, and sails. *See* canvas.

D

duffel bag   A cylindrical soft bag (usually canvas or leather) with short or long handles.

duffel cloth   A thick, heavy, napped coating fabric, usually used for duf-fel coats, hooded coats with wooden buttons that fasten through rope or leather thongs. Duffel cloth is traditionally tan or green, but can be any color.

dungaree (*duhn*-guh-ree)   A heavy, coarse cotton or blended, blue denim fabric woven from colored yarns. It is heavier than jean and used for work clothes. The term dungaree is occasionally used as a synonym for denim and the term dungarees are synonymous for the pants known as blue jeans. *See* jean.

dupion, dupioni (*doo*-pee-ahn, *doo*-pee-oh-nee)   *See* doupion.

duplex printing (*doo*-pleks *print*-ing)   A method of printing the same de-sign on both sides of the fabric to give the design additional defini-tion and clarity of color. Also called register printing.

durable finish (*door*-uh-buhl *fin*-ish)   A rather loose term for a finish added to fabric as one of the final steps to improve the "wearability" of the fabric.

durable press (*door*-uh-buhl press)   A measure of garment performance that describes a fabric or garment treated so that it should not re-quire ironing. There are two methods of creating true durable press garments: pre-curing and post-curing. In pre-curing, a chemical resin is applied to the fabric. It is dried and then cured (baked at a high temperature). In post-curing, the resin is added to the fabric, the fabric is made into the garment, and the garment is then pressed and cured. Features of durable press include shape retention, dur-able pleats and pressed creases, durable smooth seams, machine washability and dryability, wrinkle resistance, and fresh appearance without ironing.

dust ruffle   Dust ruffles were originally detachable, wide ruffles at the bottom of women's floor-length skirts that could be removed for washing before the rest of the garment. Dust ruffles are now found almost exclusively on bedspreads or as separate ruffles placed over the box spring. They can be removed for cleaning separate from the bedspread. *See* spread.

D

duvetyn (*doo*-veh-teen)   A high quality cloth that resembles a compact velvet. It has a velvety hand resulting from the short nap that covers its surface completely, concealing its twill weave. It is used for suits and coats.

dyeing   A process of coloring garments, fibers, yarns, or fabrics with either natural or synthetic dyes, or the solution from which the fiber is made. Common dyeing methods include the following entries:

batik (bah-*teek*)   A form of resist dyeing using wax. *See* resist dyeing.

cross dyeing   Refers to a method of coloring fabric made of more than one fiber. The different fibers or types of fiber take the dye in different ways, producing special effects, such as heathers or patterns.

dope dyeing (dohp *dy*-ing)   In dope dyeing, the solution for man-made fiber is colored before making it into fiber. Also called solution dyeing and spun dyeing.

piece dyeing   The dyeing of a finished fabric. Cross-dyeing is a type of piece dyeing. *See* cross-dyeing.

resist dyeing   In resist dyeing, areas that are to be colored are left exposed to the dye, whereas other areas, not to be colored, are covered with something impervious to dye. Batik is a form of resist dyeing in which wax is used to cover the area where dye is not wanted.

solution dyeing   *See* dope dyeing.

spun dyeing   *See* dope dyeing.

tie dyeing   A form of resist dyeing. Items to be dyed are tied or knotted so that the folds of the fabric form barriers to the dye to create patterns or designs on the fabric.

vat dyeing (vat *dy*-ing)   Vat dyeing refers to the type of dye rather than to the way in which the dyeing is done. Vat dyes are oxidized after they combine with the fibers to form the color, and are considered more wash-fast than most other dyes.

yarn dyeing   In yarn dyeing, fiber already made into yarn to be used for the manufacture of fabric is dyed, usually on a spool, under heat and pressure. Yarn-dyed fabrics are considered more colorfast than piece-dyed fabrics or fabrics that are printed.

D

Dynel (dy-*nel*)   Trademark of Union Carbide for modacrylic fiber.

Defect	Explanation	Severity
Damaged	The condition of a fabric rendered unusable.	Major
Dead Colors	Decorations or motifs that have been deadened, killed, or subdued during the scouring, or other more or less rigid treatments in finishing. If cotton colors, for example, have been used in woolens and worsteds, or in blended fabrics, they may be brought back to life by the use of a mild scouring treatment. If wool colors were used, an ammonia bath would likely brighten the colors and tend to bring them back to normal.	Major
Dirty or Soiled Ends	Obvious as to origin; usually caused by soiled, dirty, or old harnesses or reeds.	Minor
Doctor Streaks	Seen on printed goods as narrow, oscillating, lengthwise streaks, they occur because of some irregularity of the doctor blade on the printing machine. This is a metal scraper-blade on the frame that removes the excess color from the engraved print roll before it comes in contact with material.	Major
Double End	The result of wrong drawing-in of two or more warp ends, usually drawing an extra end through the heddle eye where there should be only one end. The effect is also observed by a swollen dent in the reed where there are more ends in the split than there should be. Forms a "flat effect" or out-of-line effect in the warp direction	Major or Minor (depending on severity)
Double Pick	This is the result of two filling picks working into the same shed in the loom weaving (where only one is called for by the design of the fabric), and causes a sort of ribbed effect in the filling, readily noted when the cloth is perched after being taken from the loom. A double-pick often occurs when	Major or Minor (depending on severity)

Defect	Explanation	Severity
	the weaver starts up the loom after attending to some error in the weaving of the goods. Carelessness is often the cause of this type of faulty pick.	
Doubling	A filling yarn twice the normal size because of two ends of roving running together into a single end of spinning. The same occurrence in warp yarn results in a coarse end.	Major
Dragging End	In warp knits, an end knitted under erratic tension because of being entangled and/or trapped on the warp beam.	Major
Drawbacks	Caused by excessive loom tension gradually applied to a number of warp yarns by some abnormal restriction. When the restriction is removed, the excess slack is woven into the fabric. Usually the ends are broken.	Major
Drop Ply	Yarn that does not have the correct or uniform number of plies; caused by faulty twisting or mixed bobbins, warp, or filling.	Major
Dropped Pick	Caused by the filling insertion mechanism on a shuttleless loom of not holding and releasing the filling yarn. This allows the yarn to snap into the body, leaving a missing pick part-way across the width of the fabric. The released pick is then woven into the fabric in a somewhat tangled mass. The filling yarn appears "kinky." There are also areas of "endout."	Major
Dropped Stitches (or Run)	Results from malfunctioning needle or jack. Appears as holes or missing stitches.	Major
Dye Streak	An irregular stain, or dispersed color stripe, or area in the cloth. Faulty dyeing, foreign matter in the dye, or defective or irregularly set guide bars or rollers in the dye bath cause these streaks.	Major

Defect	Explanation	Severity
Dye Streak in Printing	Results from a damaged doctor blade or a blade not cleaned properly. Usually appears as a long streak until the operator notices the problem.	Major
Dyestain	Any discoloration on a cloth caused by faulty dyeing, poor handling, foreign matter in the dye, or poor timing in drying as relates to time and temperature.	Major or Minor (depending on severity)

GARMENT AND TEXTILES

easy care (*ee*-zee kehr)   An extremely loose term implying that a limited amount of ironing will be necessary after the item is washed. Easy care fabrics seem to be most successful when they are made of at least 65% polyester, or have had a special finish applied to them. Durable press is a more reliable indication that garments or other items require little or no ironing.

Egyptian cotton (ee-*jip*-shun *kot*-uhn)   A fine, long, staple cotton generally grown in Egypt along the Nile Delta. Egyptian cotton fibers average more than $1^1/_2$ inches in length and produce a strong, lustrous yarn. *See* cotton.

eiderdown (*eye*-der-down)   The softest, shortest feathers, originally only from ducks, but used today to refer to any very soft feathers.The term also refers to a feather-filled bed covering and goose down.

elastic (ih-*las*-tik)   The word elastic implies stretch, recovery, and spring (a certain amount of bounce). For years, the word was limited to items made of rubber, but in recent years man-made elastics (anidex, spandex) have been developed. Woven elastic and braided elastic in fairly narrow widths are used in clothing on edges where it is desirable to have a certain degree of stretch and recovery. Woven elastic remains the same width when it is stretched; braided elastic becomes narrower when stretched.

elastic recovery   The ability of a fiber, yarn, or fabric to return to its original length after the tension that produced the elongation is released.

elastique (ih-las-*teek*)   A firmly woven, clear-finished worsted with a steep double twill that is used for riding breeches, army uniforms, and slacks. It is similar to cavalry twill.

elongation (ee-lawn-*gay*-shun)   The amount of stretch or extension that a fiber, yarn, or fabric will accept.

embossing (im-*bawss*-ing)   A method of producing an indented design on a fabric. Embossing usually is done with a heated roller with a raised section that forms the design as part of the finishing process. Today, it is mostly permanent, if heat-set. *See* finishing.

E

embroidery (im-*broyd*-er-ee)   The term for a group of decorative, usually ornamental and nonfunctional needlework done with thread or yarn on fabric. Most machine embroidery is done by the Schiffli machine which can imitate many different hand embroidery stitches. Although embroidery is usually thought of as being done in several colors, white work (white embroidery on white fabric) and black work (black embroidery on white fabric) are fairly common. Embroidery terms are tremendously variable, with different words being given to the same stitches in different countries, and even different sections of the same countries. Some of the most common embroidery stitches are beading, buttonhole stitch, chain stitch, chevron stitch, satin stitch, stem stitch, back stitch, and straight stitch.

embroidery floss (im-*broyd*-er-ee flawss)   A fine, low twist yarn made of silk, rayon, cotton, or man-made fibers used for embroidery. *See* thread.

embroidery thread (im-*broyd*-er-ee thred)   A fairly loose term for a thread used in embroidery. Buttonhole twist is often referred to as embroidery thread. *See* thread.

Encron (*en*-kron)   Trademark of American Enka Company for polyester fiber.

end-to-end   A colored warp yarn alternating with a white warp yarn; fillings are white. There is end-to-end broadcloth and end-to-end chambray, frequently sold as end-to-end madras. It is synonymous with end-on-end or end-and-end.

envelope purse   A flat, rectangular, or square purse with a folded flap opening; the size is variable. It may be clutch or have handles.

enzyme (*en*-zym)   Organic catalyst used to speed soil removal from a fabric, and to speed decomposition of starch during desizing of fabric preparatory to dyeing or finishing.

epaulet (*ehp*-uh-let) An elongated tab used at the shoulder (from neck to top of arm) as decorative trim.

espadrille (*ehs*-puh-dril) A canvas shoe with a thick braided rope sole.

ester (*ess*-tur) A technical chemical term for a compound formed by substituting a hydrocarbon radical for the hydrogen of an acid.

even plaid A plaid in which the arrangement of stripes is the same both on the cross and on the length of the grain. Also called balanced plaid.

even twill Filling passes over the same number of warps it passes under.

Everglaze (*eh*-ver-glayz) Trademark of Bancroft Licensing for certain finishes, most notably a permanent glazed finish applied to chintz.

extract printing (*eks*-trakt *print*-ing) Another name for discharge printing. *See* discharge printing.

extra-long-staple cotton Fibers $1^3/_8$" and longer.

eyelash Term used to describe clipped yarns that lie on the surface of a fabric, giving the effect of eyelashes.

eyelet (*eye*-lit) Fabrics embroidered with openwork patterns created with holes that are reinforced with buttonhole stitches. The entire fabric is called eyelet and it comes in various widths, from narrow widths trimming to wide widths for entire garments. White eyelet embroidery on a white ground is also called Broderie Anglaise, but other color combinations for eyelet embroidery are also used. The term eyelet is also used to refer to the holes in open knitted fabrics.

Defect	Explanation	Severity
End Out	1. Caused by a warp end that has snapped or broken (and loom continued to run) in weaving of cloth, thereby causing a light area or thin line to appear in the fabric. This streak effect is quickly noted on inspection. The ends that have become broken are sewn into the fabric by the sewers or experienced sewers in the dry-finishing department of the mill, if the blemish cannot be fixed by the weaver.	Major
	2. Occurs in warp knit. Results from the knitting machine continuing to run with missing end.	Usually Major

fabric   A material formed of fiber or yarns, either by the interlacing method of weaving, by the interlooping of knitting, by braiding, felting, bonding, laminating, or even nonwoven material, including not only cloth but also hosiery and lace. Fabric is also referred to as cloth, goods, material, and stuff.

fabric softeners   Chemical solutions added to the final rinse to improve the hand of terry cloths and infants' fabrics.

face (fayss)   The right side of the fabric; the side of the fabric meant to be seen.

face cloth   A piece of terry toweling, usually square in shape. It is used to wash the face and body and may also be called a wash cloth.

face-finished fabric   A fabric finished (napped or brushed, for example) only on the right side. *See* finishing.

faconne velvet (*fass*-oh-nay *vel*-vit)   A cut velvet made by the burn-out method of printing. *See* cut velvet. *See also* burn-out printing.

fade-ometer (fayd-*ahm*-uh-tur)   A standard laboratory device for testing a fabric's fastness to sunlight.

faille (fyl)   A soft, slightly glossy silk, rayon, acetate, cotton, wool, or a mixture of these, in a rib weave, that has a light, flat, narrow crosswise rib or cord. It is made by using heavier yarns in the filling than in the warp, and has more ribs to the inch than bengaline. Ottoman is similar to faille but has a wider rib. Faille is considered a dressy fabric, and is used for evening clothes, tailored dresses, coats, suits, ties, handbags, shoes, and draperies. *See* ottoman.

faille crepe   A silk, rayon, acetate, or other man-made fiber dress fabric with a decided wavy (crepe) cord fillingwise. It is used for negligees, blouses, daytime and evening dresses, handbags, and trims.

F

fake fur   A slang term for pile fabrics and garments that imitate animal pelts. The most popular fake furs are probably those made from modacrylic fiber. *See* modacrylic and pile.

false fur   Another term for fake fur. *See* fake fur.

fashion fabric (*fash*-un *fab*-rik)   A general term describing any fabric made into apparel. The term is also used as a name for material sold to the consumer by the yard. Fabrics used in home furnishings are not fashion fabrics but decorative fabrics. *See* decorative fabrics.

fashioning   A shaping process in making flat-knit fabrics by adding stitches or by knitting two or more stitches as one to narrow the fabric.

fast dyes   Those dyes that are fast for the purpose for which the fabric is intended.

feathers   The plumage of birds, feathers were once an important fashion accessory and ornamentation used profusely on hats and as trimming. With time, however, an awakened social conscience resulted in the passage of laws protecting the birds. Today, although the names of the original birds are still used, almost all feathers come from domesticated fowl (chickens, turkeys), and are treated to resemble the feathers of the most exotic, protected birds. Man-made imitations are also used. Among the most important feather names are the following entries.

aigrette (*ay*-gret)   A spray of feathers or jewels. Feathers from the egret, a heron. True aigrette feathers are no longer available.

coq (kohk)   A term used to describe feathers, usually fairly short ones, used in trimming.

down   The softest, shortest feathers are called down. Types of down include eiderdown, originally only from ducks, but now used to refer to any very soft feathers. The term also refers to a feather-filled bed covering and goose down.

marabou (*mayr*-uh-boo)   Short fluffy feathers now taken from domesticated fowl, usually dyed to match the garments on which they are used as trimming. They were originally taken from the stork.

osprey (*oss*-pree)   Osprey feathers are, like marabou feathers, usually taken from domesticated fowl. The term is used for feathers that form a plume.

ostrich (*oss*-trich)   Ostrich feathers are long, usually coiled feathers, often dyed to match a garment.

peacock (*pee*-kahk)   Peacock feathers are extremely long and can be recognized by the eye-like design at the end of the feather. They are rarely used in fashion but occasionally become popular as a room accent.

fedora (or Homburg) [(feh-*dohr*-uh) or (*hahm*-burg)]   A soft felt hat with a rolled-up brim and a crown creased lengthwise.

felt   A nonwoven fabric or interlocked fiber made from wool, fur, and hair fibers that mesh together when heat, moisture, and mechanical action are applied. Processes of spinning, weaving, or knitting are not employed. The fibers develop a tight bond and will not ravel. Some percentage of wool is necessary in the manufacture of true felt to achieve the felted effect. It is used for coats, hats, and many industrial purposes.

festoon (fess-*toon*)   A decorative cord usually accented by tassels. It forms a decoration for the edge of such items as tablecloths.

fiber   The basic unit used in the fabrication of textile yarns and fabrics. Fibers are much longer than they are wide. The term at one time was limited to materials that could be spun into yarn, but now is used to include filaments that do not require spinning, such as silk and man-made fibers.

fiber content   Amount of basic unit (raw material), such as cotton, polyester, wool, nylon, and so on, listed as a percent of the whole.

fiber dye   Dyeing of fibers before spinning into yarn. It is synonymous with raw-stock dyeing.

fiber morphology (*fy*-ber mawr-*fowl*-uh-je)   The form and structure of a fiber, including its biological structure, shape, cross section, and microscopic appearance.

Fiber Products Identification Act (*fy*-ber *prahd*-ukts eye-dent-ih-fih-*kay*-shun akt)   This act is a ruling by the Federal Trade Commission requiring that certain textile items, including garments and fabric sold to the consumer by the yard, be labeled to show fiber content by generic name, proportions of each fiber by weight, the manufacturer of the item, and, if the fabric was not made in the United States, the country where it was made. The requirement of the manufacturer's name is modified so that instead of a name, the manufacturer can use an anonymous number, called an RN number.

fiber rug   A floor covering made of tightly twisted strips of paper, finished to repel friction and moisture.

fiberfill (*fy*-ber-fil)   A man-made fluffy material used, among other things, to pad brassieres, stuff pillows, and make quilts.

Fiberglas (*fy*-ber-glass)   Trademark of Owens-Corning for glass fiber.

fibrils   Bundles of fiber cells.

Fibro (*fy*-broh)   Trademark of Courtaulds for rayon fiber.

filament (*fil*-ah-ment)   Extremely long continuous fibers that can be measured in meters or yards, or in the case of man-made fibers, in kilometers or miles. Filaments do not require spinning to form yarn. Examples are rayon, nylon, acrylic, polyester, and other man-made fibers. Silk is the only natural filament; man-made fibers can be filament or staple (short, to be spun into yarn). Filaments usually produce a fabric that is smooth and shiny; this can be changed in various ways, including crimping the yarn or changing the shape of the filament itself. Man-made filaments are often grouped into a filament bundle for a more effective final yarn.

filament yarn   Yarn made from long continuous man-made filaments.

filling   Yarns that lie crosswise from selvage to selvage, and interlace with the warp threads on a woven fabric. Also called weft, woof, shoot, and shute. Filling, however, is the most common term used in the textile industry in the United States, partly because it describes the function of the yarn so well.

filling pile method   Extra fillings are floated over four or five warps. The floats are cut after weaving, then the cut ends are brushed up to form the pile. *See* corduroy.

findings   Findings is a term for such items as buttons, interfacings, pockets, belts, snap fasteners, and zippers used in making garments. It is used in the fabric and fashion industry primarily. Notions is the common term for these items. They are normally purchased in a notions department but sometimes can be found in smallwares or haberdashery.

fine fabric   A fabric that usually requires hand washing or dry cleaning.

fingering yarn   A two-ply or three-ply yarn, usually made of wool or acrylic. Fingering yarn has an even thickness, is light or medium in weight, and is popular for hand-knitting such items as baby sweaters. *See* ply.

finished worsted (*fin*-isht *woor*-stid)   Fabric with a softened finish. It is synonymous with semifinished.

finishing   An overall term that usually refers to all processes, with the exception of coloring, to make fabric more acceptable (some experts also include coloring). Much of the look, feel, and behavior of a fabric is determined by the finishing steps taken. Finishing can be mechanical (as in calendering) or chemical, or both. Special treatments are applied to fabrics during finishing to make them perform better, shrink less, resist flames, and repel water. Calendering refers to a process in which the fabric is passed through heated cylinders. This gives the fabric a lustrous surface and can also emboss it. Another important step in finishing, and usually the final process, is tentering; it gives the fabric its final shape by passing it through heat while it is in a stretched position.

F

fire resistant   Fire resistant refers to a fabric or fiber that has been treated to discourage the spreading of flames. *See* flame retardant fabric.

fireproof   Fireproof means that a fabric literally will not burn. To be labeled fireproof, the Federal Trade Commission requires that a fabric must be 100% fireproof. If the fiber or fabric has been treated to prevent flames from spreading, it must be labeled as fire resistant. *See* fire resistant and flame retardant fabric.

fish-eye   A large woven geometric pattern, similar to birds-eye. *See* birds-eye.

fishnet   A large, novelty, coarse mesh fabric of cotton, linen, acrylic, or polyester, made to resemble fishing nets in white or colors. It has knots in each corner of a geometrically shaped hole and is sometimes used for curtains and hosiery as well as for fishing. *See* net.

fitted sheets   Sheets whose corners are made to fit the mattress. Both bottom and top fitted sheets are available.

flameproof   Flameproof is a synonym for fireproof. *See* fireproof.

flame retardant fabric (flaym ree-*tar*-dent *fab*-rik)   A fabric that resists or retards the spreading of flames. A flame retardant fabric can be made by using fibers that are themselves flame retardant, or by using special finishes on fabrics. Below is a list of some flame retardant fabrics.

Many companies produce similar items but have not given them names referring specifically to their flame retardant nature.

Cordelan (*kohr*-deh-lan) Kohjin Company's biconstituent, flame retardant fiber of 50 percent vinyl and 50 percent vinyon. *See* biconstituent fiber.

Fire Stop (fyr stop) Name given by Cotton Incorporated to 100 percent cotton or cotton blend fabrics treated to meet government or industry flammability standards.

Fire Foe (fyr foh) Spring Mills' name for their flame retardant fabrics.

Kevlar (*kehv*-lar) DuPont's flame resistant aramid fiber.

Nomex (*no*-meks) A flame resistant aramid fiber made by DuPont.

Sayfr (*say*-fer) Name for flame retardant rayon and acetate made by the FMC Corporation.

Sef (sayf) Monsanto's modacrylic flame retardant fiber.

Flammable Fabrics Act A law passed by the eighty-third Congress and signed by President Eisenhower on June 30, 1953, prohibiting the introduction or movement in interstate commerce of clothing fabrics flammable enough to be dangerous when worn. Amended in 1967.

flange (flanj) A flat border. In fabrics, the term usually applies to a flat border on a pillow. *See* pillow.

flannel (*flan*-el) Originally an all-wool fabric, usually with a brushed surface, of woolen or worsted yarn and a soft napped finish that practically obliterates the weave. It is a catch-all designation for a great many otherwise unnamed fabrics in the woolen industry. Now, it is often a rayon or cotton fabric slightly napped on both sides to resemble woolen or worsted. The brushing of the fabric weakens it to a certain degree, but this is not considered undesirable in most applications. A wide range of weights is available: an 11-ounce flannel is made for suits, and there are tissue-weight flannels for dresses. It may be twill or plain weave. Viyella flannel is a Williams, Hollins and Company trade name for a cotton and wool flannel made in England. *See* flannelette and outing flannel.

flannelette (flan-el-*et*) Theoretically, a soft, plain- or twill-weave, fairly lightweight fabric, traditionally cotton with nap on only one side. The fabric can be dyed solid colors or printed. The terms flannel and flannelette are used interchangeably, with flannelette more commonly used for cotton or man-made flannels intended for use in children's garments, especially sports shirts, and lounging and sleeping wear.

flat   A description of a loom or knitting machine and the finished product. A flat machine weaves or knits a fabric all in one plane as opposed to circular looms and machines that produce tubular fabrics.

flat collar   A collar attached at the neckline and which lies flat against the garment along its entire length and width.

flat crepe   A firm, medium-weight silk crepe with a soft, almost imperceptible crinkle. It has creped fillings alternating with two S and two Z twists. The surface is fairly flat. Flat crepe may also be made of man-made fibers. It is used for dresses, negligees, and blouses. *See* crepe de chine.

flax (flakz)   Fibers of the flax plant that are spun into linen yarns and woven into linen cloth. The word linen is derived from "linum," part of the scientific name for the flax plant. *See* linen.

fleck   A spot, usually of color, included in a fabric to add visual and textural interest. Flecks are often made by the addition of small pieces of colored fiber to the base fiber during the process of spinning it into yarn.

fleece   The wool of any animal, usually a sheep. Fleece is also used to describe certain coating fabrics that have a deep, thick pile that imitate this wool. It may be made of cotton, Orlon acrylic, nylon, Verel modacrylic, Dynel modacrylic, Dacron polyester, or other synthetic piles. *See* pile.

fleece wool   Wool shorn from the live sheep and superior to pulled wool. *See* pulled wool.

fleece-lined (fleess-lynd)   A term used to describe items in which the leather of a sheep and its wool make a naturally lined garment. Also, items lined with an artificial fleece, such as sweat shirt fabrics.

flexibility   The property of bending without breaking.

flimsy (*flim*-zee)   Description of a fabric that lacks body and wearing ability. The term flimsy is almost always used in a derogatory sense.

float   In a satin weave, the number of fillings a warp skips over before interlacing. In a sateen weave, the number of warps a filling skips over before interlacing.

flock 1. Weight added to woolens by steaming fibers into the back of the fabric. 2. A method of adding design with texture to a fabric. Flocking involves the use of either electrolysis or adhesive (either on its own or as part of a printing dye) printed onto a finished fabric in a pattern. Small pieces of fluffy or short fibrous materials are then sprinkled over the fabric and stuck to the glue in the desired pattern. Flocked fabrics are often intended to imitate more expensive fabrics, such as cut velvets. Dotted swiss today is often made with the dots flocked rather than woven. Flocking is traditional for college seals on pennants and some floor coverings. Hosiery often has flocked clocks. The flock should be able to be cleaned in the same way as the fabric, but occasionally it wears off in time. *See* clock.

flock-dotted Designs of short fibrous materials printed in or onto the fabric with the aid of an adhesive. Electrostatic and lacquered applications of designs are two methods used. The former is durable for washing and dry cleaning; the latter may be nondurable.

flocked carpet *See* nonwoven floor coverings.

floss silk Tangled silk waste. Floss is also a twisted silk yarn used in art needlework.

flounce (flowns) A very wide ruffle (strip of fabric gathered on one side).

fluorescent fabric (floor-ess-*ent fab*-rik) A fabric that glows with a more vivid color than usual under daylight, headlights, and ultra-violet light. Fluorescent fabrics are important, especially in colors such as orange, where high visibility is essential for safety in hunting clothes, clothes for crossing guards, and outfits for school children. Occasionally, fluorescent fabrics become fashionable for other items of clothing.

fly closing A rectangular overlap of fabric in a garment that covers a buttoned or zippered opening on the front of men's trousers and women's pants.

foam (fohm) Materials with bubbles as part of their basic structure. Foam rubber and foam polyurethane are two of the most common. The foam structure gives a springy, bouncy effect to the basic material, making foam items suitable for pillows, floor padding, backings, and upholstery. *See* polyurethane.

foam laminate A construction made by laminating a synthetic foam to a woven or knitted fabric.

foam rubber   Rubber made in foam form and used for pillows, floor padding, backings, and upholstery.

foam-back   A layer of foam (usually polyurethane) laminated to another fabric. *See* laminating; *see also* polyurethane.

footwear   All types of wearing apparel for the feet, including shoes, boots, and slippers.

Ford   The term Ford, a hold-over from the days when the best-selling car in the United States was the Model-T Ford, is used to describe best-selling fashions, accessories, and fabrics.

Fortrel (fohr-*trel*)   Trademark of Fiber Industries Incorporated for polyester fiber marketed by Celanese Fibers Marketing Company.

F

Foulard (foo-*lard*)   A lightweight, soft, plain- or twill-weave fabric made of silk, mercerized cotton, rayon, acetate, or thin worsted wool. Foulard has a high luster on the face and dull on the reverse side. It is often printed, and the patterns range from simple polka dots to small, allover elaborate designs on light or dark grounds. It is also made in plain and solid colors. Foulard has a characteristic hand that can be described as light, firm, and supple. It is used for spring and summer dresses, scarves, robes, and neckties, and frequently sold as surah. *See* surah.

foundations   The general term for women's supporting undergarments such as bras, girdles, and panty-girdles.

frame   Denotes the number of colors possible in a Wilton rug; for example, five frames means five colors are possible, one frame for each color yarn. Frame holds spools of colored pile yarn in Axminster construction. *See* harness.

French cuff   A wide sleeve cuff that is folded back at the wrist and fastened through four buttonholes with buttons or cufflinks.

friction towel   A terry cloth made with linen pile. It may be made into a mitt used to develop friction after bathing.

frieze (freez)   A heavy pile fabric used primarily for upholstery, slipcovers, and draperies. Frieze is looped, and the loops are often sheared to varying heights to form the pattern. Originally made of cotton (and still often referred to as cotton frieze), the fabric is now usually made of mohair, wool, cotton, and blends of cotton and man-made fibers. Also called frise.

fringes   Thread or cords of any fibers grouped or bound together and loose at one end. In the true sense, fringe is a border, but when it refers to fabrics for clothing and home furnishings it means a shaggy edging. It is used for trimming clothing, draperies, and upholstery. *See* trimming.

frise (free-*zay*)   *See* frieze.

frog   A form of garment closure. An Oriental style braid or cord fastening. It is often designed with three circles and a knot on one side of a garment and three circles and a loop at the other side. *See* trimming.

F

fugitive dye   Those colors that are not fast to such elements as light, washing, perspiration, and crocking.

full-fashioned (fool-*fash*-und)   A method of knitting in which stitches are increased and decreased as necessary to fit the item to the desired shape . Full-fashioned is used for sweaters, dresses, and hosiery. The opposite of full-fashioned is cut-and-sewn. *See* cut-and-sewn and fashioning.

fulling   A shrinking process to make wool fabrics more compact and thicker. *See* felting.

fun fur   A term used in the sale of furs, originally designed to overcome an image of furs for rich ladies only. The term is applied to highly styled, comparatively inexpensive furs such as raccoon and rabbit. Fun fur is sometimes used as a synonym for fake furs. *See* fur and fake fur.

functional finish (*funk*-shun-uhl *fin*-ish)   A special finish added to a fabric as one of the final steps in its manufacture that alters the performance and contributes a specific attribute to the fabric in some way. A water repellent finish, for example, is a functional finish because it prevents water from penetrating the fabric, thereby changing the function of the fabric. Other examples of special finishes are soil release and crease resistant.

fur   The coat of an animal, usually shorter and thicker than hair. The following entries are some of the most common furs.

  beaver   The fur of the beaver is naturally brown but occasionally is dyed other colors.

  broadtail   Broadtail is a form of lamb fur. It is usually black and has a flat, curly appearance.

chinchilla (chin-*chil*-ah)   Chinchilla, a soft bluish-white fur with dark tips, is one of the most expensive furs.

coney   *See* rabbit.

ermine (*ur*-min)   Ermine is lustrous, thick, and white with dark tips. It is the traditional royal fur and is often dyed other colors, except when used as trimming.

fox   Fox is a soft, long-haired fur, dyed or bred in various colors and used for both coats and trimming.

leopard   Leopard, with its small, dark, irregular spots on a tan ground, is one of the shortest haired furs.

F

mink   Mink is soft and glossy and one of the most popular of all furs available in many colorings. Mink are raised for fur on mink ranches.

rabbit   Rabbit is an inexpensive fur often dyed to resemble other furs or for fashion impact. It is also called coney and lapin.

raccoon   Raccoon, the traditional bulky coat fur, is long, warm, and striped. It is also used for trimming.

sable (*say*-buhl)   Sable is usually dark brown. It is warm, dense fur, and extremely expensive.

seal   Seal is thick, warm, long-lasting, and shiny. It is naturally black or dark brown.

fur-fiber fabrics   Cloths woven of hair or fur fiber intended to resemble fur. In order for a manufacturer to use this term, the T.F.P.I.A. states that the fiber content of a fabric must be hair, fur fibers, or any mixture of animals (other than wool-producing animals) in excess of 5% of the total fiber weight of the textile fiber product. No direct or indirect reference to the animals' name is permitted.

fusible fabric (*fyou*-zi-buhl *fab*-rik)   A fabric that can be joined to another fabric in a fairly permanent bond through the application of heat, moisture, and pressure with an iron. A fusible fabric has dots of polyamide resins (polyamids are the bases of many synthetic fibers) on the wrong side. The wrong side is placed against the wrong side of the outer fabric and the fusing agent melts and fuses it to the other fabric when the iron is applied.

fusing   A heat pressure process whereby parts of a garment are merged (fused together) instead of being stitched together. *See* fusible fabric.

Defect	Explanation	Severity
Filling Band Mixed Filling	A visually perceptible band across the width of the fabric directly attributable to a difference in the chemical or physical characteristics of the filling.	Major
Filling Floats	Picks of filling extending unbound over or under warp ends with which they should have been interlaced.	Major
Filling Splits	They appear inside the selvages because of crowded reed dents, crammed warp ends due to incorrect reeding, warp and/or filling tensions being too high, improper setting of the temples on the loom, selvage yarns that are not conductive to even weaving of fabric, damaged reed splits or wires, and dull pins in the temple cases.	Minor
Fine Ends	They give a streaked line appearance to cloth because of their finer diameter or fewer plies in the yarn than required.	Major
Fine Filling Pick	This is caused by the filling yarn being of finer diameter than it should be. This streak or shade bar runs across the entire fabric, and is usually the result of mixed filling bobbins taken from the bobbin pin by the tender boy.	Major
Fine Yarn	In knits, a yarn whose diameter is noticeably smaller than that normal to the fabric, usually resulting in fine line cracks in the course or widthwise direction.	Major
Finger Mark	Irregular, off-cast areas in cloth caused by variation in the picks as they are inserted into the material. Timing action of the pick wheel is the most common cause for this defect.	Minor
Finishing Bar	An uneven line or bar that runs the width of the cloth. This finishing defect is caused by machine stoppage or an irregular roller setting.	Major

Defect	Explanation	Severity
Flat	The strict meaning is that two filling picks have been woven together in the same shed in the loom, thereby causing the imperfection. A warp flat occurs in plain fabric when one end is missing and the ends on either side of the missing yarn come together to give the "flat-effect." A flat is the bane of weavers in some low-quality, low-priced cottons.	Major
Floats (*see* Warp Float, Filling Float, and Skip Stitch)	These are caused by an end, or ends, failing to weave into the cloth the way they should have. The loom, when not functioning in the proper manner, also causes floats. The weaver, because of laxity in fixing the ends affected, is a source of this trouble. Incorrect drawing-in or reeding-in of the warp may cause one or more ends to form float areas in the goods. Floats are remedied in the dry finishing department of the mill as a last resort.	Major (or Minor, if remedied)
Fly, Loom Fly	Usually caused by the spinning process, small waste fibers, or "blizzards" of defect, but waste stocks that somehow seem to be spun into yarn of another stock. Often caused by lack of precautions to prevent contamination. Much of this waste stock comes from a loom that has not been cleaned well by the weaver. In many instances, the stock, while floating in the air, becomes embedded in the fabric.	Usually a Minor Defect, but severe size and color contamination could make it Major
Foreign Fiber	Fiber, other than that common to a fabric, existing as contamination; it may be confined to a single yarn or distributed randomly.	Major
Foreign Matter	Contamination by some substance other than fiber.	Major

Defect	Explanation	Severity
Fray	When a shifting or slipping of one set of yarns over the other occurs in the woven cloth, or at the cut or unfinished edges.	Minor
Fuzz Balls	Balls of fiber encircling the warp yarn formed by the abrasion of the loom. These usually result from the lack of sufficient sizing material on the warp yarns, causing what generally is referred to as a "soft warp."	Major

gabardine (*gab*-r-deen)   A strong, hard-finished, clear-surfaced, medium-to heavy-weight, tightly woven steep-twilled fabric with rounded wales and a flat back. The diagonal wales are fine, close, and steep, and are more pronounced than in serge. The wales cannot be seen on the wrong side of the fabric. Gabardine goes in and out of fashion; when it is in fashion, it is made in wool, cotton, rayon, polyester, or mixtures. It is used for sport shirts, slacks, coats, suits, and tailored dresses. *See* twill.

galloon (ga-*loon*)   A narrow edging or braid, or a narrow (up to eighteen inches wide) lace made with scallops on both edges. *See* trimmings, and lace.

garnetting (*gahr*-net-ing)   Shredding wool fabrics into a fibrous state, prior to remanufacture into woolen yarn.

garter belt   A fabric belt to which garters are attached.

gas fading   The loss of color some fabrics suffer because of nitrogen in the atmosphere rather than exposure to sunlight. Certain dyes (blues and greens, for example) are often more susceptible to gas fading than others, as are certain fibers (acetate). Special dyes can be used on these fabrics and colors to reduce or eliminate this problem. Also called atmospheric and pollution fading.

gathers   Small, soft folds created when fabric is drawn between large stitched threads.

Gaucho hat (*gow*-choh hat)   A felt hat with a short flat crown, a fairly wide, slightly rolled-up brim, and a cord that ties under the chin.

gauge (gayj)   A measure of fineness or coarseness in knitting, gauge refers to the number of needles per unit length (i.e., inch) on the machine used in making a fabric, such as tricot and Raschel. The higher the gauge, the greater the number of needles used and the finer the fabric. Gauge is usually used to describe hosiery, and the term cut, which means much the same, is more common when describing other knit fabrics.

gauntlet   A short glove that flares at the wrist because of a triangular insert.

gauze (gawz)   A thin, sheer, open, loosely woven, plain-weave cotton fabric with widely spaced yarns, used for diapers and surgical dressings. It can also be made of wool, silk, rayon, or other man-made fibers. Some weights are stiffened for curtains, trimmings of dresses, and other decorative or apparel purposes.

generic name (jih-*nair*-ik naym)   A name that describes a class of items, such as soap or polyester. Ivory is a trade name for a type of soap as Dacron is for a type of polyester. In textiles, a generic name is the name of a family of fibers of similar chemical composition. *See* trademark.

georgette (jor-*jet*)   A soft, sheer dull-textured silk fabric, similar to chiffon, made with a crepe yarn to give the fabric a crepe appearance. The crepy surface is obtained by alternating right-hand and left-hand twist yarns in warp and filling. It is used for summer and evening dresses. *See* chiffon and crepe.

germ resistant   Fabrics treated with compounds to protect the wearer against fungi and germs.

Germantown yarn (*jur*-men-town yarn)   A four-ply medium-weight yarn usually made of wool or acrylic. It is soft and thick and used for hand-knitted items such as afghans, sweaters, and socks.

ghiordes (gee-*ohr*-dis)   Type of knot used to make pile in Turkish hand-tied rugs.

gigging   A process of raising nap (fibers on the surface of a fabric) to make it softer and increase its warmth. It is done by teasels. *See* napping.

gillie (*gih*-lee)   A low-cut women's pump with decorative lacing up the front.

gimp or guimp (gihmp)   An edging, often with small scallops of fine cord along its edges. Gimp was originally designed to hide such things as upholstery tacks on chairs and sofas, but is now used for other decorative purposes.

gingham (*ging*-um) A light- to medium-weight, plain-weave cotton fabric. It is usually yarn-dyed and woven to create stripes, checks, or plaids. The fabric is mercerized to produce a soft, lustrous appearance; it is sized and calemdered to a firm and lustrous finish. The thread count varies from about 48x44 to 106x94. Traditionally made of cotton (although other natural fibers have been used in ginghams and given that name), today gingham is usually made of a blend or a man-made fiber. When the pattern is checked it is called checked gingham; when plaid it is called plaid gingham. Plain-weave fabrics are sometimes printed with gingham patterns, such as checks, and are also called ginghams. When the gingham look is in fashion, even knits in checked patterns are called ginghams. Gingham patterns are available in a wide range of colors, and checked ginghams are the most popular. It is used for women's and children's dresses, blouses, men's sport shirts, curtains, and bedspreads. *See* check.

ginning A process of separating fibers from the seeds.

girdle A foundation garment extending from the waist or bust to below the buttocks. It has all-elastic webbing or inserts of webbing and fabric, with or without bones.

glacé or glazed (glah-*say* or glayzed) Both terms, glacé and glazed, are used to refer to a shiny finish applied to leather or fabric. At one time, the glaze was often not permanent and came out in the first washing or cleaning; today, however, most glazes are permanent. *See* finishing.

glass curtains Sheer window coverings that hang in front of a window, affording a degree of privacy without cutting off an excessive amount of light. Glass curtains are often used behind draperies. *See* curtains and draperies.

glass fiber Very fine flexible fiber made from glass. It is used extensively for curtains and draperies. Glass fiber fabrics are very strong and wash well, but care should be taken to avoid getting small splinters of the glass yarns in the hands. Glass fiber is stiff and has poor resistance to wear and abrasion. It is also fireproof. *See* fireproof.

glass towel A towel made of linen crash, cotton, or mixtures suitable for drying drinking glasses, glass plates, and silver because it is lint free. Glass towels are often checked red and white and may have the word "Glass" woven into the fabric.

glazed (glayzd)   *See* glacé.

glazing   A finishing process consisting of treating the fabric with glue, starch, paraffin, shellac, or resin, then moving it through hot friction rollers.

glitter   The name, sometimes used in place of lamé, for any fabric woven or knitted with all metallic yarns or with a combination of metallic and other fiber yarns. Today, most glitter is made from one of the nontarnishable metallic fibers, a great improvement over lamé of the past that tended to darken with age.

godet (go-*day*)   A piece of fabric, tapering from wide to very narrow, inserted into another fabric section, often at a seam, for additional fullness for function or appearance. Godets move in and out of fashion and are often used in home decorating at corners of beds, chairs, sofas, and slipcovers.

golf umbrella   A straight-handled umbrella that typically has a striped canopy with a wide spread. Originally designed for use while golfing, it is sometimes considered a man's or woman's fashion umbrella.

good middling   The best grade of cotton—lustrous, silky, clean fibers.

good ordinary   The poorest grade of cotton. Contains leaf particles, sticks, hulls, dirt, sand, and the like.

goods   Another name for fabric. *See* fabric.

goose down   Down from a goose, the softest and shortest feathers.

gore   A tapering piece of cloth that is one of several such panels in a gored skirt.

gossamer (*gahs*-uh-mer)   Any sheer, fine fabric may be given the name gossamer, although the term was traditionally used to describe silk fabrics.

graded (or sloped)   Scaled adjustments that meet the dimensional requirements of each size in which a style is made.

grading   Determining, by touch, the fineness of the diameters of individual fibers. Wool tops are graded in this fashion. Efforts are now being made to grade wool in the grease by this method.

grain   The direction in which the yarns run in weaving. The straight grain is the direction of the warp yarns; the crosswise grain is the direction of the filling yarns. Off-grain is a term used to describe a fabric in which these yarns are not at right angles to each other.

Off-grain fabrics can be corrected by wetting them with water, then pulling the fabric until the two grains are at right angles. This straightening of the grain, however, is only successful if a pattern has not been printed off-grain on the fabric and if the fabric has not been given a permanent press finish.

grain leather (grayn *leth*-er)   A common name in leather *See* leather.

grass bleaching   Whitening fabrics by laying them on the grass in the sun.

grass cloth   A plain-weave, loosely woven fabric made from such fibers as hemp, ramie, and even nettle. Today, true grass cloth is relatively rare, but the appearance of grass cloth is copied in wallpaper and fabrics of man-made fibers. *See* hemp, ramie, and nettle.

grass rug   Made of cured prairie grass.

gray goods   A textile industry term referring to fabric after it has been manufactured but before it has been colored or finished. It is also spelled grey and greige.

grease   Natural grease adhering to the wool fiber that must be removed by scouring.

greige (grehj) [correct pronunciation]; (gray) [common pronunciation]   The state of a fabric as it comes from the loom (after it has been constructed) but before it has been colored or finished. *See* gray goods.

grenadine   A tightly twisted ply yarn composed of two or three singles.

grey goods   Textile merchandise as it comes from the loom (after it has been constructed) before it is finished. *See* greige.

gripper (snap)   An interlocking (or snap) metal socket and stud used as a closure for clothing.

groove markings   Rather heavy line markings running lengthwise of the acetate fiber; a mark of identification.

gros de londres (groh duh *lahn*-dray)   Ribbed or corded fabric. The flat, fillingwise cords alternate wide and narrow. It is used for dresses and millinery.

gros point (grow pwanh [correct pronunciation]; (grow poynt) [common pronunciation])   A synonym for regular needlepoint most commonly worked on canvas with 10, 12, or 14 holes to the inch. *See* needlepoint.

grosgrain (*grow*-grayn)   A fairly heavy, closely woven, firm, corded or ribbed fabric, made in silk or rayon warp with cotton cords. The cords are round and firm, heavier than in poplin, rounder than in faille. Grosgrain is often made in narrow widths for use as trimming. The most common use of grosgrain is for ribbons in which the ribs are usually narrow, but it can be made with larger ribs for academic gowns. It is really a bengaline in narrow goods and is used for ribbons, neckties, and lapel facings.

ground   The background of a fabric design or print, as when red flowers are printed on a black ground.

guanaco (gwah-*nah*-koh)   A wooly, reddish-brown wild animal of the llama family. *See* llama family.

guest towels or finger-tip towels   Lightweight and smaller than hand towels. They are made of lightweight linen crash, huck, damask, and terry, in white, solids, and designs.

gun club checks   Double check designs in which large checks are superimposed on smaller ones. The name is rarely used in the United States, but the design is a popular one. *See* check.

Defect	Explanation	Severity
Gouts	Really neps in goods, but appears in larger bunches of foreign matter or waste that have been woven into the fabric. This defect differs from slubs in that slubs generally are symmetrical in shape and gouts appear as undrafted lumps.	Major

GARMENT

AND

TEXTILES

habutai (*hah*-boo-ty)   Soft, lightweight silk dress fabric originally woven in the gum on hand looms in Japan. It is sometimes confused with China silk, which is technically lighter in weight.

hackling (*hak*-ling)   A combing process that prepares the flax fibers for spinning by removing short lengths of fiber, leaving only longer ones and laying them parallel. It may be done by hand or by machine.

haircloth   A stiff, wiry fabric made from a combination of natural or man-made fibers with animal hair filling, usually mohair (goat) or horsehair. It is used in upholstery and as interfacing and stiffening because of its strength.

hairpin lace   A delicate, narrow lace worked over a hairpin or a special hairpin-shaped, loom-like tool.

halter neck   A neckline formed by bodice fabric below the arm, reaching up the front to encircle the back of the neck. The bodice is typically backless.

hand or handle   The way a fabric feels. One of the important elements in fabric selection is the subjective judgement of the feel of a fabric and whether or not it will work well for its intended purpose. To make this judgement, the fabric must be felt, and the resulting decision is based on the hand or handle. Fabrics may be described as having a crisp, soft, drapeable, smooth, pliable, springy, stiff, cool, warm, rough, hard, or limp hand. *See* texture, crisp, and drapeable fabrics.

hand-blocked print   Fabrics printed by hand with blocks made of wood or linoleum.

handkerchief (*hang*-ker-chif)   A small rectangular piece of fabric that traditionally had a hand-rolled hem. Today, handkerchiefs are made of plain-weave fabric (combed cotton, blend of cotton, and man-made fibers), but were usually made of linen in the past. Handkerchiefs are available in many colors, but the most popular are all white or a woven design of plaids or checks surrounding a white center. *See* bandanna.

handkerchief hemline   An irregular hemline falling in a series of points.

handkerchief linen (*hang*-ker-chif *lin*-uhn)   A well-hackled, sheer, lightweight, fine linen fabric in plain weave that is used for handkerchiefs, blouses, summer dresses, and clothing where a batiste-like fabric is considered desirable. Today, the term is rarely used, but when it is, it usually refers to a woven fabric made of a blend of polyester and linen. It is synonymous with lawn. *See* lawn, linen, and batiste.

handkerchief sleeve (or kerchief sleeve)   A full sleeve with the bottom edge draping in one or more diagonal peaks; this type of sleeve comes in short to long lengths.

hand-knotted rug   Hand-knotted rugs, including Oriental and Persian rugs, are among the most expensive made. Intricate designs are possible. The higher the number of knots to the inch, the finer the rug.

hand-loomed (hand-loomd)   Synonymous to hand-woven. *See* handwoven.

hand-rolled hem   A hand-rolled hem is an extremely narrow hem made by turning under a small edge of fabric and securing it with small hemming stitches. It is most often used on scarves and full skirts of sheer fabrics such as chiffon and georgette. *See* stitches.

hand-woven   A self-explanatory term, referring to a woven fabric that has been made by hand on a loom rather than on a power loom.

hank   A measure of yarn loosely coiled upon itself rather than wound onto a spool or into a ball.

hard-finished   A term applied to woolen, worsted, and cotton fabrics that are finished without a nap. *See* clear-finished.

harness   The frame holding warp yarns that are threaded through the eyes of its heddles. *See* heddles.

Harris Tweed (*hayr*-iss tweed)   Fabric identified by the label "Harris Tweed," required as a protective device by the British association of that name. A tweed that is hand-woven from yarns spun on the islands of the Outer Hebrides off the coast of Scotland; the Isle of Harris is one of these islands. Originally, hand-woven and dyed with color pigments that were cooked over peat fires by cottagers, hence its distinctive odor. The yarns may now be spun by hand or machine. *See* tweed.

haute couture (oat koo-*tour*)   The business of designing, making, and selling high fashion, custom-made clothing.

hawser cord (*haw*-zur kohrd)   The result of twisting together singles with various directions of twists.

headboard (*hed*-bord)   A board or frame at the pillow end of a bed. The headboard stands perpendicular to the floor. Headboards may be made of wood or slipcovered or upholstered to match a bedspread or other decorative areas of a room. The term bed head is a synonym.

heading (*hed*-ing)   The top portion of a curtain or drapery. Headings are usually decorative and are often made from trimmings such as braid. *See* trimmings.

hearth rug   A hand-tied Oriental rug characterized by designs in the form of arches, one at either end.

heat setting   Although practices similar to heat setting are used in the finishing of almost all fabrics, the term heat setting, strictly speaking, refers only to thermoplastic man-made fibers. Because of the thermoplastic nature of most man-made fibers (they change their shape when heat is applied), certain features, such as pleats, can be made permanent by treating them under very high heat. Heat setting usually gives a smooth appearance to a fabric and sets its final measurements. Boarding, a process in the manufacture of stockings, is a type of heat setting.

heat transfer   A form of printing in which elaborate colors and designs are printed onto a special type of paper. The paper is placed over the fabric and the designs and colors are transferred to the fabric through the application of heat. *See* sublistatic printing.

heather (*heh*-ther)   A misty coloration in a fabric achieved by cross dyeing or by using one color for the warp yarns and another color for the filling yarns. It can also be achieved by the addition of certain soft fibers such as rabbit hair to the basic yarn, which, because of their fluffy nature, give a misty appearance to the fabric. *See* cross dyeing.

heat-set finish   The stabilization of synthetic fabrics to ensure no change in size or shape. Methods of setting fabrics of nylon and polyester fibers include treatment of fabrics at boiling or near boiling temperatures

H

one-half hour to one hour, treatment with saturated steam, and application of dry heat. Heat setting also secures maximum dimensional stability of acrylic fibers.

heavy-duty soap   Pure and mild, but has special alkalies added to improve its cleaning power.

heavy-duty synthetic detergent   One that has a builder for improved cleaning power. A suds-making ingredient is added primarily for automatic washers. A low-sudsing detergent is often recommended for the front-loading type of automatic washer.

heddles (*hed*-uhlz)   Series of wires held by the frame or harness. Each wire has an eye, similar to a needle, through which a warp yarn is threaded. Heddles are raised to form the shed. *See* shedding.

hem   A finish on the edge of a fabric or garment designed to prevent it from running or raveling. A hem is made by turning the fabric up to the inside and stitching it in place. A hem may be finished by adding a decorative trimming of some kind to protect the edge.

hemline slit   A split or cut at the seam of a dress or skirt from the bottom of the hem to any point above it.

hemmed extension sleeve   A rectangular-shaped extension of the shoulder line; can be cut in one piece with the garment or stitched separately.

hemp   A plant grown in the Philippines, Mexico, Central America, the West Indies, and India. Outer fibers are used for cordage, inner fibers for cables and canvas.

Herculon (*her*-kyu-lon)   Trademark of Hercules Incorporated for olefin fiber.

herringbone (*her*-ing-bohn)   A fabric in which the pattern of weave resembles the skeletal structure of the herring. It is a twill weave in which the wale runs in one direction for a few rows and then reverses, forming a "V" pattern. It is made with a broken twill weave that produces a balanced, zigzag effect and is used for sportswear, suits, and coats.

hessian (*hesh*-uhn)   The word hessian is occasionally used as a synonym for burlap. *See* burlap.

hexamethylene-diammonium-adipate (hek-suh-*meth*-uh-leen dy-uh-*mohn*-nee-uhm *ad*-uh-payt)   A solution of a salt that is polymerized and hardened into a solid and cut into flakes, then melted and extruded into nylon fibers.

high tenacity   High strength of modified rayon and acetate fibers as a result of chemical treatment while the fibers are in the plastic state. *See* modified rayon and modified acetate fibers.

high-bulk yarn (hy-bulk yarn)   Although the term high-bulk yarn is definitely a technical one, it is used occasionally in advertising. High-bulk yarns are processed so that, through a form of shrinkage in the processing, they are thicker and bulkier than they would be otherwise.

hill dropping   A method of planting cotton seeds by dropping them in hills.

hit-or-miss rug   A floor covering made of many colored twisted rags bound together.

holland (*hol*-und)   A plain-weave fabric used in the home primarily for window shades.

homespun   Originally, fabrics made from yarns spun by hand. Today, homespun is used for fabrics that imitate this look. It is a very coarse, rough, plain-weave fabric, loosely woven with irregular, tightly twisted, and nubby, unevenly spun yarns. It is made from linen, wool, cotton, or man-made fiber, or blends in varied colors and is used for coats, suits, sportswear, draperies, upholstery, and slipcovers.

homopolymer (hoh-moh-*powl*-ee-muhr)   A polymer composed of one substance or one type of molecule.

Honan (*hoh*-nan)   A heavy silk, pongee-type, but a finer weave, originally the product of wild silkworms of Honan, China. A fabric of the best grade of Chinese silk, it is sometimes woven with blue edges. It is now made to resemble a heavy pongee, with slub yarns in both warp and filling. Honan is manufactured from silk or from man-made fibers. It is used for women's dresses. *See* silk, pongee, and wild silk.

honeycomb (hun-ee-*kohm*)   A weave that results in fabrics that have diamonds or other geometric shapes resembling a honeycomb. Waffle weaves are identical to honeycomb weaves, and many weaves called thermal are honeycomb weaves. *See* thermal.

hooked rug   A rug made by hand or machine using a large hooked needle to pull loops of yarn or bias-cut fabric through a coarse burlap backing or canvas to form a pile. Some types are made on the Jacquard loom in round wire construction to imitate the hand-hooked type.

hopsacking   A coarse, loosely woven, ply-yarn fabric in basket or novelty weave. Originally a word for certain types of burlap bagging used for sacking hops, hopsacking is now used interchangeably with the term basket weave. Now made to resemble the original of linen, spun rayon, or cotton and used in blends. It is used for dresses, coats, jackets, skirts, and blouses.

horsehair   Fibers that are hair from the mane and tail, for the most part, of Canadian and Argentine horses. It is occasionally used for upholstery, but is more commonly used in interfacings for stiffening and strength. It is always combined with other fibers. True horsehair is rare and fabrics loosely called horsehair are often made from other hairs (such as goat) or man-made fibers.

hosiery   Stockings and socks for men or women.

houndstooth   (*howndz*-tooth)   A broken check, regular in pattern. This check is extremely popular. It shows up periodically on everything from woolens to shower curtains. *See* check.

huarache (huh-*rah*-chee)   A low-heeled Mexican sandal with the upper portion made of interwoven leather.

huck   A type of toweling fabric with a honeycombed surface made by using heavy filling yarns in a dobby weave. It has excellent absorbent qualities. It is woven with a pattern, most often with a dobby attachment on the loom and may have Jacquard borders. Huck is traditionally made of cotton, linen, or rayon, or a mixture of these, although today, other fibers may be used. In a mixture it is called a union fabric. Face or hand towels are made in white or colors and are used for drying dishes, glasses, and kitchen utensils. Huck is also called huckaback. Embroidery enthusiasts often use huck as a ground for their work. *See* dobby.

huckaback (*huk*-uh-bak)   *See* huck.

hydrophilic fibers (hy-druh-*fil*-ik *fy*-berz)   Fibers that absorb water readily, take longer to dry, and require more ironing. The opposite of hydrophobic fibers.

hydrophobic fibers (hy-druh-*foh*-bik *fy*-berz)   A nonabsorptive fiber with no affinity for water. It has a low degree of moisture attraction. *See* hydrophilic fibers.

Defect	Explanation	Severity
Hair-in-Filling	This is often caused by poor winding and gives a flatness to the material since the yarn that has been affected by hair will give a slight refraction.	Minor
Halo	A light place encircling a defect resulting from dye migration to the defect during drying.	Minor
Hang Pick Hang Shot (also Loopy Filling)	This is when a pick is out of line for a short distance and produces a small angular hole in the fabric. This results in a short loop of filling appearing on the face of the fabric. Foreign matter in the yarn, such as shives, motes, knots, or burrs are often the cause for the defect.	Major or Minor (depending on the size of the hole); Minor if loops can be manicured
Hang Thread	A thread left hanging on the face of a fabric. The most common cause is the failure of a weaver to clip the excess yarn after repairing a broken end and/or the cloth inspector's failure to remove the excess yarn.	Major
Hard Size	A place in a fabric characterized by a harsh, stiff hand and cloudy, uneven appearance. This is most common in mill-finished yarn-dyes and is the result of a slasher stop that allows excessive amounts of sizing material to harden on the yarn. This generally appears in bands across the width of the fabric.	Minor
Harness Balk	An isolated failure of a loom harness to move in its prescribed sequence, causing a pick of filling to float over certain warp ends with which it should have interlaced.	Major
Harness Breakdown	Caused by the harness straps breaking on a conventional loom, resulting in the ends drawn through that harness, floating either to the face or back of the fabric. There will be a definite pattern change in the weave.	Major

Defect	Explanation	Severity
Harness Misdraw	Where one or more ends are drawn through the harness contrary to the design of the weave.	Major
Harness Skips	Breaks in the weave or the failure of the harnesses to work properly. Skips are often caused by harness straps that slip, snap, or break, and work out of the plane and place provided for them to perform their functions. Skips form varying length floats on either the face or the back of the cloth.	Major
Heavy Filling Bar	A shaded streak that runs the width of the goods caused by several adjacent picks whose yarn is of greater diameter than should be used in the fabric. Usually the result of carelessness, but the beating-up action of the loom should be checked carefully. Mixed bobbins also contribute to this defect.	Major
Hitch-backs	Defects noted in cloth caused by improper starting up of the loom by the weaver after a "pick-out" caused by some irregularity. The blemish gives bright and dim areas to the material; loose filling pickage or undertension of the warp are conducive to hitch-backs.	Minor
Holes	Caused by broken needles. Small perforations, weak areas, perforations, or actual holes in fabric are caused by any number of things. Knots, perforations, weak yarn areas, foreign matter, irregular loom action, and finishing operations such as shearing and cropping all tend to produce these areas. Shuttles, shuttle-smashes, poor action by the feeler stop-motion in the raceplate of the loom, and sheer carelessness also contribute to this blemish. Holes are fixed in the dry-finishing department of the plant.	Major

illusion (il-*oo*-zhun)   Very fine net or mesh fabrics such as those used in bridal veils. Illusion usually is made of either silk or nylon. *See* mesh and net.

India rug   Hand-tied rugs made in India in the province of Lahore. Numdahs and druggets are two styles of India rugs.

Indian blanket (*inn*-dee-un *blang*-kit)   A woolen blanket hand-woven by American Indians in the western part of the United States. Indian blankets are usually made in bright colors or in earth colors. The term has come to be used for any blanket that resembles an authentic Indian blanket.

Indian muslin (*inn*-dee-un *muz*-lin)   Muslin is the name for a very large group of plain-weave fabrics originally made of cotton. Most muslin used for purposes other than sheets is unbleached, which means that bits of trash, usually appearing as brown flecks, add color to the fabric. Occasionally, unbleached muslin becomes popular in fashion, even for wedding gowns. Indian muslin is a very fine muslin from India, often printed with gold and silver and is an expensive luxury fabric. *See* muslin, trash, and flecks.

indigo (*in*-dee-goh)   A type of dyestuff, originally obtained from the indigo plant, now produced synthetically. Blues are brilliant. It is colorfast to washing and light.

indoor-outdoor carpeting   Floor coverings suitable for both inside the house and outdoors.

informative label   A tag that gives a description of qualities inherent in the merchandise in order to aid consumers to select properly for their needs and give instructions for proper care of their purchase.

ingrain   A knitted or woven fabric made of yarns dyed before knitting or weaving.

insertion (inn-*sur*-shun)   A narrow fabric—lace is probably the most common—that is finished on both edges and can be sewn to another fabric for decoration.

intarsia (inn-*tar*-see-uh)   A pattern knitted into a fabric. The term usually refers to a design on only one part of the fabric; knitted patterns that cover the entire fabric are usually called Jacquards. *See* Jacquard.

interfacing (*inn*-tur-fayss-ing)   A stiffening fabric made of horsehair (often goat hair, wool, man-made fibers, or combinations of these fibers). Interfacing is used to give additional body and strength to certain parts of garments. Areas that usually require interfacing include the front opening edges, collars, pocket flaps, and any piece where stretching or a loss of crispness would be a disadvantage.

interlining   A layer of fabric placed between the outer fabric and the lining of the garment to add warmth. It is most commonly found in coats and jackets. Interlinings are often made of reprocessed wool, but other materials such as polyester fiberfill may be used. *See* fiberfill, reprocessed wool.

interlock (*inn*-tur-lok)   A fine gauge, compound knit fabric with a smooth surface on both front and back, composed of two separate 1 x 1 rib fabrics interknitted to form one cloth, made on an interlock machine. The fabric was traditionally used for underwear, but today is being used for apparel. Despite the name of the fabric, poorly made interlock develops runs at the edges and all interlock knits should be reinforced or finished in some way at these edges.

intimate apparel   A term for women's foundations, lingerie, and lounge wear.

inverted pleats (inn-*vur*-tid pleetz)   Pleats formed by turning the folded edges toward each other in the same way as box pleats, but the edges meet on the right side of the garment. *See* box pleats.

iridescent (ir-ih-*dess*-ent)   Fabric woven with yarns of one color in the warp and another color in the filling so that the fabric seems to change color as the light strikes it. Other names for this type of fabric are changeable and shot.

Irish lace   The term Irish lace can be used to refer to any lace made in Ireland, but crocheted laces are those most often given the name. Embroidered nets are another type of Irish lace. *See* crocheted lace.

Irish linen   Linen products that come from Ireland, mainly Belfast in Northern Ireland, but also from Eire.

Irish tweed   Tweed made in Ireland, Northern Ireland, or Eire. These tweeds generally are distinguished by a white warp and colored filling threads. Donegal is a type of Irish tweed.

irregulars   Goods that have defects affecting the appearance, but not the wear of an item.

I

Defect	Explanation	Severity
Imperfect Selvages	These include balky, beaded, broken, corded, curled, cut, doubled, folded, looped, loose, rolled, scalloped, slack, tight, torn, and turned.	Major or Minor

jabot (zhah-*boh*)   A decorative ruffle or pleated cloth or lace at the center front of a neckline of a blouse or dress; a single or tiered fall of lace attached to the front of a neckband. Also, a ruffled drapery heading.

Jaquard (*jak*-ard)   A term used to describe fabrics with a woven or knitted pattern, whether or not they are made with a Jacquard attachment on the loom. The Jacquard attachment for weaving and knitting machines makes possible the manufacture of complicated, repeated geometrical designs in knits and wovens. *See* dobby.

Jacquard cards   Oblong punched cards used to control the raising of warp yarns on a Jacquard loom.

Jacquard patterns   Fancy patterns knitted in articles made by a special attachment on the knitting machine.

Jacquard weave   A construction characterized by very intricate woven-in designs. A special Jacquard loom makes these designs by controlling each warp yarn.

jap silk   Another name for China silk. *See* silk, China.

jean (jeen)   In theory, a sturdy, solid-colored or striped twill-weave cotton fabric, softer and finer than denim and drill. In practice, the term denim is almost always used for the fabric, whereas the term jeans is used for pants made of denim. Jean is used for sport blouses, work shirts, women's and girl's pants and shorts, and children's overalls and playclothes.

jersey (*jur*-zee)   A single knit fabric with plain stitches on the right side and purl stitches on the back. A weft-knitted rayon, acetate, or two-bar tricot-knitted rayon or acetate used for slips, gowns, and blouses. Jersey is also made of wool, cotton, silk, nylon, or blends of the newer synthetics. As an elastic knitted wool fabric, usually in stockinette stitch, jersey was first made on the Island of Jersey off the English coast and used for fisherman's clothing. It is also used for blouses, dresses, and basque shirts. The word jersey is also occasionally used as a synonym for any knit. *See* knitting, single knit, and purl knit.

jig dyeing Passing the cloth through a jig-dyeing machine (a large tub holding dye). It is used particularly for dark, direct dyes.

jumpsuit A one-piece garment consisting of a blouse or shirt and trousers or shorts.

jute (joot) One of the natural fibers still used extensively for fabrics. It is a bast fiber that comes from jute plants grown primarily in India, Pakistan, and Bangladesh. Jute is used for many purposes, including the manufacture of burlap, gunny sacks, bags, cordage (twine and rope), trimmings, binding threads, and backings for rugs and carpets.

J

Defect	Explanation	Severity
Jerk-backs	Any loose, straggly length of filling yarn that hangs at the side of the selvage and is cast back into the cloth as it is being woven. Filling that catches on the side fork or (front box plate is often jerked back) into the body of the fabric.	Major or Minor (depending on how close the patterns are cut to the selvage edge)
Jerk-in	Caused by an extra piece of filling yarn being jerked part way into the fabric by the shuttle, along with a regular pick of filling. On conventional looms, they generally are confined to the battery side. The most common cause is the failure of the thread-holding mechanism to hold the filling from the outgoing bobbin long enough for the temple thread cutter to cut the yarn after a filling change. The defect appears at the selvage.	Major or Minor (depending on how close the patterns are cut to the selvage edge)

kapok (*kay*-pahk)   A fluffy fiber that comes from the seed pods of the kapok tree found in the tropics. Kapok at one time was extremely popular for stuffing pillows and was also used in life preservers as it is naturally buoyant. Today, man-made fibers have replaced kapok in many cases.

karakul (*kayr*-uh-kuhl)   Curly and fairly heavy fleece from karakul lambs used to produce wool called astrakhan. *See* astrakhan.

kashmir (*kash*-meer)   Another spelling for cashmere. Kashmir is also an alternate spelling for the name of the goat from which cashmere wool comes. *See* cashmere.

kemp (kemp)   Short-fibered, harsh wool, used principally in carpets.

keratin (*ker*-uh-tin)   A protein substance that is the chief constituent of the wool fiber.

kersey (*kur*-zee)   A thick, heavy, pure wool and cotton twill-weave fabric similar to melton. It is well fulled, with a fine nap and a close-sheared surface. Kersey is used for uniforms and overcoats.

keyhole neck   A rounded neckline with an opening in the shape of a circle, teardrop, or inverted wedge.

khaki (*kak*-ee)   A term used for both an earth color or olive green color (yellow-brown color with a greenish tint) and for fabrics made in these colors, whether of wool, cotton, linen, or man-made fibers. Khaki is a classic uniform color and material. It is also used for sportswear and leisure clothes.

kick pleat   A small pleat at the bottom of a straight, fairly long skirt to give room for walking.

kidskin   Fine grain leather from young goats, used for gloves, shoes, clothing, purses, and purse accessories. Suede is generally made from kidskin.

kilim (ghi-*leem*)   Near Eastern oriental fabric woven with a shuttle or needle, with no pile. Kilims are used by the Orientals as portieres, couch covers, and table covers.

kimono (kuh-*mohn*-uh)   A loose rectangular-shape, Japanese-style robe with wide sleeves. Originally designed with a broad sash at the waist, modern variations often omit the sash.

knee-highs   Men's, women's, or children's socks or stockings that reach almost to the knee. They come in a variety of styles and colors.

knickers   Fairly loose-fitting short pants gathered below the knee.

knife pleats (or side pleats)   Narrow, single folds of fabric all turned in the same direction.

knit terry cloth (nit *tayr*-ee kloth)   Terry cloth is a soft, absorbent fabric with loops on one or both sides. When this fabric is knit rather than woven, it is called knit terry. Knit terry is especially popular for bathrobes and beach wear because of its absorbency. Stretch knit terry (usually made stretchable by the addition of a synthetic elastic fiber) is popular for baby clothes because of its absorbency and comfort.

knitted pile fabrics   Fabrics containing extra yarn that may be drawn out in loops to form the pile that may or may not be cut.

knitting (*nit*-ing)   The process of constructing an elastic, porous fabric by interlocking a series of loops of one or more yarns with needles. It may be done by hand or by machine. These yarns form a series of connecting loops that support one another like a chain. Almost any textile item can be and has been knitted, including rugs. A warp knit is made on a machine in which parallel yarns run lengthwise and are locked into the series of loops. Warp knits have a good deal of crosswise stretch. Weft knits are made on a machine that forms loops in a circular direction and have one continuous thread running across the fabric. The following entries are common knit terms.

> **double knit** (*duh*-buhl nit)   A weft knit fabric produced in two layers which cannot be separated. Its appearance is the same on either side with a characteristic fine vertical wale. *See* wale.

> **Jacquard knit** (*jak*-ard nit)   A knit with a design knit into the fabric in a regular allover pattern. Most Jacquard patterns are closely knitted, but it is possible to make some pattern knits with a Jacquard machine. *See* pattern knits.

pattern knit   Knit made on a weft knit machine by dropping, adding, rearranging, and crossing various stitches to create intricate designs.

plain knit   A flat-surfaced even knit made by hand or machine knitting. In hand knitting it is called stockinette stitch. The face of the fabric is smooth and the reverse is looped. *See* purl knit.

purl knit (purl nit)   A term used to describe alternating rows of knit and purl stitches (purl is the reverse of a plain knit fabric with the loops showing) forming a pattern with considerable crosswise stretch.

raschel knit (ra-*shell* nit)   A knit made on a raschel machine, a warp knitting machine that uses bulky yarns to form designs to imitate crochet or net.

rib knit   A knit that consists of groups of alternate plain and purl stitches (the reverse of a plain knit with loops showing). Rib knit fabrics are stretchier and have a snugger fit than plain knits. Rib knit is frequently used at wrists, waists, and necklines of plain or patterned knit garments where it is called ribbing.

single knit   Single knit, made on a weft knitting machine, is another term for plain knit. *See* plain knit.

stable knit   Any knit unlikely to stretch excessively. Double knits are usually stable knits.

stretchable knit   Any knit that has a good deal of give or "stretch." Most single knits are considered stretchable knits.

knitwear   Knitted apparel, including hosiery, underwear, outerwear, and sportswear.

knotting (*naht*-ing)   A process of forming an openwork fabric or net by tying yarns together where they cross one another.

Defect	Explanation	Severity
Kinks	These occur when yarn recedes upon itself forming a series of extra loops in the goods. Kinks may be caused by poor shuttle tension or action, irregular stop motion action of the loom, and improper timing of the shed as the warp ends raise and lower to form this shed.	Major
Kinky Filling	Short filling yarn loops caused by tension release of the filling before the loom turns over for the proper timing of the shed of the warp yarns. The three actions of a loom (shedding, picking, and beating-up) must synchronize to the decimal part of a second, otherwise kinks are likely to occur. Poor shuttle lining also causes yarn kinks.	Major
Knots	Caused by tying spools of yarn together.	Usually Minor

lace   A decorated openwork fabric created by looping, interlacing, braiding, or twisting threads. It is made (either on a background fabric of net or without a background fabric) with a design formed by a network of threads made by hand or on special lace machines, with bobbins, needles, or hooks. The pattern in lace is usually open and most often floral in design. Machine-made lace is most commonly seen today and many patterns formerly only made by hand, are imitated by machine. Lace is the traditional bridal fabric, but it is also used for other nonformal clothing such as sports clothes. The following entries are some of the major types of lace.

ajour lace (ah-*zhur* layss)   An open lace design with the pattern scattered on the ground.

Alençon lace (ah-*len*-sun layss)   Lace with a fine, solid, floral design outlined by cord or heavy threads. It may have one scalloped edge. This lace is made on a sheer net fabric.

allover lace   Lace in which the pattern covers the entire fabric, rather than being isolated on one section of background net.

aloe lace (*al*-oh layss)   Usually a bobbin or tatted lace made from aloe plant fibers, a group of plants that includes the agave. *See* bobbin lace and tatting.

antique lace   A heavy lace made on a square knotted net with designs darned onto the net. Machine-made antique lace is often used for curtains. *See* embroidery and darn.

Argentan lace (*ahr*-jen-ten layss)   Argentan lace is similar to alençon, but the designs usually are not outlined with cord and are often larger and bolder than those of alençon.

Battenberg lace (*bat*-en-berg layss)   A lace similar to Renaissance lace with a pattern formed by tape or braid joined by bars. *See* Renaissance lace.

beading   A type of lace made by the bobbin lace method. Also, an openwork lace or embroidery containing holes designed for the insertion of decorative ribbon. *See* bobbin lace.

Belgian lace (*bel*-jin layss)   Any lace made in Belgium. Originally, the term meant a bobbin lace worked on a machine-made net. *See* bobbin lace.

Binche lace (beench layss)   A lace in which hand-made lace motifs are appliqued to a machine-made net ground. The name comes from Binche, a town in Belgium, where the lace is said to have originated.

bobbin lace (*bob*-in layss)   Lace made using a pillow to hold pins around which thread is arranged. Bobbins are used to hold and feed the thread. Bobbin lace is also called bobbinet lace and pillow lace.

bobbinet lace (bob-in-*et* layss)   *See* bobbin lace and pillow lace.

bourdon lace (*boor*-dohn layss)   Lace made by machine, usually in a scroll design. The design usually is outlined with a heavy thread.

Breton lace (*bret*-uhn layss)   Lace made on open net, usually embroidered with very heavy, often brightly colored, yarns, Breton is the area in France where the lace is said to have originated.

Brussels lace (*bruss*-uhlz layss)   Brussels lace may be either a bobbin lace or a needlepoint lace. It is usually worked on a machine-made ground and sometimes the designs are appliqued onto the ground. Because of the importance of Brussels, Belgium, in the history of lace-making (many patterns developed there), several different laces are called Brussels lace. *See* bobbin lace and needlepoint lace.

Chantilly (shan-*til*-ee [incorrect pronunciation, but the only one used])   One of the most popular of bridal laces often used for the trimming on bridal veils. It is made by the bobbin method and has designs outlined by thick cords. *See* bobbin lace.

Cluny lace (*kloo*-nee layss)   A heavy lace, often made of thick cotton or man-made fibers using the bobbin method. It is the traditional lace for doilies and place mats, but is also used in apparel. *See* bobbin lace.

crocheted lace (kroh-*shayd* layss)   Lace made with a single yarn. A crochet hook is used to form loops joined to other loops to form the design.

hairpin lace   A delicate, narrow lace worked over a hairpin or a special hairpin-shaped, loom-like tool.

Irish lace (*eye*-rish layss)   The term Irish lace can be used to refer to any lace made in Ireland, but crocheted laces are those most often given the name. Embroidered nets are another type of Irish lace. *See* crocheted lace.

needlepoint lace (*need*-uhl-poynt layss)   Lace made with a sewing or embroidery needle to form buttonhole stitches as the basis of the design.

Nottingham lace (*not*-ing-um layss)   One of the first of the machine-made laces. It originated in Nottingham, England. Today, the term Nottingham lace is often used for any lace made by any machine.

pillow lace   Lace made by using a pillow to hold pins around which thread is arranged. *See* bobbin lace.

reembroidered lace (ree-im-*broyd*-erd layss)   Lace with designs outlined with embroidery stitching. *See* embroidery.

Renaissance lace (*rehn*-uh-sahns layss)   A lace made of woven strips of fabric joined by flat stitches. *See* Battenberg lace.

tatting (*tat*-ing)   A method of lace-making worked with the fingers and a shuttle that holds the thread. Tatting forms a narrow, knotted lace, often used for edging.

Val lace (val layss)   *See* Valenciennes lace.

Valenciennes lace (vah-len-see-*enz* layss)   A flat bobbin lace worked with one hand forming both the background and the design for the lace.

Venetian lace (veh-*nee*-shun layss)   *See* Venise lace.

Venice lace (*veh*-niss layss)   *See* Venise lace.

Venise lace (veh-*neess* layss)   A needlepoint lace usually in a floral pattern connected by picot edgings. It is also called Venice lace and Venetian lace. *See* picot.

lacing (or fagoting)   String, cord, or ribbon strung through eyelets or over hooks in order to bring together and fasten parts of an item such as a blouse, belt, or shoe.

lambrequin (*lam*-ber-kin)   A structure at the top and sides of a window that frames it and is usually part of the window decoration. Lambrequins are often covered with fabric and trimmed. They are usually made of wood and may be simply painted.

lamb's wool   Soft, resilient wool clipped from sheep less than eight months old. It is used in fine-grade woolen fabrics.

lambskin   A common name in leather for the hide of an animal with the fur removed.

lamé (lah-*may*)   Brocade, damask, or brocatelle fabrics in which flat metallic yarns (or with a combination of metallic and other fiber yarns) are woven or knitted in warp and filling for a luxurious effect. Today, most lamé is made from one of the nontarnishable metallic fibers, a great improvement over lamé of the past that tended to darken with age. Lamé is also a trademark term for a nontarnishable metallic yarn. Glitter is sometimes used to describe this type of fabric and is used for evening dresses, blouses, and trimmings.

laminating (*lam*-ih-nayt-ing)   The sticking of a fabric to a plastic foam or sheet of plastic. A method of joining one fabric to another by means of an adhesive. Polyurethane is often laminated to the back of an outerwear coating fabric for warmth. The term laminating is occasionally used as a synonym for bonding, but this is incorrect. *See* bonding.

lansdowne (*lans*-down)   A lightweight twill fabric made from natural or man-made fibers and usually used for dresses.

lapel (luh-*pehl*)   The front part of a garment that is folded back on the chest and forms a continuation of the collar. A notched lapel joins the collar at a seam and its outer point slants downward; a peaked lapel joins the collar at a seam and its outer point slants upward.

lappet (*lap*-it)   An ornamental embroidery effect woven into a cloth by a series of needles. The design, often in zigzag effect, is not clipped.

lariat (*lar*-ee-uht)   A woven belt that looks like a cowboy's rope; it is generally made of leather.

lastrile (*las*-trel)   Generic name for a made-made elastic fiber. There is not now, and has never been, any commercial production of this fiber in the United States. *See* generic name.

latex (*lay*-teks)   The name for the liquid form of natural or man-made rubber. It can be formed into thread for use as an elastic yarn. Latex is also used extensively as part of the backing in the manufacture of rugs and at one time, was used extensively in corsets and brassieres. Now, however, although some latex foundation garments are still made, it has been largely replaced by spandex. Solid latex is sometimes referred to as rubber. *See* spandex.

launder-ometer (*lawn*-duhr-ahm-uh-tuhr)   A standard laboratory devise for testing a fabric's fastness to washing.

lawn   A light, well-hackled linen fabric first made in Laon, France. Now, it is a lightweight, fairly sheer, fine, plain-weave cotton or linen muslin fabric generally more sheer and with a higher count than nainsook. It can be given a soft or crisp finish and is sized and calendered to produce a soft, lustrous appearance. Linen lawn is synonymous with handkerchief linen. Cotton lawn is a similar type of fabric. Lawn is slightly stiffer than batiste, but can be used for similar purposes. It is white, solid colored, or printed and is used for dresses, blouses, curtains, lingerie, and as a base for embroidered items. *See* batiste, nainsook, and handkerchief linen.

leather   The hide of an animal with the fur removed. It has been used throughout history for clothing and other purposes. Today, man-made fabrics that imitate leather are widely available. Common leather names include alligator, buckskin, calfskin, chamois, cordovan, cowhide, crocodile, doeskin, grain leather, kid, lambskin, morocco, nappa, patent, peccary, pigskin, pin seal, reptile, reversed leather, Russian, shearling, skiver, snakeskin, and suede.

L

leather converter   A business that buys hides and skins, has them processed in contract tanneries, and then sells the finished product.

leatherette (leth-uh-*ret*)   A term used for imitation leathers. More correctly, these should be described by their actual construction, such as vinyl-coated fabric.

Leaver's lace (*lee*-verz layss)   Machine-made lace named for the inventor of the machine on which it is made. Many hand-made lace patterns can be copied on this machine. The term is sometimes used in preference to machine-made lace to imply quality.

leg warmers   Bulky knit, footless socks that extend from ankle to mid-thigh. They can be worn over stockings, boots, and pants, and also with skirts.

leghorn straw   A braided straw popular for hats and is made from wheat grown in Italy. *See* straw.

leno (*lee*-noh)   An open, lacy woven fabric made with a special loom attachment. In a leno weave a pair of filling yarns twist around the warp yarns in various patterns to achieve the lacy effect. A leno weave is also made by twisting adjacent warps around each other like a figure eight. The filling passes through the twisted warps. Leno fabrics are popular for curtains and summer dresses.

letting off   Releasing warp yarns from the warp beam as the weaving operation proceeds.

Liberty prints (*lih*-ber-tee prints)   Liberty, a shop founded in London in 1875, has been noted almost since its beginning for the unusual printed fabrics it sells. The prints are also available in other stores. These prints are often in muted colors and feature floral and other patterns, often on dark grounds. Liberty prints have traditionally been printed on lawn and on a blend of wool and cotton. The type of print Liberty has come to stand for over the years moves in and out of fashion. When these prints are popular the term "Liberty prints" is often used incorrectly for prints that resemble those made by this company.

limp fabric   A fabric that is too soft because of inadequate amounts or improper application of finishing materials.

line   Longest flax fibers used for fine, even linen yarns. Shortest flax fibers are called tow.

line yarn   Well-hackled, even linen yarn made of long fibers.

linear polymer (*lin*-ee-uhr *powl*-ee-muhr)   A polymer formed by end-to-end linking of molecular units. The resulting polymer is very long and narrow. It is typical of fibrous forms.

linen (*lin*-uhn)   A vegetable fiber obtained from the inside of the woody stalk of the flax plant. It is one of the oldest fabrics known. It is strong, and today's man-made fibers are often blended with it to improve its wrinkle resistance and give the fabric other desirable qualities. Linen is woven in various weights for different purposes and is occasionally used in knit blends. The following entries are common linen names.

> **art linen**   A plain-weave, medium-weight linen or blended fabric, bleached or left its natural color, used for embroidery. It can be found in art needlework (embroidery) departments and stores.

Belgian linen (*bel*-jin *lin*-uhn)   Any linen produced in Belgium.

embroidery linen (im-*broy*-der-ee *lin*-uhn)   Another name for art linen. *See* art linen.

handkerchief linen (*han*-ker-chif *lin*-uhn)   A fine, sheer linen used for handkerchiefs, dresses or blouses, or whenever a lightweight cloth is desired.

Irish linen (*eye*-rish *lin*-uhn)   Irish linen refers to linen items from Northern Ireland and Eire.

linen straw   A type of straw made to resemble woven linen. *See* straw.

linen tester   A magnifying glass for counting cloth, also called pick glass or pick counter.

linens and domestics (*lin*-uhns and doh-*mess*-tiks)   The term used in stores to describe various household items which, at one time, were made of linen. Today, most linens and domestics are made of cotton and man-made fibers. The following entries are some of the items found in the linens and domestics sections of stores. *See* blankets, towels, and bedding.

antimacassar (ann-tih-me-*kass*-er)   A piece of cloth originally pinned to the back of a chair to protect the upholstery from hair oil (macassar). Today, although antimacassars are still available, changes in hair grooming and the development of fairly easy-to-clean upholstery fabrics have made their purpose primarily decorative.

batting (*bat*-ing)   Batting is usually stocked in linens and domestics departments although it is used today primarily for crafts. Batting is a filling material used to stuff pillows, toys, and quilts. At one time, batting was made of cotton; today, it usually is made of polyester fiberfill. Batting may be sold in bulk form or in true batting form, in which case it is a long flat sheet. Correctly, only the sheets should be called batting, but the term has come to be used for this type of stuffing in all forms.

doily (*doy*-lee)   A piece of fabric, round, square, or rectangular in shape, used under plants and decorative objects partly to protect furniture surfaces and partly as decoration. Doilies are often crocheted. *See* crocheted lace under entry for lace.

mattress cover (mat-*ress kuv*-er)   A quilted, fairly thick pad placed on top of a bed mattress and beneath a bottom sheet to protect the mattress and to make the bed more comfortable. A mattress cover often has elastic at all corners to hold it on the bed and it should completely cover the top of the mattress.

napkin   A rectangular piece of fabric or paper used to wipe the mouth and hands in the course of eating. Napkins are often matched to the tablecloth or placemats.

pillow cover   A fabric cover which is placed over the bed pillow before the pillowcase. Pillow covers are designed to give more protection to pillows than is provided by pillowcases alone. *See* pillowcase.

pillowcase   Pillowcases are washable covers for bed pillows that usually match the sheets and protect the pillow from soil. Most American pillowcases are made in a rectangular form with one open, hemmed edge. They occasionally are decorated on one of the narrower ends.

placemat   A piece of cloth or other material (often foam-backed plastic) placed on a table between the table and the place setting to protect the table and to decorate it during meals. Placemats are available in a variety of sizes, shapes, and colors.

rubber sheets   Sheets used on a bed to protect the mattress more than a mattress pad alone. Although relatively few rubber sheets today are actually made of rubber, the term is still used. These sheets, because they are impervious to water, tend to hold perspiration. They are more comfortable for sleeping if covered by a mattress cover and sheet. *See* mattress cover and sheet.

runner   A rectangular piece of fabric used with placemats to decorate and protect the dining table. It is placed in the center of the table under condiments (salt, pepper, mustard) and any decorations such as flowers or candles. Runners frequently match the placemats and are also used on chests of drawers to protect the top from spills.

sheet   A rectangular piece of fabric used to cover and protect the top and sides of a mattress. This is usually referred to as a bottom sheet. A top sheet is placed over a bottom sheet to protect the skin from a sometimes scratchy blanket and to protect the blanket from soil. Traditionally, sheets were made of linen or cotton; today, they are more likely to be made of cotton and polyester blends for easy care qualities. At one time, sheets were white; today, they are available in many colors and patterns.

silence cloth   A cloth put on a dining table to protect it and (as the name suggests) to prevent the clatter of dishes against the table. A silence cloth is usually a napped, fairly heavy fabric. Silence cloths are placed beneath tablecloths and are also called silencers.

silencer   Another name for silence cloth. *See* silence cloth and table pad.

table pad   A table covering used to protect the table and prevent clatter. Table pads are usually heavier and stiffer than silence cloths and are usually made with a felt back and a plastic top. *See* silence cloth.

tablecloth   The traditional table covering for protection and decoration. Tablecloths range from informal ones made, for example, of checked fabrics, to formal, such as double damask. Napkins are usually matched to the tablecloth. *See* double damask and napkin.

lingerie (*lahn*-jeh-ree)   Another term for women's underwear and nightwear, including panties, slips, petticoats, camisoles, pajamas, and nightgowns. Lingerie implies delicate fabric, often lace-trimmed. The term lingerie fabrics is occasionally used for very delicate fabrics. Formerly, the finest lingerie was made of muslin, lawn, or silk; today, fabrics of man-made fibers, especially nylon tricot, are dominant.

lingerie crepe (*lahn*-jeh-ree crayp)   Formerly called French crepe because it was originally made in France. The creped surface was made by embossing (pressing cloth over a fleece blanket). Because it is no longer pressed, it is not a crepe and it is used for lingerie and spring and summer dresses.

lining (*lyn*-ing)   Fabric made in the same shape as the outer fabric, a lining supports and protects the outer fabric and hides seams as well. Linings are found not only in apparel, but also in draperies and occasionally curtains and bedspreads. Items that are lined tend to wear better and last longer than unlined items and the appearance of a lined item is usually better than that of an unlined one. Special lining fabrics include those sold under the trademarks Si Bonne and Earl-Glo. Linings should be of the same construction as the outer fabric; wovens should be lined with wovens and knits with knits.

linsey-woolsey (*lin*-zee-*wuhl*-zee)   When linen and wool were woven together in the 18th century, the resulting coarse, loosely woven, and rather scratchy fabric, was called linsey-woolsey. Although linen and wool blends are occasionally made today, the use of finer finishing techniques makes them extremely comfortable and the name linsey-woolsey is limited to historical references.

linters (*lin*-tuhrz)   Very short fibers that cover the cotton seeds after the long fibers have been removed by ginning. These short, fuzzy fibers, after removal from the cotton seeds, are a source of cellulose for rayon and acetate.

Linton tweed (*lin*-ton tweed)   The trademark of Linton, Ltd., Carlisle, England. These tweeds are noted for their softness and subtle or vivid colorings.

lisle (lyl)   A hard, usually long-staple cotton or wool yarn of defined length in two or more ply and with a minimum twist for a given count specified by the Federal Trade Commission (FTC) rules for hosiery.

llama (*yah*-ma [correct pronunciation]; *lah*-muh [common pronunciation]   An animal found in parts of Latin America, it is believed to be a member of the camel family. Llama wool is used to make some expensive coating fabric.

llama family   A large family of South American camels. It includes the llama, alpaca, huarizo and misti, guanaco, and vicuna.

loafer   A slip-on shoe with a separate sole and heel; similar to, but providing more support than, a moccasin.

loden cloth (*loh*-den kloth)   A thick, heavy, napped fleecy coating fabric woven of coarse grade wool in Austria and the German Tyrol. It is similar to duffel cloth if made of wool or the occasional man-made fibers. Since the wool has some grease, it is naturally water-repellent. It is usually a light forest green color, called loden, from which it gets its name. Loden cloth moves in and out of fashion everywhere except in those parts of Germany and Austria where loden jackets, suits, and coats are considered basic dress. Loden cloth is sometimes gray in color. *See* duffel cloth.

loft   The springiness or fluffiness of a fiber.

longcloth   A fine, soft, cotton cloth woven of softly twisted yarns. It is similar to nainsook but slightly heavier, with a duller surface. Longcloth is so called because it was one of the first fabrics to be woven in long rolls. It is also a synonym for muslin sheeting of good quality. The fabric is used for underwear and linings. *See* nainsook and muslin sheeting.

loom   A machine for weaving cloth. It is operated either by hand or by machine.

loom-figured fabrics (loom *fig*-yerd *fab*-riks)   Fabrics that have the design or pattern woven or knitted in as opposed to those which, for instance, have patterns printed on finished cloth.

loom finished (loom *fin*-isht)   A term referring to certain fabrics sold without most of the steps mentioned in the entry under finishing. Loom finished fabrics are relatively rare because the consumer has grown accustomed to finished fabrics. *See* finishing.

loop   Any material (braid, fabric, and so forth) that is shaped into an oval and topstitched to a garment or encased into a seam and used as a buttonhole.

loop rug   Usually, a rug with an uncut loop pile. Types of loops include high-low loop (a rug in which some loops are higher than others giving a sculptured effect), one-level loop, and random-sheared loop (a rug with some loops cut and others uncut to create a sculptured effect). *See* pile.

loop yarn   The slack-twisted strand is twisted to form loops or curls. This strand is held in place by one or two binder yarns.

loose cover   Another term for slipcover. *See* slipcover.

lounge wear   Intimate apparel that includes robes, housecoats, and bed jackets.

L

lumen (*loo*-muhn)   The open structure or canal from which the protoplasm has disappeared.

Lurex (*loor*-eks)   Trademark of Dow Badische Company for metallic fiber.

luster (*lus*-tehr)   The gloss, sheen, or shine of a fiber, yarn, or fabric.

luster rugs   Rugs that are chemically washed to give them sheen. They may be Wilton, Axminster machine-made rugs with oriental designs or velvet construction, and are frequently referred to as sheen-type rugs.

Lycra (*ly*-krah)   Trademark of DuPont for spandex fiber.

Lyons velvet (*lee*-ohn *vel*-vit [correct pronunciation]; *ly*-onz *vel*-vit [common pronunciation])   Velvet originally made of silk in Lyons, France. Lyons is a thick, rather stiff velvet with a short pile. It may be silk pile and cotton and rayon backed. Today, this type of velvet (often called Lyons-type) is made totally from man-made fibers. It is used for home furnishings as well as for evening wear.

Defect	Explanation	Severity
Loom Bar	A change in shade across the width of a fabric, resulting from a buildup of tension in the shuttle before a filling change. This is most common on yarn-dyed fabrics.	Major (can be Minor)
Loom Waste	A place in a fabric where accumulated waste off the loom has found its way into the fabric, either by air currents or loom shuttle.	Minor
Looped Selvages	These come from poor or uneven shuttle tension, improperly twisted filling yarn, poorly wound filling bobbins, poor or unbalanced timing of the harness frames of the loom, or waste accumulation, chiefly among the loom dropwires on the respective warp yarns.	Minor (can be Major)
Loopy Filling (also Hang Pick)	A pick of filling hanging for a split second on a warp knot or other protrusion until freed by the stroke of the reed. This results in a short loop of filling appearing on the face of the fabric.	Minor (can be manicured without serious damage.)
Loose Course	In knits, a course whose loops are more extended than normal, because of a lack of correct tension on the yarn.	Major
Loose Picks	Actual loose picks do not weave into the cloth the same as regular picks. Easily noted, they are caused by irregular filling motion, faulty shuttle action, poor winding, or yarn that is not what it should be as to diameter, ply, twist, or yarn count.	Major
Loose Selvages	Listing that has worked loose because of uneven filling tension and action against the yarns in the material that make up the selvage. The term also includes selvage ends that have become broken and not been repaired; this condition will likely cause the other end to snap and break within a very short time. Selvages of this type impair appearance of finished fabric, and they will definitely give trouble when the fabric is being made into a garment.	Major

Macclesfield silk (*mak*-les-feeld silk)   Hand-woven silk or rayon fabric with small overall Jacquard patterns. Macclesfield, England, is the town of origin. Today, the name applies to small, yarn dyed, dobby designs used in men's neckties. *See* Spitalfields.

Macintosh (*mak*-en-tosh)   Fabric named for its inventor, Charles Macintosh. It is coated with rubber to make it water-repellent. As a result, the name refers not only to the fabric, but also the raincoats made from it. Although the process has been almost replaced by other methods of making water-repellent fabrics, the name is still used occasionally for raincoats. *See* water-repellent.

Mackinac (*mak*-en-naw)   Another spelling for Mackinaw. *See* Mackinaw.

Mackinaw (*mak*-eh-naw) A thick, heavy, usually coarse fabric with a certain degree of natural water repellency. It was originally made of wool, but other fibers such as acrylics are being used today. It was named for the blankets made by the Mackinaw Indians in Michigan. Mackinaw and similar fabrics are extremely popular for hunting jackets and are usually plaid or checked. Mackinaw is also spelled Mackinac.

Mackintosh (*mak*-en-tosh)   Another spelling for Macintosh. *See* Macintosh

macramé (*mak*-rah-may)   An ancient method of forming open fabrics by knotting string, yarn, or other threads. Macramé can be used to make anything from delicate trimmings to sturdy items such as hammocks. Recently, wall hangings of macramé have also become popular.

macromolecule (mak-ruh-*mowl*-uh-kewl)   A large molecule formed by hooking together many small molecule units. The term is used synonymously with polymolecule or polymer. *See* polymer.

madder (*mad*-uhr) A root from which a vegetable dye called Alizarin was obtained originally. It is now produced synthetically. *See* Alizarin dye.

Madras (*mad*-rehss) 1) Called Indian Madras. A fine, hand-loomed cotton imported from Madras, India. The Federal Trade Commission has ruled that it is deceptive to apply this term to a fabric that does not meet this description. In addition, the FTC definition requires that any dyes used on this fabric must be vegetable dyes that will bleed (the colors run into each other). The fact that the FTC felt called upon to make such a definition is some indication of the popularity of Madras and imitation Madras fabrics in recent years. The authentic Madras and its imitations usually have checked or plaid designs; with time, as the colors bleed into each other with washing, true Madras develops extremely soft colorings. It should, of course, be washed by hand separately from other fabrics. 2) A finely woven, soft, plain- or Jacquard-weave muslin shirting with a woven-in pattern or stripe in balanced count in the lengthwise direction and Jacquard or dobby pattern woven in the background. White-on-white Madras has a white figure on a white ground. Some Madras is made with woven checks and cords. It can be used for blouses, dresses, and shirts.

maillot (my-*yoh*) A one-piece, typically strapless, woman's bathing suit.

maline (mah-*leen*) A gauze-like veiling of net used to trim hats. *See* net.

Mandarin collar (*man*-duh-rin *kowl*-uhr) A small (two- to three-inch deep) collar standing on a high, close neckline; the collar does not quite meet in front.

man-made fibers (*man*-mayd *fy*-berz) An overall term referring to all fibers not found naturally. This includes rayon and acetate made from cellulose, a natural product. The term synthetic fibers also applies only to man-made fibers made entirely in the laboratory from such things as petroleum (polyester).

mantilla (man-*tee*-yuh) A lace scarf worn over the head.

marabou (*mayr*-ah-boo) Short, fluffy feathers now taken from domesticated fowl, usually dyed to match the garments on which they are used as trimming. They were originally taken from the stork.

marl (mahrl) A technical term that refers to a yarn made of different colored fibers. The word is used descriptively for fabrics to indicate randomly or uniformly colored slubs that appear on the surface giving added textural and design interest to the fabric.

marquisette (mahr-kwi-*zet*) A light, strong, sheer, open-textured curtain fabric in leno weave, often with dots woven into the surface. The thread count varies from 48 x 22 to 60 x 40. Marquisette, extremely popular for curtains and mosquito netting, is made of cotton, rayon, acetate, nylon, polyester, acrylic, glass, silk, or mixtures.

Marseilles (mahr-*say*) A firmly woven reversible fabric with raised geometric designs. Marseilles was originally made of cotton, but is now usually made from man-made fibers or blends.

Marvess (mahr-*vess*) Trademark of Phillips Fibers for olefin fiber. *See* olefin.

Mary Jane A low-heeled girl's or woman's pump with a strap across the instep and a rounded toe.

mat Another spelling for matte. *See* matte.

matelassé (mat-leh-*say*) A soft double or compound fabric with a quilted appearance. One of the fabrics that, like cloqué, has a blistered or quilted look to the design. Officially, the word matelassé implies the use of two different yarns that, when finished, react differently to the finishing resulting in a puckered effect in the fabric. In practice, the term matelassé is usually applied to luxury fabrics for evening wear, while a word such as cloqué is used for a similar fabric made from cotton. The heavier type is used in draperies and upholstery, whereas crepe matelassé is popular in dresses, semiformal and formal suits and wraps, and trimmings.

M

material (muh-*teer*-ee-ul) Another word for fabric. *See* fabric.

matte (mat) A dull surface on a fabric. Since one of the characteristics of fabrics made from man-made fibers is a shiny surface, matte-finished fabrics have become popular and matte looks for man-made fabrics are achieved in yarn processing or finishing. *See* finishing.

mattress cover (*mat*-ress *kuv*-er) A quilted, fairly thick pad placed on top of a bed mattress and beneath a bottom sheet to protect the mattress and to make the bed more comfortable. A mattress cover often has elastic at all corners to hold it on the bed and it should completely cover the top of the mattress.

mechanical finishes Those finishing processes done by copper plates, roller brushes, perforated cylinders, tenter frames, or any type of mechanical equipment.

mechanical picker   A device with vertical drums equipped with spindles that remove the cotton from the boll.

medium-staple cotton   Fibers 1" to 1^1/$_8$" long.

medulla (mih-*dul*-uh)   Honeycombed cellular section found in medium and coarse wools.

melamine resins (*mell*-uh-meen *reh*-zins)   Finishes used to give wrinkle resistance and other desirable qualities (including a degree of shrinkage resistance) to fabrics, primarily those made from natural fibers. Melamine resins are chlorine retentive which means that if fabrics with these finishes are bleached with a chlorine bleach, they will keep both the color and the odor of the chlorine.

melton (*mell*-tun)   Melton, usually called melton cloth, is a thick, heavily felted or fulled wool fabric in a twill or satin weave, with clipped surface nap, felt-like in feeling, and lustrous, similar to a dull broadcloth. The close weave means that the fabric appears to be completely smooth. Melton was originally made of all wool or cotton and wool, but today is made of other fibers. It is used extensively for coats and also for uniforms. *See* nap.

mercerization (mur-ser-eh-*zay*-shun)   A finish applied to cotton yarn or fabric or to a blend of cotton and other fibers to make it stronger, more absorbent, and to give the fabric additional luster and increased ability to take dye. Mercerization can be done at the yarn stage or the fabric stage. In common with several other textile processes, mercerization involves the use of caustic soda (sodium hydroxide or lye).

merchandise beam   Cylinder in the loom on which finished cloth is wound (taken up). It is synonymous with cloth beam.

merino (meh-*ree*-noh)   Wool from the merino sheep that produces a short staple fiber of extremely high quality. Merino sheep are raised in the United States, Australia, South Africa, and South America. Occasionally, the term merino is used as a synonym for Botany. *See* Botany.

mesh (mehsh)   A term for a large class of open fabrics made by almost all methods except felting. It can be made of any fiber, mixture, or blend. Mesh fabrics are used for bags, summer sport shirts, underwear, foundation garments, and hosiery. Mesh hosiery is knitted in such a pattern that, when one yarn is snagged, the stocking will not develop a long, vertical run, but a hole instead. Mesh stockings and panty hose are believed to wear better than other constructions.

M

metal complex dyes   A class of dyestuffs that is ionic and premetallized (chemically coupled with nickel, copper, and cobalt salts to make the dye on the fiber).

metallic (meh-*tal*-ik)   A generic name for a manufactured fiber that may be metal, metal coated with a synthetic, or a man-made fiber core covered with metal. When the metal is coated with a man-made film, the metal does not tarnish.

metallic cloth   Any fabric, such as lamé, woven with gold, silver, tinsel, or other metal threads.

micronaire fineness (*my*-kruh-nayr *fyn*-nihs)   The weight in micrograms of one inch of fiber.

middy twill (*mid*-ee twill)   The term middy twill is used for many fabrics that are sturdy and have a twill weave. Traditionally made of cotton, middy twill today is likely to include at least some man-made fibers in its construction. When middy blouses are in fashion (a loose-fitting, hip-length overblouse with a sailor collar) the most popular color for this twill is navy blue. It is used also for school uniforms.

Milan straw (mih-*lahn* straw)   A type of straw.

milanese (mihl-uh-*neez*)   A kind of warp knitting with several sets of yarns. Characteristic is its diagonal argyle-type pattern.

mildew resistant (*mill*-doo ree-*zis*-tent)   Among the many properties that can be given to fabrics in the finishing is resistance to traditional enemies. Waterproofed fabrics and fabrics treated with metallic compounds and certain organic compounds will resist mildew. Fabrics such as canvas, that are exposed to the damp conditions that encourage the growth of mildew fungus, can be treated with finishes to resist this fungus, making them mildew resistant. *See* finishing.

military braid (*mil*-ih-tayr-ee brayd)   A flat, ribbed braid used for decorating military and other uniforms. It is also used as a trimming on clothing when the military look is popular.

Milium (*mil*-ee-um)   Trademark of Deering Milliken for a finish that involves the application of aluminum to a lining fabric to make it retain and reflect heat. It is often used as a lining in winter coats eliminating the need for an interlining. *See* interlining and lining.

millinery (*mihl*-uh-nehr-ee)   Women's hats.

minaudière (mihn-ohd-*yayr*)   A small evening bag made from precious metals and often studded with precious or semiprecious gems.

M

mineral fibers   Textile raw material obtained from minerals in the earth, such as asbestos, silver, gold, copper, and the like.

mirror velvet (*mihr*-er *vel*-vit)   Velvet with the pile pressed flat in one or several directions to impart a shimmering appearance.

mixture (*miks*-chuhr)   Although the word mixture is often ignored in favor of the word blend, it should be used to describe fabrics made from a combination of two or more fibers in which one of the fibers is used for the filling thread. *See* blend and biconstituent fiber.

moccasin (*mahk*-uh-suhn)   A soft suede or leather slip-on shoe with no heel and a flat sole.

mock crepe (mahk krayp)   A term for fabrics that have the appearance of crepe, but are not made from crepe yarns. *See* crepe.

modacrylic (mahd-uh-*krill*-ik)   A generic name for modified acrylic fibers derived from thirty-five to eighty-five percent of acrylonitrile units. It differs from acrylic in its chemical structure. Modacrylic is used most commonly to make fake furs and wigs. Modacrylic fibers are naturally flame-retardant (slow-burning). *See* acrylic.

modern style   A style in home furnishings that emphasized simplicity, angularity, and straight lines in furniture.

modified acetate fibers (*mahd*-uh-fyd *ass*-uh-tayt *fy*-berz)   Fibers that are stretched and then treated with alkali.

modified cellulose fibers (*mahd*-uh-fyd *sel*-you-lohs *fy*-berz)   Cotton fibers treated with caustic soda to give strength, increased luster, and improved affinity for dye. Modification of a fiber changes its physical and chemical properties within the limits of a generic family.

modified fibers (*mahd*-uh-fyd *fy*-berz)   Fibers that are treated to eliminate characteristics considered undesirable and to add characteristics considered desirable. Some treatments improve a fiber's ability to take dye, whereas others give a fiber stretch it does not naturally have.

modified rayon fibers   Chemical treatment while fibers are in the plastic state to give them high tenacity (high strength). Changes in the molecular structure of the fiber have been made.

modified yarns (*mahd*-uh-fyd yarnz)   *See* modified fibers.

mogadore (mahg-uh-*dohr*)   A corded silk or rayon fabric with wide ridges and often with wide stripes used for ties.

mohair (*moh*-hayr)   The long, lustrous hair of the Angora goat. It is used, mixed with other fibers, to make mohair fabrics.

mohair rug (*moh*-hayr rug)   Floor covering with mohair pile and jute back.

moiré (mwa-*ray* [correct pronunciation]; moh-*ray* [common pronunciation])   A wavy, rippling pattern similar to a watermark produced in the finishing of certain fabrics by calendering, usually on a ribbed textile fabric. On acetate, moiré made this way is permanent; on most other fabrics it is not. Moiré fabrics go in and out of fashion and are usually popular when taffeta is popular. Moiré effects can also be made by printing and in the weaving of fabrics, but the finishing method is the most common one. *See* calendering under finishing.

moiré taffeta (mwa-*ray taf*-eh-tah)   Taffeta with a moiré finish. *See* taffeta and moiré.

moiréing (mwa-*ray*-ing)   A finishing process by engraved rollers that produces a waved or watered effect on a textile fabric. Design is permanent when heat-set.

moisture regain   The moisture in a material determined under prescribed conditions and expressed as a percentage of the weight of the moisture-free specimen.

molding (*mohl*-ding)   The thermoplastic nature of most of the man-made fibers means that they change their shape under heat, thereby enabling the molding of items instead of knitting them or cutting and sewing them to the desired shape. Although this method of manufacture has great promise, so far it has been successful primarily in brassieres (most seamless brassieres have molded cups) and in upholstery applications.

M

molecular orientation   The degree to which fiber molecules are parallel to each other and to the longitudinal axis of the fiber.

moleskin finish   A cotton fleece lined with close, soft, thick nap that is used in underwear for cold climates.

momie cloth (*mahm*-ee kloth)   A fabric made with a weave that produces a pebbled effect, similar to crepe.

momme (*mahm*-ee)   A Japanese unit of weight used for weighing silk. A momme is slightly less than 4 grams (about .034 ounces).

monk shoe   A plain-toed shoe that closes on the side with a strap and buckle and has a heel.

monk's cloth (mungks kloth)   A heavy, coarse, loosely woven basket weave (4 x 4 or 8 x 8) fabric in solid colors or with stripes or plaids woven into the fabric. Traditionally, this fabric is a natural color, brownish beige, and is made of cotton with, sometimes, the addition of flax or jute; today, it may be made of man-made fibers, also. Monk's cloth is most popular for home furnishings such as draperies, couch covers, and slipcovers, but it is occasionally used in clothing. *See* basket weave under weaving.

monochromatic scheme   The use of a combination of different shades of one color.

monofilament (mahn-eh-*fill*-eh-mint)   A single, fine thread of continuous man-made fiber (as in nylon hosiery). *See* multifilament, staple, and tow.

monogram   Initials of a name combined in a single design and used on clothing, ornaments, stationery, and the like.

monomer (*mahn*-oh-mehr)   A single unit or molecule from which polymers are formed.

mordant (*mahr*-duhnt)   A substance that acts as a binder for the dye. A mordant has an affinity for both the dyestuff and the fabric.

Morocco (meh-*rock*-oh)   A type of leather. *See* leather.

M

mosquito netting (mehs-*keet*-oh *net*-ing)   A coarsely meshed, net fabric used to make mosquito nets to place over windows and beds to keep mosquitoes out. *See* net.

moss crepe (mawss krayp)   Officially, moss crepe is made in a plain or dobby weave with rayon yarns that produce the moss-like effect. In practice, however, the term refers to any crepe, including polyester, considered to have a moss-like surface. *See* weaving.

moss fringe (mawss frinj)   A short, thick fringe usually made of fluffy yarns of wool or acrylic.

moth repellency (mawth ree-*pell*-en-see)   An example of the desirable qualities that can be given to fabrics in the finishing process. Some fabrics are treated with colorless chemicals, similar to dyestuffs, added to the dye bath. Another method atomizes the fabric with mothproofing chemicals. Fabrics that attract moths, such as woolens, can be treated for repellency. The treatment also repels other insects, such as carpet beetles. Wool rugs are almost always treated for moth repellency today.

motif (moh-*teef*)   A design or color used alone or repeated on a fabric.

Mousquetaire (moos-kuh-*tayr*)   A long glove, eight to sixteen buttons in length. It has a vertical opening with buttons near the wrist, so that the wearer can remove the finger section and tuck it into the arm section without having to remove the entire glove.

mousseline (mooss-eh-*leen*)   The name for a broad category of fabrics, usually fairly sheer and lightweight and made in a variety of fibers, including man-mades, silk, cotton, and wool. Mousseline usually has a crisp hand. The word mousseline is often used today for a fabric resembling de soie. *See* mousseline de soie and hand.

mousseline de soie (mooss-eh-*leen* deh swah)   Literally, "muslin of silk." The words de soie mean "of silk" which may explain why the fabric similar to this made from man-made fibers is usually called mousseline. Mousseline de soie (silk organdy) is a lightweight, sheer, plain-weave silk fabric similar to chiffon in its appearance and uses, but a little crisper.

Moygashel (*moy*-gah-shehl)   A trade name representing excellent quality in imported Irish linen.

muff   A tube of fur, wool, or velvet covering used to warm the hands outdoors. It is occasionally supplied as a matching accessory with an outerwear costume.

muffler   A long woven or knitted scarf worn around the neck for warmth.

multicomponent fabric   A fabric in which at least two layers of material are sealed together by an adhesive.

multifilament yarn (mul-tih-*fil*-eh-mint yarn)   A yarn made of two or more filaments (long threads) of man-made fibers (monofilaments) that are joined together, usually by twisting.

multilobal (mul-tih-*loh*-buhl)   A fiber with a modified cross section exhibiting several lobes.

mushroom hat   A hat with a turned-down brim and a round crown.

muslin (*muhz*-lin)   The name for a large group of plain-weave fabrics, originally made of cotton. It ranges in weight from the sheerest batiste to the coarsest sheeting. Muslins include such fabrics as voile, nainsook, lawn, and percale. The sizing may also be light or heavy. Muslin can be solid colored or printed. It is used for dresses,

M

shirts, sheets, and other domestic items. When muslin looks are popular they are usually made of blends of cotton and man-made fibers. When muslin sheets are made of cotton and man-made fiber blends, they are said to approach the softness of percale sheets after a few washings. Muslin is also used for interfacings in ready-to-wear coats and suits and is extremely popular in dressmaking for testing garment appearance and fit before cutting an expensive fabric. It is used as a furniture covering on expensive furniture that is subsequently covered with upholstery fabric or with sets of selected slipcovers. Muslin sheets are bleached; most muslin used for other purposes is unbleached, which means that bits of trash, usually appearing as brown flecks, add color to the fabric. Occasionally, unbleached muslin becomes popular in fashion, even for such uses as wedding gowns. Indian muslin is a very fine muslin from India, often printed with gold and silver. It is an expensive luxury fabric. *See* trash and flecks.

muslin sheeting   A carded muslin for bed sheets in white or colors made in types 140 (A grade), 128 (B grade), and 112 (C grade).

M

Defect	Explanation	Severity
Machine Stop	A term used to describe the visible evidence of a fabric having been stopped in some machine during the dyeing and finishing process. Generally it appears as glaring shade changes across the width of the fabric.	Major
Mat-up	A place where the warp yarns have become entangled so as to disrupt the proper interlacing of warp and filling. This can be caused by a loom failing to stop when an end breaks, or the introduction of a piece of wild yarn from some other source. Mat-ups may range in severity from minor to very damaging.	Major
Misdraw (Color)	In wovens, the drawing of colored yarns through the loom harness contrary to the color pattern and/or weave design. In warp knits, the drawing of colored yarns through the guide bars contrary to the pattern design.	Major
Misdraw (Harness)	Where one or more ends are drawn through the harness contrary to the design of the weave.	Major
Misdraw (Reed)	Where one or more ends are drawn through the reed contrary to the design of the weave.	Minor (can be Major)
Mispick	A filling yarn pick that has not gone all the way through the shed of the loom when weaving. The pick may have been left out altogether, or a short or long portion of the pick may have been deposited in the shed. Caused chiefly by mechanical defects such as filling running out of the bobbin, breakage of the yarn, not interlacing with the warp yarn, poor action by the picker stick, and so on.	Major
Missing Yarn	Occurs in circular knits. Caused by one end of the yarn missing from the feed as the machine continues to run.	Major

Defect	Explanation	Severity
Miss-selection	In knits, where the design is corrupted by the random dropping of stitches. This can result from sticking jacks or the erratic behavior of a yarn feed.	Major
Mixed End (Yarn)	Yarn of a different fiber blend used on the warp frame, resulting in a streak in the fabric.	Major (usually)
Mixed Filling	A visible widthwise band resulting from the placing of improper color on the filling bobbin, thereby impairing the color pattern. It may also be caused by a bobbin of lightweight yarn or different fiber blend used in filling. It appears as a distinct shade change. Often the result of carelessness by the bobbin boy, and by the filling winder or quiller.	Major
Mixed Warp Ends	These come from ends of varying thickness or plies. Attributed to mixed yarn spools during the warp dressing operation.	Major (usually)
Mixed Yarn	Occurs in warp knit. Results from wrong fiber yarn (or wrong size yarn) placed on warp. Fabric could appear as thick end or different color if fibers have different affinities for dye.	Major
Mottled or Cloudy Fabric	A blotchy or spotty appearance resulting from the uneven application of color to a fabric, or the uneven acceptance of color by a fabric. Faulty printing, dyeing, or finishing may also cause this blotched, cloudy, or mottled effect; an irregularity in some process or treatment is the reason for this blemish, often slippage or inaccuracy in a roller setting.	Major (usually)

nacré velvet (na-*kray vel*-vit)   A velvet with a changeable appearance created by using one color for the pile and another for the backing.

nainsook (*nayn*-sook)   A fine, soft, plain-weave cotton muslin fabric made from combed or carded yarns. Better grades have a polished finish on one side. When it is highly polished, nainsook may be sold as polished cotton. In low-priced white goods, cambric, longcloth, and nainsook are often identical before converting; the finishing process gives them their characteristic texture, but it is often difficult to distinguish one from the other. Nainsook is heavier and coarser than lawn. It is usually found in white, pastel colors, and prints and is used primarily for baby clothes, blouses, and lingerie. It has a soft or a crisp finish. With the increasing importance of manmade fibers, nainsook has declined in significance.

naked wool   A relatively new term, much promoted by the International Wool Secretariat, the advertising and promotion organization for wool producers, as a description for sheer, lightweight woolen fabrics that can be worn throughout the year.

nap   Technically, a fuzzy or soft, down-like surface produced by brushing the fabric, usually with wire brushes. However, the term nap has come to mean any hair-like surface including ones which, more correctly, should be termed pile, including velvet. The term nap is also occasionally used to describe the surface of a fabric that reflects light differently from different angles, even though the fabric has no nap. The word nap is used in home sewing to describe all fabrics that must be cut with the pattern pieces facing in the same direction, whether or not these fabrics have a true nap.

naphthol dye (*naf*-thohl dy)   Insoluble azoic dyes formed on the fiber by impregnation of the cotton fabric with beta-naphthol that has been dissolved in caustic soda and then immersed in a basic dye. It is used primarily on cotton and gives brilliant scarlet and red at relatively low cost.

napkin   A rectangular piece of fabric or paper used to wipe the mouth and hands in the course of eating. Napkins are often matched with the tablecloth or placemats.

nappa (*nap*-ah)   A common name for the hide of an animal with the fur removed.

napping (*nap*-ing)   The finishing process used to produce a true napped surface. The fabric is passed over fine wires, brushes, burrs, or revolving cylinders with wire brushes that raise some of the fibers to the top and produce the characteristic soft or fuzzy napped surface. Shearing may be part of the napping process; it cuts the raised nap to a uniform height, similar to the way a lawn mower cuts grass. This process is used primarily on fabrics in which a stripped nap effect is considered desirable.

narrow carpet   Narrow carpet is used as the opposite of broadloom carpet. Narrow carpet is woven in narrow widths (thirty-six inches) and is popular for stair coverings. *See* rugs and carpets.

narrow fabrics   The term narrow fabrics refers to items such as braids and tapes that are woven on a very narrow loom and have a selvage at each side. Officially, ribbons are not considered narrow fabrics, but in practice they are often included.

natural color   A term used loosely to describe the color of a natural fiber fabric as it comes from the loom before bleaching or dyeing. Natural also is used for many colors from off-white to a pale brown. *See* neutral color.

natural fibers   Fibers found in nature that can be made into yarn with relatively few steps. The most commonly known fibers include cotton, silk, wool, linen, hemp, jute, ramie, kapok, nettle, and hair fibers. The term natural fibers only came into use with the development of man-made fibers to distinguish one from the other. *See* entries for above-listed fibers.

Navajo rug (*nah*-vuh-hoh rug)   A rug tapestry woven in a geometric pattern by Navajo Indians in the western part of the United States. Navajo rugs are usually brightly colored and have become true collectors' items. *See* tapestry.

neckerchief (*nek*-uhr-chif)   A small scarf or handkerchief tied around the neck.

needlepoint A form of embroidery worked on an open fabric (called needlepoint canvas) that is unusable until the embroidery covers the openings. Although many different stitches can be worked on needlepoint canvas, the most commonly used are the basket weave, continental, and half-cross stitch. Needlepoint has several other names, depending on the size of the holes in the canvas. Petit point (*pet*-ee poynt), for example, is done on canvas with small holes close together. Canvas with twenty holes per inch is considered petit point canvas. Quick point (kwik poynt) is the name for needlepoint worked with thick yarns on needlepoint canvas with large, widely-spaced holes (five holes to the inch). Quick point goes faster than petit point, which is very time-consuming. Gros point (grow poynt) is a synonym for regular needlepoint most commonly worked on canvas with ten, twelve, or fourteen holes to the inch. *See* needlepoint canvas.

needlepoint canvas The fabric on which needlepoint is worked. It is a heavily sized (starched) mesh fabric. The open spaces in the mesh are filled with yarn as the needlepoint is worked. There are two kinds of needlepoint canvas. Penelope canvas has double threads used in the weave. These threads can be split so that certain areas can be worked in extremely small stitches (petit point) and other areas worked in larger stitches. The second type of canvas is called mono canvas; it is woven with single threads. The color of needlepoint canvas is usually white or light beige and the sizes of the holes vary from those requiring as many as 200 stitches to the square inch up to those requiring only sixteen stitches to the square inch. Rug canvas used to hook rugs closely resembles needlepoint canvas but has larger holes. *See* needlepoint.

needlepoint lace Lace made with a sewing or embroidery needle to form buttonhole stitches as the basis of the design.

needle-punched carpeting A nonwoven, nonpile carpeting with a felt-like surface. A lap, web, or batt of loose fibers is applied to a base of cotton fabric, burlap, plastic, rubber, and the like. Needles having downward-facing barbs are forced into the base, causing the tufts of fiber to adhere to the base.

negligee (neg-lih-*zhay*) A loose, robe-type garment, worn in the boudoir, made of sheer fabric and often lace or fur trimmed.

N

Nehru hat (*nay*-roo hat)   A fabric cap with a crown that folds inward; designed after the style worn by India's late Prime Minister Nehru.

net   A geometrically shaped, figured mesh fabric made in nylon, rayon, silk, or cotton. The size of the mesh varies as well as the weight of the net. Net and mesh are often used as synonyms and the fabrics themselves can be used for the same purposes. Net ranges from the delicacy of hair net, often made of human hair and used to hold hair in place, to mosquito nets, used for protection from insects, to fish nets, used to catch fish and drain the water from the catch. Net is either made on a warp-knitting machine or knotted by hand and often forms the ground on which lace is made. It is used for veils, evening dresses, and trimmings. Tulle, a favorite for bridal veils, is another form of net, and is made from silk or nylon.

nettle (*net*-uhl)   A plant found primarily in Europe that is sometimes used to produce a fiber by much the same method as that used to make linen from flax. The word nettle is sometimes used for fibers which are actually ramie. *See* ramie and linen.

neutral color (*noo*-trul *kul*-er)   A color that can be used with many other colors as an accessory color. Black, brown, gray, beige, and white are the most common neutral colors, but navy blue, burgundy, and red are often used as neutral colors for accessories.

new wool   Wool not previously woven, knitted, or felted into a wool product.

newsboy hat   A full, flat fabric cap with a headband and front brim.

ninon (*nee*-nahn)   A smooth, transparent, lightweight, closely woven fabric originally made of silk. It is a voile with warp yarns grouped in pairs available in plain or novelty weaves. It is now usually made in synthetic fibers such as nylon, polyester, acetate, and others, and is used for dresses and curtains.

nitrocellulose rayon (ny-truh-*sel*-you-lohs *ray*-on)   The first type of synthetic fiber discovered, but no longer made in the United States. This type of rayon is made from a solution of nitrated cellulose solidified into filaments.

noil silk   Short fibers of waste silk produced in the manufacture of spun silk.

noils (noyls)   Short fibers, often those taken out by combing or carding. They may be used with other, longer fibers, to form yarn, producing

N

a fabric with textural interest. Occasionally, the noils are colored differently from the other fiber in the fabric. *See* combing and carding.

nonpermanent finish   A finish that is removed when subjected to such agents as friction, laundering, light, and heat.

nonthermoplastic (nahn-thuhr-muh-*plas*-tik)   Not capable of being softened by heat.

nonwoven (nahn-*wohv*-uhn)   A word to describe a fabric that is neither knit nor woven. The category of nonwoven fabrics usually includes those that are felted as well as those in which fibers are joined by glue or heat. Occasionally, a distinction is made between felted fabrics, paper, and other nonwovens. *See* felt.

nonwoven fabrics   Webs of fibers held or bonded together with plastic, heat, pressure, or solvent.

nonwoven floor coverings   Carpets with tufts that are usually punched through a burlap backing. Flocked carpets are made of precut electronically charged fibers stuck to a backing coated with adhesive.

notched collar   A collar made of two pieces of fabric that form a V-shaped indentation at the lapel.

notions   The consumers' term for findings, such as buttons, interfacings, pockets, belts, snap fasteners, and zippers used in making garments. They are normally purchased in a notions department, but sometimes are found in smallwares or haberdasheries.

Nottingham lace (*not*-ing-um layss)   One of the first of the machine-made laces, it originated in Nottingham, England. Today, the term Nottingham lace is often used for any lace made by machine.

N

novelty (*nahv*-el-tee)   Anything a little different from the usual. Novelty yarns, for example, are often those with slubs. Novelty fabrics often have textural interest and novelty prints include just about anything except such classics as florals. In natural fibers, novelty yarns are formed when natural lumps form from uneven spinning. In man-made yarns, similar effects are produced by deliberately manufacturing filaments of varying thicknesses.

novoloid (*noh*-vuh-loyd)   A generic name for a man-made noncellulosic fiber made from a cross-linked polymer derived from carbon, hydrogen, and oxygen.

no-wale (no-wayl)   Wale describes the pile ribs on corduroy fabrics. No-wale corduroy has an all-over pile shorter than the pile on velveteen. *See* corduroy, velveteen, and pile.

nub   A synonym for slub. An uneven area in a yarn that gives the fabric a degree of texture. Nubs can be produced naturally (as in hand-spinning which often has nubs) or artificially (deliberately making them in spinning). Nubs in man-made fibers are usually produced by making parts of the fiber thicker than others. Short staple fibers mixed with other fibers in the yarn will produce nubs.

numdah rug (*nuhm*-dah rug)   A rug from India, made of felted goat's hair. Designs are embroidered on the rug by hand.

nun's veiling (nunz *vay*-ling)   A plain-weave, lightweight, quite sheer fabric, traditionally used by nuns for veils as part of their habits. It is made of woolen, worsted, silk, man-made, or mixed fibers dyed black, brown, or white for religious garb and dyed in colors for dresses.

nylon (*ny*-lon)   Nylon, the first of the synthetic fibers, is very strong and resists abrasion and wrinkles. It has a natural luster, holds body heat, and resists moths. Nylon dyes well, but fades in the sunlight, may pill, and melts under high heat. Nylon is naturally mildew resistant, which has led to its popularity for such things as mosquito netting used in the tropics. Nylon is a thermoplastic man-made polyamide fiber derived largely from petroleum, chemically combined with air and water. *See* thermoplastic and man-made fibers.

N

nytril (*ny*-tril)   The generic name for a man-made fiber containing at least eighty-five percent vinylidene dinitrile derived from ammonia and natural gas. Nytril is no longer produced in the United States. It was used with other fibers to form soft fabrics for such things as sweaters. *See* generic name and man-made fibers.

Defect	Explanation	Severity
Narrow Goods	Fabric that has not been finished in the proper width. Usually caused by excessive treatment in one or more finishing operations. Narrow width can be traced to many causes. One of the main reasons for this defect is in tentering, where for some reason or other, the cloth is not brought out to the specified width.	Major
Needle Line	In knits, a vertical crack resulting from a bent needle. The design is intact but the uniform placement of wales is distorted.	Usually Major (can be Minor)
Neppiness	An excessive amount of tangled masses of fibers (neps) appearing on the face of a fabric. Neps are detrimental to cotton manufacture and are dead, tangled, immature, and loose waste particles that roll into little balls as the stock is being processed. Over-opening in the opener pickers and poor carding are causes for neps. Sometimes ginning will also produce its share of this waste. Nep specks are detrimental to most cotton fabrics, regardless of whether they are white or dyed.	Usually Major (can be Minor depending on severity)

GARMENT

AND

TEXTILES

obi sash (*oh*-bee sash)   A wide sash worn with a Japanese-style kimono.

off-grain   A term used to describe a fabric in which the straight grain and the crosswise grain are not at right angles to each other. Off-grain fabrics can be corrected by wetting them and then pulling the fabric until the two grains are perpendicular to each other. This straightening of the grain, however, is only successful if a pattern has not been printed off-grain on the fabric.

oil repellency   The ability of a fabric to prevent or retard the penetration of oil. This ability is the result of a finish added to the fabric. The finish is used on some man-made fibers (notably polyester) and tends to hold oil-based stains once the stains penetrate the cloth.

oilcloth (*oyl*-kloth)   Any fabric treated with oil to make it waterproof. Oilcloth was used extensively at one time for kitchen tablecloths. Oiled silk was used for shower curtains and other areas that required a waterproof fabric. Oilskin, also an oilcloth, was a term usually used to describe oilcloth used for making raincoats. Today, the name oilskin is used for a variety of waterproof coating fabrics, most commonly those with a thick synthetic coating on the right side of the fabric.

olefin (*oh*-leh-fin)   The generic name for fibers derived from polyethylene or polypropylene. Olefin is primarily used in home furnishings for inexpensive rugs and upholstery because it has good bulk and coverage and resists chemicals, mildew, and weather. Its sensitivity to heat has limited its use in clothing and special care has to be taken to clean it. Olefin is occasionally, and incorrectly, called polypropylene. *See* generic name.

oleophilic (oh-lih-uh-*fihl*-ik)   Tending to absorb and retain oily materials.

oleophobic (oh-lih-uh-*foh*-bik)   Tending to repel oily materials.

ombré (*ohm*-bray [common pronunciation]; *ahm*-bra [correct pronunciation])   The word ombré is used to describe a design that changes, usually in rainbow-like gradations, from one color to another. Ombré patterns can be shades of one color or several different colors.

ondulé (ohn-dyou-*lay*)   The wavy appearance that certain fabrics, especially sheer fabrics hung as curtains, have when looked at from a distance.

one hundred (100) denier crepe   A 100-denier viscose rayon yarn made in a flat crepe construction.

opacity (oh-*pass*-eh-tee)   The opposite of transparency. This quality has become increasingly important as a fabric consideration with the development of man-made fibers. For their weight, most man-made fibers, unlike most natural fibers, have little opacity (they are more transparent than natural fibers). This is not objectionable in most cases, but in such things as white slacks, it can prove to be a problem. Opacity can be increased at many different points in the manufacture of a fabric or a garment, from the way the fiber is produced and the processing of the yarn to the way the fabric is dyed and finished and the way the garment is made (with or without a lining). Opacity in hosiery is more a fashion matter. At a time when very sheer stockings are fashionable, opacity is relatively undesirable. When, on the other hand, it is fashionable for legs to be colored, opaque hosiery becomes important. *See* opaque.

opaque (oh-*payk*)   Something is opaque when what is behind or under it cannot be seen. *See* opacity.

open fabric   A fabric in which the yarns are spaced far apart. Most curtain fabrics, for example, are open fabrics that allow light to filter through the fabric.

open width   Fabrics that come off a flatbed machine (horizontal or V bed).

openwork stitch   A construction of open spaces purposely made at regular intervals across the knitted cloth. It is a variation of a basic stitch.

opera length gloves   Evening gloves that extend above the elbow, intended for wear with bare-armed formal fashions.

optical brightener (*ahp*-tee-kuhl *bryt*-ehn-er)   Optical brighteners convert invisible ultraviolet light to visible light in the blue region, making fabrics appear to reflect more light than they really do. This makes them appear brighter and, perhaps, cleaner. Optical brighteners are used in the manufacture of fabrics and included in the formulas of some synthetic detergents sold for use by the consumer. *See* detergent.

optical dye (*ahp*-tee-kuhl dy)   Dye used to produce fluorescent fabrics. *See* fluorescent fabric.

optical whitener (*ahp*-tee-kuhl *whyt*-ner)   *See* optical brightener.

organdie (*ahr*-guhn-dee)   Another spelling of organdy. *See* organdy.

organdy (*ahr*-guhn-dee)   At one time, organdy was a thin, transparent, lightweight, open, plain-weave, wiry cotton muslin fabric with a stiff finish; organza was the same fabric made of silk. Today, those former distinctions have almost disappeared and the names organdy and organza are used almost as synonyms. The natural fibers have been replaced by man-made fibers for their manufacture. Permanent finishes on natural fiber organdy and man-made fiber organdy have eliminated the largest objection to this fabric: its tendency to wrinkle easily and lose its crispness. Shadow organdy has a faint printed design in self-color. Organdy is always popular for curtains and is often used in blouses, summer dresses, neckwear, collars and cuffs, trimmings, and evening wear.

organza (ahr-*gan*-zah)   *See* organdy.

organzine (ahr-guhn-*zeen*)   A yarn of two or more plies with a medium twist.

O

Oriental rugs (ahr-ee-*en*-tuhl rugz)   Hand-made rugs produced in the Near East, India, or China. They are hand-woven (the tapestry method) or are hand-knotted. True Oriental rugs are extremely expensive and are collectors' items. Machine-made imitations are available. *See* tapestry and hand-knotted rug.

orientation   *See* molecular orientation.

Orlon (*ahr*-lon)   Trademark of DuPont for their acrylic and modacrylic fibers.

Osnaburg (*oz*-neh-berg)   Named for the town in Germany where it was first made, Osnaburg is a coarse cotton or blended fiber fabric in a plain weave that resembles crash. It is quite strong and was originally used unbleached for bags, grain and cement sacks, and other industrial purposes. Osnaburg is also occasionally used for drapes, upholstery, slacks, and sportswear.

osprey (*oss*-pree)   The term is used for feathers that form a plume. Osprey feathers, like marabou feathers, are no longer authentic, and these feathers usually come from domesticated fowl.

ostrich (*oss*-trich)   Ostrich feathers are long, usually coiled feathers, often dyed to match a garment.

ottoman (*aht*-uh-mehn)   A heavy corded wool, silk, rayon, or synthetic fabric with wide horizontal ribs similar to faille, but with larger and rounder ribs. The cords are heavier than bengaline and are widely spaced. Fillings of the cloth are usually cotton or wool, and they should be completely covered by the silk or man-made fiber warp. It is primarily used for evening clothes, coats, skirts, and trimmings. It also appears in upholstery and draperies. *See* faille.

outing flannel (*owt*-ing *flan*-el)   A soft, lightweight, plain- or twill-weave cotton fabric, usually napped on both sides. Most outing flannels have colored yarn stripes. Outing flannel soils easily, and the nap washes and wears off. It is traditionally used for sleepwear, diapers, underwear, and interlinings. *See* flannel.

overplaid (*oh*-ver-plad)   A plaid design made of two or more plaids woven or printed so that one appears to be on top of the other.

overprinting (*oh*-ver-print-ing)   Printing new colors or designs on a fabric already printed. *See* printing.

Oxford (*ahks*-fuhrd)   A flat-heeled shoe for men, women, and children that laces across the instep.

O

Oxford cloth   A cotton fabric or blend with man-made fibers, in basket weave (2 x 1, 2 x 2, 3 x 2, 4 x 4, or 8 x 8), first made in Oxford, England. It often has a colored warp and a white filling. This fabric is given a smooth finish and is a popular fabric for sport dresses, blouses, shirts, and sportswear.

Oxford gray   A popular color that is very dark but not quite black. It is especially common in wool flannel and is often used for men's suits and slacks and occasionally for women's clothing.

oxidation (ack-seh-*day*-shuhn)   The joining of oxygen and another substance. In the case of fabrics, the term is usually used in reference to fibers or dyes that weaken or change when they come in contact with oxygen.

oxidation dyes   A class of dyestuffs formed in the fiber substrate. These dyes are applied to the fabric as an oxidation base in the form of water-soluble salts and thereafter oxidized to a pigment.

oxygen-type bleach (*ahk*-sih-jehn-typ bleech)   Oxygen-type bleaches, milder and less effective than chlorine bleaches, are frequently recommended for laundering when bleaching is desirable, but chlorine bleaches would cause fabric deterioration. Perborate bleaches are oxygen-type bleaches. *See* bleach.

O

Defect	Explanation	Severity
Off-Register Printing or Out-of-Register	A jumbled motif or mottled color effect that comes from improper alignment of the printing machine rollers. The effect shows blank areas that should have been printed, but because of poor settings, are white or discolored.	Major
Off-Shade	Color in fabric that matches only in areas and seems to be irregular throughout the piece. A peculiar or poor cast will result in off-shades. This effect is sought in cloth from side-to-side, side-to-center, and from end-to-end.	Major
Oil Stains	Stains, spots, and marks that are detrimental to cloth. They are acquired in several ways and should be removed in scouring. Many oil spots are the result of carelessness by the operators as the cloth cut is moved from machine to machine, and from room to room in the finishing.	Major
Open Reed	Results from a bent reed wire causing warp ends to be held apart, exposing the filling yarn. It is characterized by a fine-lined thin place in the warp direction, and will be conspicuous on fabrics that use different colored yarns on warp and shuttle.	Major
Out-of-Register	*See* Off-Register Printing.	Major
Overshot	A pick of filling deflected from its normal path through the shed and extending unbound over warp ends with which it should have interlaced. This condition is most common within twelve to fifteen inches of the selvage and results from improper loom setting.	Major
Over-width	Fabric that is too wide for proper manipulation. Extra washing and proper shrinking may bring the cloth to the proper width, or retentering may do this to perfection.	Minor

GARMENT
AND
TEXTILES

pad dyeing   A process of passing the cloth through a trough containing dye, then squeezing it between heavy rolls to remove excess dye.

padding (*pad*-ing)   Any item that provides a degree of support to a fabric. It usually describes the layer of fabric placed underneath a carpet or rug to provide it with longer life and to give it a more luxurious appearance and feeling. Carpet padding has been made from cattle hair, rubberized hair, rubber, and combinations of jute and cattle hair, as well as some of the man-made fibers. Some rugs and carpets have a bonded foam, sponge rubber, or man-made backing and no separate padding is needed. Padding is also called cushion and underlay. *See* rugs and carpets.

paillette (pal-*yet*)   Another name for sequin. A shiny, usually metallic, decoration or spangle. Paillettes are sewn to clothing, especially evening dresses because they shimmer and sparkle in the light. Paillettes usually have a single, central hole for fastening to the garment or fabric. Fabric covered with pailettes is available by the yard.

paisley (*payz*-lee)   Paisley is usually used to describe a design developed for use on fine wool shawls made in Paisley, Scotland. The shawls were originally woven to imitate the woven shawls of Kashmir which had a cone design. The woven shawls proved too expensive to produce and the design was adapted for printing. The Paisley design itself changed to the scroll-like form it now has. Paisleys, both large and small, are almost never out of fashion and may be knitted into fabrics, woven into, or, more usually, printed on fabrics.

Panama (*pan*-uh-mah)   A fairly lightweight summer suit fabric usually made of wool worsted. Before man-made fibers were available, it was used extensively for men's suits because of its coolness and wrinkle resistance. *See* tropical suiting.

Panama hat   A hat with a deep, creased crown and a wide brim turned up at the back. It is typically made from jipijapa plant leaves, but is also produced using man-made material.

panne velvet (pan *vel*-vit [correct pronunciation]; pan-*ay vel*-vit [incorrect but common pronunciation])   Velvet with the pile flattened in one direction. *See* mirror velvet.

pants suit   A two-piece garment consisting of jacket and long pants.

panty   A woman's or girl's undergarment with an elastic waistband that is bound, scalloped, or lace-trimmed at the bottom.

panty girdle   An elasticized, form-fitting panty. A foundation garment with legs attached. *See* girdle.

paper fabric (*pay*-per *fab*-rik)   Most paper fabrics are not, strictly speaking, paper at all, but nonwoven fabrics. This area holds great promise for the future because of anticipated savings in cost in the manufacture of these fabrics and the development of varied applications that new fabrics bring. This promise is, as yet, largely unrealized. Paper clothing had a brief popularity but now is rarely seen. Items such as disposable underwear, baby diapers, industrial clothing, hospital gowns, and napkins are being made of these fabrics today.

paper taffeta (*pay*-per *taf*-eh-tah)   A lightweight, crisp taffeta used for evening clothes.

paper yarn   A strand made of paper slit and twisted in web form.

passementerie (or braid, or spaghetti) (pas-*mehn*-tree)   An ornamental trimming or edging made of intertwined strips of fabric, cord, beading, or metallic thread.

patch pocket   A pocket sewn entirely on top of the garment fabric. Patch pockets come in different styles:

cargo pocket   A long pocket generally placed at the hip.

kangaroo pocket   A pocket similar to a large pouch that stretches across the midriff.

spade pocket   A pocket with a diagonally peaked bottom edge.

patchwork   A fabric that results from joining small pieces of fabric together in a pattern or in random fashion to make one large piece. It was important in Colonial America as a means of utilizing fabric scraps and remnants when fabric was scarce. Patchwork was originally sewn by hand and often a completed piece of patchwork became the top of a quilt. Patchwork has become an art form in and of itself, and patchwork quilts are a traditional American folk craft and collectors' item. Today, patchwork can be made by machine and is available by the yard for clothing and home furnishing items. Printed patchwork fabric is made to imitate the real thing. *See* quilt. *See also* patchwork quilts.

patchwork quilts   Quilts made from small pieces of cotton or silk fabric cut in various shapes and sewn together to form patterns. They are quilted on a frame when done by hand. Modern patchwork quilts may be printed to resemble those that are hand-sewn. *See* quilt. *See also* patchwork.

patent (*pat*-uhnt)   A common name in leather for the hide of an animal with the fur removed.

patent back   Carpeting that has its tufts locked in place by a mixture of latex or pyroxylin.

pattern (*pat*-uhrn)   Any design that is repeated. A pattern on fabric is the design that is repeated several times in every yard of fabric. The word pattern is used as a synonym for design and motif. Pattern also refers to a printed paper guide that shows how a particular garment style is to be cut from fabric. A step-by-step instruction sheet is included which shows how to sew the garment together. *See* motif.

pattern knit (*pat*-uhrn nit)   Knit made on a weft knit machine by dropping, adding, rearranging, and crossing various stitches to create intricate designs.

pearl cotton (purl *kot*-uhn)   A mercerized cotton thread with a loose twist used primarily in embroidery, crochet, knitting, and weaving.

P

peasant sleeve   A long, full, gathered sleeve generally finished at the wrist with a band or elastic casing.

peau de soie (*poh* deh swah)   Originally, a luxurious fabric made of silk (*soie* is the French word for *silk*). It is a rather heavy, smooth, reversible, silk fabric usually woven in a variation of the satin weave with rib-like fillings. Peau de soie has a dull sheen. Today, most of this fabric is made of polyester or other man-made fibers and is referred to simply as peau. It is especially popular for formal uses including wedding gowns. *See* weaving and satin weave.

pebble (*peb*-uhl)   Pebble is used to describe a fabric with a somewhat bumpy, grainy appearance. It is commonly used to describe crepes. *See* crepe. *See also* pebble crepe.

pebble crepe   Usually woven of abraded yarns (rayon and acetate) warp and filling. It is a plain weave with skips of warp over two fillings and two fillings over two warps at intervals, to give a pebbled surface.

pecarry (*pek*-uh-ree)   A common name in leather for the hide of an animal with the fur removed.

peignoir (payn-*wahr*)   A loose robe worn in the boudoir or a coat worn over a bathing suit at the beach. It is often made of terry cloth to absorb water after bathing.

Pellon (*pel*-lahn)   Trademark of the Pellon Corporation for a group of nonwoven fabrics used primarily for interfacings.

pelt (pelt)   The stripped skin of a furry animal.

peplum (*pep*-luhm)   A short, full flounce sewn into the seam of the waist of a blouse or jacket

pepper and salt (*pep*-ehr ehnd sawlt)   A fabric made of a combination of white and black yarns. The term usually is used to describe tweed fabrics. *See* tweed.

perborate bleach (per-*bohr*-ayt bleech)   An oxygen-type bleach. *See* bleach and oxygen-type bleach.

percale (per-*kayl*)   Originally, a plain weave, medium-weight, closely woven, muslin cotton fabric with a smooth finish. Most percale today is a blend of cotton and man-made fibers. It is similar to cambric, but dull in finish. It is generally printed for apparel. Calico prints are often printed on percale rather than on calico. Heavy grades in higher counts are used for sheeting. Dress percale runs 80 square (80 x 80) or 160 yarns to the inch. Percale sheets are high quality, smoother, and softer than muslin as the yarns are combed as well as carded. Most percale sheets have a thread count of at least 180 (84 x 96) threads per inch. Some fine percale sheets count over 200 threads per inch (96 x 104 or 96 x 108). Besides sheets, percale is used for shirts, shorts, pajamas, curtains and bedspreads. *See* calico, combing, carding, and percale sheeting.

percale sheeting   A combed muslin (may be carded in poorer grade) for bed sheets, in white or colors, made in type 200 (A grade) and 180 (B grade). *See* percale.

perching   Visual inspection of wool fabrics.

perle cotton (purl *kot*-uhn)   Another spelling of pearl cotton. *See* pearl cotton.

permanent finish   A substance applied to fabric during the final or finishing step in manufacture that lasts throughout the life of the fabric and withstands whatever effects it in its use. *See* finishing.

permanent press   Another term for durable press, although it is used more loosely than durable press. It is a misnomer because almost all fabrics so treated tend to need a minimal amount of pressing, and the press is not permanent. *See* durable press and easy care.

permanent starchless   A process that impregnates a cloth with compounds that are not dissolved in laundering. When ironed, the cloth returns to its original crispness.

Persian (Iranian) rug (*pur*-zhehn [eye-*ray*-nee-uhn] rug)   A hand-tied oriental rug made in Iran. Names of Persian rugs include Kirman, Kashan, Shiraz, Teheran, Saraband, Isfahan, Sarouk, Hamadan, Meched, Tabriz, Nain, and Qum. *See* Oriental rug and rugs and carpets.

perspiration resistant (pur-speh-*ray*-shun ree-*sis*-tuhnt)   The ability of a fabric to resist the effects of perspiration that causes some fabrics and dyes to deteriorate. Perspiration resistant finishes are occasionally applied as part of the finishing process. *See* finishing.

Peter Pan collar   A small, flat collar, two or three inches deep, with rounded ends that meet at the center front.

petersham (*pee*-tehr-shehm)   Petersham is a ribbon-like fabric similar to grosgrain. *See* grosgrain.

petit point (*pet*-ee poynt)   A form of embroidery worked on a needlepoint canvas with small holes extremely close together. Canvas with 20 holes per inch could be considered petit point canvas. *See* needlepoint.

P

photographic printing (foh-toh-*graf*-ik *print*-ing)   Printing in which either rollers or silk screens are made from photographs. In roller photographic printing, the photograph is engraved on the rollers. In the silk screen process, the photograph is transferred to the screens. Exact reproductions of pictures are possible with photographic printing. *See* roller and screen printing listed under printing.

pick   Man-made fibers tend to develop pills (the formation of small balls of fiber that appear on the surface of certain fabrics) and picks (small loose threads which can snag). The tendency of man-made fibers to pill and pick is reduced by steps taken in the processing of the yarn or the finishing of the fabric. *See* pilling.

pick glass   A magnifying glass for counting cloth, it is also called a linen tester or pick counter.

pickage   The number of fillings that pass between two rows of pile yarns plus the number of fillings under the pile loops. Two fillings shot through the same pile shed and one filling shot through to interface with the ground warps (2 + 1) equal 3 picks.

picker   A mechanical device with vertical drums equipped with spindles that remove cotton from the boll.

picking   Carrying the filling through the shed.

picot (*pee*-koh)   A series of small decorative loops placed along the edge of a fabric in the manufacturing or by hand crochet or embroidery. Picot trimming is also available by the yard. *See* trimming.

piece dyeing (peess *dy*-ing)   The dyeing of a fabric after weaving, knitting, or other method of construction. Cross-dyeing is a type of piece dyeing. *See* cross-dyeing.

pigment dyes   Dye emulsion made with certain kinds of fine synthetic pigment in a solution of synthetic resins in an organic solvent. Water is stirred in with a high-speed mixer. Often applied by pad dyeing, they have good colorfastness to light, washing, acids, and alkalies. When resin binder is ineffective, dye may crock or have poor resistance to washing.

pigmented fibers and yarns   Delustered or, occasionally, colored with pigment to a desired hue. White or colored pigments added to a fiber-forming substance before spinning.

pigskin (*pig*-skin)   A common name in leather for the hide of an animal with the fur removed.

pile (pyl)   A fabric surface formed by yarns that are brought to the right side of the fabric in the course of making the fabric. Some fabrics have pile surfaces on both sides. Looped fabrics, such as terry cloth, tufted fabrics including candlewick and many rugs, and fabrics such as velvet, made by the double cloth construction method in which the heavy joining yarns are subsequently split to make two fabrics, are all pile constructions. In certain specialized areas, notably home sewing, pile fabrics are considered to have a nap. *See* nap, terry cloth, candlewick, and velvet.

pile warp   The warp yarn in a carpet that forms the looped pile.

pillbox   A stiff, short, round, brimless hat.

pilling (*pil*-ing)   The formation of small balls of fiber that appear on the surface of certain fabrics. Pills develop on woolen fabrics, but tend to disappear when the fabrics are cleaned; man-made fiber pills remain on the fabric. Man-made fibers also tend to develop picks (small loose threads that can snag). The tendency of man-made fibers to pill and pick can be reduced by steps taken in the processing of the yarn or the finishing of the fabric.

pillow (*pill*-oh)   A cloth bag (often made of ticking) stuffed with feathers, down, kapok, rubber, synthetic foam, fiberfill, or a similar substance used to support some part of the body and to make furniture comfortable. *See* entries for materials listed. There are various kinds of pillows including:

> **bolster** (*bohl*-ster)   A long, narrow pillow of round or rectangular shape used for decoration and support.

> **box edged** (boks edjd)   A pillow with three dimensions rather than two-sided as most bed pillows. The pillow fabric covering is shaped like a round or rectangular box and has a fabric band (boxing) that covers the edges of the pillow and joins the top and bottom sides.

> **flange** (flanj)   A flat border. On pillows, it is an unstuffed decorative edging surrounding a stuffed pillow. It differs from a ruffle in that it is flat rather than shirred. *See* shirring.

pillow lace   Another name for bobbin lace and bobbinet lace. Lace made using a pillow to hold pins around which thread is arranged. Bobbins are used to hold and feed the thread used.

pillowcase   Pillowcases are washable covers for bed pillows that usually match the sheets and protect the pillow from soil. Most American pillowcases are made in a rectangular form with one open, hemmed edge. They are occasionally decorated on one of the narrower ends.

pima cotton (*pee*-mah *kot*-uhn)   American cotton grown chiefly in the irrigated lands of Arizona, New Mexico, and El Paso. Extra-long staple averaging $1\,^3/_8$" to $1\,^5/_8$".

pin check   A checked pattern in which the squares are extremely small. *See* checks.

pin seal   A common name in leather for the hide of an animal with the fur removed. *See* leather.

pin tuck (pin tuk)   The narrowest of tucks. A tuck is a small, narrow section of fabric folded and then stitched, either down the fold of the tuck or across each end. *See* tuck.

pinstripe (*pin*-stryp)   A very narrow stripe in any color. When pinstripes are white, they are often called chalk stripes. *See* stripe.

pinwale (*pin*-wayle)   In woven fabrics, wales are a series of ribs or ridges that usually run lengthwise on the fabric. Wale describes the pile ribs found on corduroy fabrics. The term pinwale describes one of the different types of ribs in corduroy. *See* wale.

piping (*pyp*-ing)   Piping and welting are synonymous. A decorative edging that lends a certain degree of strength to the area in which it is sewn. Piping is made by covering cord with bias strips of matching or contrasting fabric. It is a popular finish for seams on upholstery and slipcovers and is occasionally used on clothing. When used on clothing, it is usually called piping. *See* cord and bias.

piqué (pee-*kay*)   A fabric woven on a loom with a dobby attachment with small, raised geometric patterns. It is usually made of silk, rayon, cotton, synthetics, or a blend of cotton and synthetic and is usually a crisp fabric of medium or heavy weight. Strictly, a ribbed or corded cotton with wales running across the fabric formed by warp ends. The term is often used in the trade to refer to Bedford cord or warp piqué, in which the cords run lengthwise. In honeycomb design it is called waffle piqué; in diamond pattern, bird's-eye piqué. It is often printed with colorful designs. White piqué is a classic fabric for tennis clothes and for collars and cuffs on dresses and blouses. The look of woven piqué can be duplicated with embossing and heat-setting. *See* dobby. *See also* embossing and heat setting.

placemat   A piece of cloth or other material (often foam-backed plastic) placed on a table underneath the place setting to protect the table and decorate it during meals. Placemats are available in a variety of sizes, shapes and colors.

placket closing (*plak*-it *klohs*-ing)   A narrow piece of material used to finish an opening made in a fabric to enable the wearer to put the garment on with ease.

plaid (plad)   Any pattern of multiple stripes that cross each other at right angles forming rectangles. Originally, the word plaid was used for a length of fabric in a Tartan design, a plaid design associated with a specific Scottish clan. *See* Tartan for a listing of the names of some of the major authentic Tartan plaids. Following is a list of the most common plaids:

argyle plaid (*ahr*-gyl plad)   A plaid pattern of diamonds, often with thin stripes running over the diamond patterns in the same direction as the sides of the diamonds. Originally argyle designs appeared only in knits, but today they are also found woven and printed.

balanced plaid   A plaid in which the arrangement of stripes is the same both on the cross and on the length of the grain. Also called even plaid.

bias plaid (*by*-us plad)   A plaid design that actually forms a diamond pattern with the intersection of its lines. An argyle plaid is a bias plaid.

blanket plaid   A vividly colored plaid design usually on a napped fabric similar to those used for blankets.

even plaid   Another name for balanced plaid.

overplaid   A plaid design made of two or more plaids woven or printed so that one appears to be on top of the other.

unbalanced plaid   An unbalanced plaid is one in which the arrangement of the stripes is different on the crosswise and lengthwise grain of the fabric. In constructing a garment of this type special care must be taken when matching the plaid design.

uneven plaid   Another name for unbalanced plaid.

plain knit   A flat-surfaced even knit made by hand or machine knitting. In hand knitting it is called stockinette stitch. The face of the fabric is smooth and the reverse is looped. *See* purl knit.

plain weave   Plain weave, the best known and most basic form of weaving, is made by passing the filling thread over and under one warp thread in alternating rows.

plaiting (*playt*-ing)   Another name for braid. A method of making fabric by interlacing three or more yarns or strips of fabric. *See* braid rug and trimming.

plastic   A plastic substance is one that can be molded into another shape. The materials from which man-made fibers are made are plastic, meaning that the same substance, depending on how it is molded, can be made into fiber, buttons, or zippers.

platform sole   A very thick sole of a shoe or sandal.

pleating (*plee*-ting)   A way of folding cloth. Pleats differ from tucks in that tucks are usually stitched on the foldline whereas pleats usually are not. *See* pleats and tucks.

pleats (or plaits) (pleetz [ahr playtz])   Folds of cloth arranged in a certain way. Pleats can be made as the fabric is produced (usually through heat-setting) and are used to control fullness or provide decorative uses. The thermoplastic nature of man-made fibers (they change their shape under heat) means that permanent pleating does not have to be renewed when a pleated item is cleaned. Following is a list of common types of pleats:

accordion pleats (uh-*kor*-dee-un pleetz)   Narrow, straight pleats, similar to knife pleats, but facing in any direction desired for effect. *See* knife pleats.

box pleats   Box pleats are made by folding fabric so that the edge of two pleats face in opposite directions on the right side of the fabric.

cartridge pleats (*kar*-trij pleetz)   Unpressed, narrow pleats. They are usually used more as decoration than to control fullness.

inverted pleats (inn-*vur*-ted pleetz)   Pleats formed in the same way as box pleats, but the edges meet on the right side of the garment. *See* box pleats.

kick pleat (kik pleet)   A small pleat at the bottom of a straight, fairly long skirt to allow room to walk.

knife pleats (nyf pleetz)   Narrow, straight pleats similar to accordion pleats with each pleat facing in the same direction.

sunburst pleats (*sun*-burst pleetz)   Pleats that begin at a central point and move out to the edge of a fabric. They are often narrow at the top of the fabric and wider at the edge and are especially popular for skirts.

unpressed pleats (un-*prest* pleetz)   Pleats whose edges (the folds) have not been set by pressing. The term unpressed pleats usually is

P

used for wide unpressed pleats whereas cartridge pleats, also unpressed, is used to describe narrower, decorative pleats.

plissé (crinkle crepe) (plih-*say* [*kring*-kuhl krayp])   A puckered fabric made by printing plain fabric, usually cotton, rayon, or acetate with a chemical (caustic soda). The printed area shrinks, causing the unprinted area of the fabric to pucker. The pucker is permanent. The same effect can be achieved in thermoplastic, man-made fiber fabrics by using heat to set puckers. Plissé is used incorrectly as a synonym for seersucker. It is used for dresses, pajamas, and so forth. *See* seersucker.

plush (pluhsh)   A thick, deep, heavy-pile fabric with deeper pile than velvet or velour, found in some coating fabrics and rugs. It may be mohair, silk, rayon, acrylic, or polyester, and is used for upholstery. It is usually a cut pile. *See* cut pile and pile.

plush carpet   Floor covering with one level of cut pile made of soft twisted yarns that does not show any yarn texture.

plush velour (pluhsh veh-*loor*)   A pile weave fabric with especially long shaggy pile, used for robes and lounge wear.

ply yarn   A yarn in which two or more single strands are twisted together to form one yarn. Two yarns twisted together form a two-ply yarn, four yarns, a four-ply yarn, and so forth.

pocket flap   A narrow piece of fabric sometimes used above a pocket to add a decorative element; the bottom edge is often specially shaped.

pocket square   A small patterned or trimmed handkerchief intended to be tucked inside a pocket and worn with a portion showing.

pointillism (*pwan*-teh-liz-em [correct pronunciation]; *poynt*-teh-liz-em [common pronunciation])   A method of printing dots of color on a fabric to give an impression of being one color from a distance. This technique was first developed by French painters around the turn of the century.

point-paper design   Squared paper pattern to represent a certain weave.

polished cotton   Cotton fabrics with a shiny surface, ranging from the slightest sheen to a definite glaze. Generally, the term polished cotton refers to fabrics that have a lower sheen than glazed chintz, for example. The sheen is added to the fabric in finishing by the application of starch, wax, or synthetics. Today, the finish is almost always permanent. *See* chintz.

P

polka dots (*poh*-kah dahtz)   A popular circular design usually positioned in a regular pattern on the fabric, although the placing may appear random. Dots may be woven, knitted, or printed. Sizes usually determine the name of the dots. Aspirin dots are the size of an aspirin tablet. Coin dots are approximately the size of a nickel or quarter.

Polo Cloth   Trade name for a fine camel's hair and wool blend by the Worumbo Manufacturing Company.

polyamide (powl-ee-*am*-eyed)   A resin made by condensation (a chemical rearrangement of atoms to form a molecule of greater weight). Nylon is a polyamide.

polychromatic printing (or jet printing) (powl-ee-kroh-*mat*-ik *print*-ing [ahr jeht *print*-ing])   A process of applying (squirting) dye onto a continuous width of fabric. The movement of the various jets control the design.

polyester (powl-ee-*es*-tehr)   A generic name for manufactured fibers made from a chemical composition of ethylene glycol and terephthalic acid. Probably the most versatile and widely used of the man-made fibers. It is extremely strong, has excellent wrinkle and abrasion resistance, and resists mildew and moths. It may be warm and clammy when used as apparel because it holds body heat. It may pill and attracts lint.

polymer (*powl*-ee-mehr)   A large molecule produced by linking together many molecules of a monomeric substance.

polymerization (powl-ee-mehr-ee-*zay*-shuhn)   The way in which certain small molecules (monomers) combine into large fiber-forming molecules or polymers.

polynosic (pol-ee-*nohz*-ik)   Rayon less likely to shrink or stretch when wet because of the way in which it is made.

polypropylene (powl-ee-*proh*-peh-leen)   A man-made material used to produce fibers with the generic name of olefin. *See* olefin.

polyurethane (powl-ee-*yoor*-eh-thayn)   A man-made material used for foam that is laminated to other fabrics to provide warmth. It is also used for mattresses and stuffing. Polyurethane foam tends to yellow upon exposure to air, but it is claimed this does not affect its performance. It will not harden and is not affected by mildew, moisture, or strong sunlight. Spandex fibers are based on polyurethane. *See* foam. *See also* laminating.

polyvinyl chloride (powl-ee-*vy*-nihl *klohr*-eyed)   Often referred to as vinyon, the generic name for a man-made fiber made from units of vinyl chloride. Vinyon fibers soften at low temperatures, but resist chemicals. Its primary use is in commercial products. *See* vinyon and vinyl.

pompon (*pahm*-pahn)   A fluffy ball, usually made from yarn, and used as a decorative accent. *See* trimming.

pongee (pahn-*jee*)   (1) A plain-weave, fairly lightweight, thin, natural tan-colored, tussah silk fabric originally made of wild Chinese silk with a knotty (slight slub) rough weave. It is lighter and less slubby than shantung, and is named for the Chinese Pun-ki, meaning "woven at home on one's own loom." It is used primarily for summer suits and dresses, scarves, sport shirts, and pajamas. Plain fabrics and prints are used for decorative purposes. (2) A staple fine-combed cotton fabric finished with a high luster and used for underclothing. (3) A man-made fiber fabric simulating pongee. Today, the terms Honan and pongee are used interchangeably for fabrics with this texture although they are made from man-made fabrics. Pongee is used for draperies and casement curtains.

poodle cloth (*poo*-duhl kloth)   A heavy, looped fabric usually used for coats. Originally made of wool, today this fabric is often made of man-made fibers.

poplin (*pahp*-lihn)   A plain-weave, tightly woven, high-count cotton fabric with fine crossribs formed by heavy filling yarns and fewer, finer warp yarns. It may consist of acetate, rayon, silk, wool, nylon, polyester, or combinations of these fibers. Poplin has heavier threads, and a slightly lower count than broadcloth, ranging from 80 x 40 to 116 x 56. It is used for dresses, shirts, coats, sports jackets, ski jackets, and snowsuits (water-repellent).

positive-negative (*pahz*-eh-tiv-*neg*-eh-tiv)   The name for two co-ordinated fabrics, one of which, for example, might have white dots on a blue ground, the other blue dots on a white ground. Positive-negative effects can be made in an infinite number of designs, but are usually only of two colors.

pouch   A gathered purse with a top opening. It comes in all sizes, shapes, and styles.

power net   An elastic net fabric that stretches in one or both directions. It is used primarily for support garments such as girdles.

P

prayer rug A hand-tied Near Eastern Oriental rug characterized by a design in the form of an arch.

preshrinking (pree-*shringk*-ing) A step in the finishing of fabrics so they will not shrink (become smaller) in later cleanings. Acceptable shrinkage is less than one percent; anything more affects the fit of the garment. Unfortunately, shrinkage standards are extremely arbitrary. A term, such as shrinkage controlled (quite commonly used in the textile industry) means only that a fabric will not shrink more than a certain amount, but that may be as much as 6% in some cotton knits.

press A machine that flattens fabric. Press also refers to the act of flattening fabric.

press cloth (pres kloth) A piece of fabric placed between the press or iron and the fabric being pressed or ironed to prevent unwanted shine and other effects of excessive heat.

pret á porter (pray ah por-*tay* [correct pronunciation]; pret ah por-*ter* [incorrect pronunciation, but occasionally used]) The French name for ready-to-wear clothing. Recently, the French ready-to-wear industry has developed tremendously, and the designs that appear at showings of French ready-to-wear firms are imported to the United States and sold under the name pret á porter.

print cloths Cotton muslin fabrics ranging in counts from 48 square to 80 square (finished).

printcloth Term applied to carded, plain-weave cotton fabrics with single yarns with counts of 30 square and 40 square. Finishes may vary to produce cloths such as lawn, percale, cambric, and longcloth. For longcloth, *see* muslin sheeting.

printing A process for adding a colored pattern to fabric. Following are some of the most common printing methods:

block printing A method of printing in which a block, usually of wood or linoleum, is cut so that only the design to be printed is left on the surface. The block is inked and placed on the fabric. Block printing is limited almost entirely to the craft field today because it is very time-consuming.

burn-out printing A fabric made of two fibers with different characteristics is printed with a chemical that eats away (burns out) one of the fibers but not the other. This printing method is used to make some sculptured velvets (the pile of the velvet is eaten away) and to make fabrics with some sheer and some nonsheer areas. In making the sculptured velvets, the pile of the velvet reacts to the chemical; in making the sheer fabrics, the yarn is spun from two fibers, one of which is sensitive to the chemical and one of which is not.

calender printing   *See* roller printing.

cylinder printing (*sil*-en-der *print*-ing)   *See* roller printing.

direct printing   *See* roller printing.

discharge printing (*dis*-charj *print*-ing)   A method of obtaining light designs on a very dark ground. The fabric is piece dyed and the color is bleached from the design areas in a pattern. An additional step is often the roller printing of these design areas with patterns and colors. Also called extract printing. *See* dyeing.

duplex printing (*doo*-pleks *print*-ing)   A method of printing the same design on both sides of the fabric to give the design additional definition and clarity of color. Also called register printing.

extract printing (*eks*-trakt *print*-ing)   *See* discharge printing.

heat transfer printing   In heat transfer printing, elaborate colors and designs are printed on a special type of paper. The paper is placed over the fabric and the designs and colors are transferred to the fabric through the application of heat.

print-on-print   Another term for overprinting. *See* overprinting.

register printing (*rej*-iss-ter *print*-ing)   *See* duplex printing.

resist printing (ree-*zist print*-ing)   Printing similar to resist dyeing. In resist printing, the fabric is coated with a paste that protects it from the printing colors in certain areas. When the printing is complete, the paste is removed. *See* dyeing and resist dyeing.

roller printing   Roller printing may be the most important method of printing today. The design is etched onto a roller through which the fabric is passed. For each color in the design a different roller is used. High speed can be obtained in roller printing.

screen printing   In screen printing, a sheer fabric, such as silk or nylon gauze, is stretched over a wood or metal frame to form a screen. The entire screen, except for the design area to be printed, is coated with a substance that closes the pores of the fabric screen.

P

The dye is poured onto the screen and forced through the uncoated design areas onto the fabric below. A different screen must be used for each color in the print.

sublistatic printing (sub-lih-*stat*-ik *print*-ing)   A form of heat transfer printing. *See* heat transfer printing.

warp printing (wahrp *print*-ing)   A printing method in which only the warp yarns are printed with a design before the fabric is woven. The resulting fabric has a wavy, shadowy effect. It is also called shadow printing.

profile hat   A hat with a brim that dips down on one side and rolls up on the other.

pucker (*puhk*-er)   A bump or wrinkle in a fabric such as that found in crinkle crepe. *See* crinkle crepe.

puff   A synonym for a resilient comforter.

puff sleeve   A short, set-in sleeve with gathered fullness at the shoulder and bottom edge. The bottom of the puff sleeve is generally gathered into a narrow band or is elasticized.

pulled wool (poold wool)   Wool pulled from the hide of a slaughtered animal or taken from pelts of dead animals by means of chemicals.

pure silk   Silk containing no metallic weighting. It is synonymous with pure-dye silk. *See* weighted silk.

purl knit (purl nit)   A term used to describe alternating rows of knit and purl stitches (purl is the reverse of a plain knit fabric with the loops showing) forming a pattern with considerable crosswise stretch.

purl stitch (purl stich)   Generically, it is a weft-knit cloth and belongs in a separate class from single and double knits and weft knits. Characteristics are similar to the reverse side of jersey, mostly for sweaters, in stripes and patterns.

P

Defect	Explanation	Severity
Pattern Defector	In wovens, the formation of interlaces or the insertion of color contrary to the design of the fabric, resulting from a machine malfunction or the incorrect placement of colored yarn in the harness of the loom. In knits, the formation of stitches or the insertion of color contrary to the design of the fabric, resulting from a machine malfunction or the incorrect placement of colored yarn in the creel.	Major
Pin Holes	Holes common to a fabric run over a pin-tenter that become defective when they venture too far in from the selvage and enlarge or tear.	Major (depending on how far into body of fabric pins extend)
Press-Off	Results when all or some of the needles on circular knitting fail to function and fabric either falls off the machine or the design is completely disrupted or destroyed. Many knitting needles are broken and have to be replaced when bad press-off occurs. Bad press-offs usually start a new roll of fabric.	Major
Print Out of Register	Caused by print rollers not synchronized properly; results in various colors of the design not printed in proper position.	Major or Minor
Printing Machine Stop	Dye smudged along width of fabric as a result of a stopped printing machine.	Major
Pucker (also, Sanforize Pucker)	A warp-wise distortion resulting from the selvage being stretched in finishing or uneven wetting-out during sanforization, generally due to faulty spray heads. It may appear as a wavy selvage or affect any other area of the fabric. Confined to one spray head, the pucker generally is eight to ten inches wide.	Major or Minor

Qiana (kee-*ah*-nah)   Trademark of DuPont for nylon.

quality control (*kwahl*-ih-tee kon-*trohl*)   A term used to imply inspection of an item throughout the manufacturing process to ensure that the finished product meets high standards. Unfortunately, the term is inexact and can mean everything or nothing.

quilt (kwihlt)   A fabric construction, usually thinner and less resilient than a comforter, most often used as a bed covering for added warmth. It consists of a layer of printed cotton muslin fabric, known as the quilt top, and backing fabric, also made of printed or solid cotton muslin fabric, with a layer of cotton, wool, or synthetic batting between. All three layers are sewn together with fine quilting (running) stitches that usually create a design of its own. Quilted bed coverings filled with down feathers are called eiderdowns or comforters. A patchwork quilt has a patchwork quilt top. *See* quilting, patchwork, and batting.

quilting (*kwihlt*-ing)   Stitching through two or more layers of fabric to form a design or pattern. The most common quilting design today is a diamond pattern, but quilting stitches (usually a short running stitch) may also be done in abstract, pictorial, geometric, floral, or random patterns. Quilting stitches often are used to outline patchwork or appliqué designs on a quilt. *See* appliqué, quilt, and patchwork.

rabbit An inexpensive fur often dyed to resemble other furs or for fashion impact. It is also called coney and lapin.

rabbit hair Fur from the angora rabbit. The hair of rabbits often is added to other fibers to give softness or an interesting texture to the surface of the finished fabric. Rabbit hair is used in woven and knit fabrics.

raffia straw (*raf*-ee-uh straw) *See* straw.

rag rug A floor covering woven with strips of twisted rags made of cotton, wool, or synthetic fabrics braided, crocheted, or bound and used as the filling on a cotton or synthetic yarn warp. Rag rugs are made by hand or machine, and with the exception of some handmade antique rag rugs, usually are the most inexpensive rugs.

raglan sleeve (*rayg*-luhn sleev) A sleeve whose shoulder seam extends, slanted, from the neckline to the underarm.

raincoat A water-repellent or waterproof coat of poplin or gabardine.

rainwear Water-resistant or waterproof apparel, such as a raincoat or rain boots.

ramie (or rhea) (*ray*-mee [ahr *ray*-uhn]) A strong, lustrous, natural bast fiber from a nettle-like East Indian shrub, also produced in China, Egypt, and the United States. It is used for shirts, suitings, automobile seat covers, table covers, and in blends with wool for carpets.

ramie straw (*ray*-mee straw) A type of straw. *See* straw.

random-tip shears Carpets and rugs with a high pile sheared at random.

raschel (rah-*shehl*) A knit made on a raschel machine, a warp knitting machine that can use bulky yarns to form designs imitating crochet or net.

rattail (*rat*-tayl)   A narrow, round cord used for trimming and for macramé. *See* macramé.

rattail fringe (*rat*-tayl frinj)   A decorative edging made of rattail in which the rattail forms loops across the edging. *See* rattail.

raw silk   A term used incorrectly for wild silk or reeled silk wound directly from several cocoons with only a slight twist. Raw silk is the silk fiber before it has been processed in any way. It is silk that has not been degummed. Raw silk is coated with a glue-like substance called sericin. The sericin is removed in later processing and is not silk.

raw-stock dyeing   Dyeing of fibers before spinning into yarn. It is synonymous with fiber-dyed. *See* fiber-dyed.

rayon (*ray*-on)   The first successful man-made fiber, rayon was originally called artificial silk. It is made from cellulose and is weak when wet. Rayon is soft and comfortable and dyes well, but is weakened by exposure to sunlight. Because of its low wet strength, rayon may shrink or stretch unless treated. Two main processes are used in this country to produce rayon: viscose process and cuprammonium process. Several different modifications of these types of rayon are being made and consist of the following. *See* cellulose.

cuprammonium rayon (kyou-pre-*moh*-nee-um *ray*-on)   Rayon made by a process that allows very fine filament fibers to be formed. The fineness of its filaments is its best known characteristic.

high wet modulus rayon (hy wet *mahd*-you-les *ray*-on)   Rayon made by a modified viscose process. The resulting rayon is much stronger when wet than ordinary rayon. Zantrel and Avril are examples of high wet modulus rayon. *See* viscose rayon.

polynosic rayon (pol-ee-*nah*-sik *ray*-on)   Rayon less likely to shrink or stretch when wet because of the way in which it is made. Regular rayon shrinks and stretches when wet and is said to have poor wet strength.

saponified rayon (sah-*pahn*-eh-fyd *ray*-on)   A type of rayon made from cellulose acetate filaments, similar to the kind used in making acetate. These fibers are treated in a special way to produce a rayon that is very strong. Fortisan is an example of saponified rayon.

viscose rayon (*viss*-kohss *ray*-on)   Rayon made by the viscose process, the process used to make the majority of rayon on the market today. True viscose rayon is not strong, especially when wet. This has led to modifications of the viscose process to produce high wet modulus rayon. *See* high wet modulus rayon.

ready-to-wear (*red*-ee-to-wayr)   A term used in the fashion industry. It was developed to distinguish between manufactured items of clothing and those made from fabrics sold by the yard to the consumer. The term is sometimes shortened to r-t-w. *See* pret á porter.

real lace   Hand-made lace. *See* lace.

reclaimed textile fibers (ree-*klaymd tex*-til *fy*-berz)   Fibers made into fabric (whether sold commercially or not) and then converted back into fiber. Most reclaimed textile fibers are wool and other natural fibers because it is extremely difficult to reclaim man-made fibers. *See* reprocessed fibers and reused fibers.

recovery (reh-*kuv*-er-ee)   The ability of a fabric to return to its original shape after being stretched. This term is used most often in reference to stretch fabrics. A quality stretch fabric will recover promptly. Recovery may also be used in reference to knit fabrics because they have varying amounts of stretchability.

recycled fiber (ree-*sy*-keld *fy*-ber)   *See* reclaimed textile fibers, reprocessed fiber, and reused fiber.

reed   This frame, located directly in front of the harnesses, swings forward to batten the last filling inserted against previous fillings. *See* battening.

reeling   The process of winding silk filaments onto a wheel directly from cocoons.

reembroidered lace (ree-im-*broyd*-erd layss)   Lace with designs outlined in embroidery stitching. *See* embroidery.

regimental stripe (rej-eh-*men*-tuhl stryp)   *See* stripe.

register printing (*rej*-iss-ter *print*-ing)   A method of printing the same design on both sides of the fabric to give it additional definition and clarity of color. Also called duplex printing.

R

remnants (*rem*-nents)   Leftover pieces of fabric, including fabric originally sold by the yard and rug and carpeting material. Usually, because remnants are of odd sizes, the price is reduced and they can be true bargains. Care labeling is not required on remnants under ten yards so note fiber content if it is available in order to determine care requirements.

rep or repp (rep ahr rep)   Heavy filling-wise corded fabric, heavier than poplin. It may be silk, rayon, man-made fibers, cotton, wool, or a mixture. The fabric may be solid or striped. It is used for ties, robes, draperies, and upholstery, and in lighter weights for blouses and trimmings.

repeat   Repeat refers to a design that appears over and over again on a fabric. It also refers to the amount of space the design takes before it starts over again. Since it is desirable to center the design in a fabric on such things as sofas, the size of the repeat must be known in order to determine the yardage needed. The larger the pattern, the larger the repeat and the more fabric needed. The size of the repeat in a plaid, for example, is also important in buying fabric for home-sewn garments.

reprocessed fibers (wool) (ree-*pross*-est *fy*-berz [wool])   Fibers obtained from scraps and clips of woven and felted fabrics made of previously unused wool that have been shredded back into fiber form and then remade into new yarns. Reprocessed fibers are usually wool fibers and must be relabeled as reprocessed wool according to Federal Trade Commission standards. Reprocessed fibers are less desirable than new or virgin fibers. *See* virgin fiber.

reptile (*rep*-tyl)   *See* leather.

residual shrinkage (reh-*zij*-you-el *shring*-kij)   The amount of shrinkage remaining in a fabric or garment after all manufacturing processes are completed. More than 1% residual shrinkage is undesirable, but common because in many fabrics the removal of residual shrinkage is not always included as part of the finishing process. Because fabrics often have residual shrinkage, it is important to preshrink before cutting fabrics used in home sewing. *See* preshrunk.

resiliency (rih-*zil*-ee-ehn-see)   The ability of a fabric to return to its original shape after compressing, bending, or other deformation.

resin finish (*rez*-ehn *fin*-ish)   A finish made of synthetic resins applied to fabrics to impart certain characteristics such as wrinkle and crease resistance. *See* finishing.

resist dyeing (ree-*zist dy*-ing)   In resist dyeing, areas to be colored are left exposed to the dye, whereas other areas, not to be colored, are covered with something impervious to dye. Batik is a form of resist dyeing in which wax is used to cover the area where dye is not wanted. *See* batik.

resist printing (ree-*zist print*-ing)   Printing similar to resist dyeing. In resist printing, the fabric is coated with a paste that protects it from colors in certain areas; when the printing is completed, the paste ("resist") is removed. *See* resist dyeing and batik.

retting (*ret*-ing)   The removal, usually by soaking, of the outer woody portion of the flax plant to gain access to the fibers. This may be done by several methods: pool, dew, tank, and chemical.

reused fibers   Fibers obtained from rags and used clothing which, after sorting and cleaning, have been shredded into fiber. Products made from reused fibers must be labeled as such. Reused fibers, similar to reprocessed fibers, are less desirable than new fibers. *See* virgin fiber and reprocessed fibers.

reused wool   Old wool that has been made into a wool product and used by consumers, then cleaned, garnetted, and remade into merchandise. It must be labeled reused wool. *See* reused fibers.

reversed leather (ree-*verst leth*-er)   A common name in leather for the hide of an animal with the fur removed.

reversible fabric (ree-*vers*-eh-buhl *fab*-rik)   A fabric that can be used on either side. Generally, the term reversible is applied to two quite different fabrics joined together by such methods as laminating or double cloth construction. Reversible fabrics frequently are used for coats, less frequently for other garments. *See* laminating and double cloth.

rhinestone (*ryne*-stohn)   A faceted piece of glass (the glass is cut with faces that reflect light). Rhinestones are used in costume jewelry or as decoration on clothing or trimming. Rhinestones are also called diamante.

rib   A straight, ridged, or corded effect that usually moves vertically or horizontally on a fabric.

rib knit   A knit consisting of alternate plain and purl stitches (the reverse of a plain knit with loops showing). Rib knit fabrics are "stretchier" and have a snugger fit than plain knits.

rib stitch   A weft knit identified by vertical ribs on both sides of the fabric. A very resilient stitch. When combined with the tuck stitch, it is called rib-and-tuck stitch.

rib weave   A plain weave that forms ridges in a fabric through the way in which it is woven or by the use of thicker yarns for the filling than those used for the warp. *See* weaving, filling, and warp.

ribbed cuff   A close-fitted knit finish in ribbed pattern for the open end of a sleeve.

ribbing   Rib knit that is used at wrists, waists, and necklines of plain or patterned knit garments. *See* rib knit.

ribbon   A narrow, woven fabric with two finished edges. Both natural and man-made fibers are used to make ribbon. It is available in many patterns and colors and in such fabric constructions as velvet, satin, and grosgrain. *See* velvet, satin, and grosgrain.

rick-rack (rik-rak)   A flat braid woven in a zig-zag, serpentine shape. It is available in several widths and is an extremely popular and inexpensive trimming.

rippling   Threshing of flax to strip the seeds or bolls from the plant. This process may be done by hand or by machine.

Robin Hood hat   A felt hat with a pointed crown and rolled-up brim on the sides and in the back.

roll collar   A collar that rises from the neckline then folds over (or rolls) so that the edge of the collar touches the garment.

roller blinds (*rohl*-er blyndz)   Shades wound around a roller or dowel when the window is exposed. Originally made only in neutral colors, today these shades often are made in colors or matched and coordinated with the draperies in a room.

roller printing (*rohl*-er *print*-ing)   Roller printing may be the most important method of printing today. The design is etched onto a roller through which the fabric is passed. For each color in the design a different roller is used. High speed can be obtained in roller printing.

roller shades (*rohl*-er shaydz)   Another name for roller blinds.

romain crepe (roh-*mayn* krayp)   A semisheer fabric of abraded yarns in warp and filling. It is made of rayon and acetate or wool and is used for street and dressy dresses.

Roman shades (*roh*-men shaydz)   Shades similar to Austrian shades. When the window is exposed, the fabric of Roman shades hangs in graceful folds at the top of the window. Austrian shades are shirred throughout when they cover the window, but Roman shades hang straight and only form folds when drawn up to uncover the window.

Roman stripes (*roh*-men stryps) Narrow, multi-colored stripes that cover an entire fabric. The colors may be as vivid as those of blazer stripes or as subtle as soft ombré shadings. *See* blazer stripes and ombré.

rough crepe A heavy fabric of rayon, acetate, or mixtures made with alternately twisted fillings, two right and two left (2x2).

round-wire carpet A Wilton construction in which a round wire is used instead of a flat wire to make the pile. Pile is, therefore, uncut.

roving Intermediate stage in yarn manufacture between sliver and yarn, by which a sliver of natural fiber is attenuated to between $1/4$ and $1/8$ of its original size; also, the product of this operation, a single strand of fibers having very little twist.

roving frame A machine that puts a loose twist in the drawn-out sliver.

rows to the inch Rows of yarn tufts to the inch lengthwise.

rubber The generic name of man-made fibers in which the fiber-forming substance is natural or synthetic rubber.

rubber sheet (*ruhb*-uhr sheet) A sheet used on a bed to protect the mattress better than a mattress pad. Although relatively few rubber sheets today are actually made of rubber, the term is still used. These sheets, because they are impervious to water, tend to hold perspiration. They are more comfortable for sleeping if covered by a mattress cover and sheet. *See* mattress cover. *See also* sheet.

ruche, ruching (roosh, *roosh*-ing) A ruffle. *See* ruffle.

ruff (ruhf) A wheel-shaped collar made of several layers of fabric (usually lace) in S-shaped folds.

ruffle (*ruhf*-uhl) A strip of fabric or other material gathered on one edge and inserted into a seam and hemmed or finished on the other edge. Used as trim.

rug cushion A fabric of sponge rubber or hair felt placed under the rug to prevent the rug from slipping and to make the rug softer and more cushiony.

rug or carpet pad The layer of fabric placed underneath a carpet or rug to provide it with longer life and to give it a more luxurious appearance and feeling. Carpet padding is made of cattle hair, rubberized hair, rubber, and combinations of jute and cattle hair as well as some of the man-made fibers. Some rugs and carpets have a bonded foam, sponge rubber, or man-made backing, in which case no separate padding is needed. Padding is also called cushion and underlay.

rugs and carpets   Usually the most expensive fabrics people ever buy. They are thick, heavy fabrics that can be made of a variety of different fibers and textures. The words rug and carpet are often used interchangeably. Rug usually refers to a floor covering that does not cover the entire floor and the ends are finished with binding or fringe. Carpet is used for fabric that covers the entire floor and is fastened to it. Following are common rug and carpet terms:

area rug   A small, usually decorative rug often placed on a carpet as an accent in a room or to define an area, such as a dining section in a living room.

Aubusson (oh-boo-*sohn*)   A woven rug with little or no rib and a low pile.

Axminster (*aks*-min-ster)   A rug woven on a loom that allows the creation of fairly complicated designs.

braid rug   A rug made of strips of fabric braided together then stitched together to form a rug. *See* braid.

broadloom carpet (*brawd*-loom *kar*-pit)   A carpet woven on a loom at least nine feet wide or wider. It is incorrectly used to suggest carpet quality. The term is also used to describe wide, tufted carpeting in which tufts of yarn are pulled through a backing to form the rug surface. *See* tufted rug, pile, cut pile fabric, and shearing.

brocade (broh-*kayd*)   A rug in which a pattern is formed by using yarns of the same color with different twists. The light strikes the yarns differently, giving a shaded design effect. *See* twist.

drugget (*drug*-it)   A coarse, felted floor covering made from mixtures of such fibers as cotton, jute, and wool. Drugget is usually napped on one side and is a traditionally inexpensive floor covering used by institutions.

hand-knotted rug   Hand-knotted rugs, including Oriental and Persian rugs, are among the most expensive made. Intricate designs are possible. The higher the number of knots to the inch, the finer the rug.

R

hooked rug A rug made by hand or machine using a hook to pull loops of yarn or fabric through a coarse backing or canvas to form a pile.

indoor-outdoor carpeting Carpeting that can be used outdoors where it will be exposed to weather conditions, as well as indoors. Most of this type of carpeting is made of olefin. *See* olefin.

loop rug Usually, a rug with an uncut loop pile. Types of loops include high-low loop (a rug in which some loops are higher than others giving a sculptured effect), one-level loop, and random-sheared loop (a rug with some loops cut and others uncut to create a sculpted effect). *See* pile.

narrow carpet Carpet made on a loom about three feet wide. The term is used to distinguish this carpeting from broadloom carpeting. Narrow carpet is often used on stairways. *See* rugs and carpets and broadloom carpet.

Navajo rug (*nah*-vuh-hoh rug) A rug woven in a tapestry weave in geometric patterns by Navajo Indians in the western part of the United States. Navajo rugs usually are brightly colored and have become true collectors' items. *See* tapestry.

Oriental rugs (*ahr*-ee-en-tuhl rugz) Hand-made rugs produced in the Middle and Far East. They are hand-woven in the tapestry method or hand-knotted. True Oriental rugs are extremely expensive and are collectors' items. Machine-made imitations are available. *See* tapestry, rugs and carpets, and hand-knotted rug.

Persian rug (*pur*-zhen rug) An Oriental rug made in Iran (formerly Persia). *See* Oriental rug.

rag rug A rug woven with strips of cotton, wool, or synthetic fabrics used as the filling on a cotton or synthetic yarn warp. Rag rugs are made by hand and machine and, with the exception of some hand-made antique rag rugs, are usually the most inexpensive rugs.

random-sheared rug (*ran*-dum-sheerd rug) A pile rug in which some sections of the pile are cut and other sections are not. *See* pile and shearing.

rya rug (*ry*-ah rug) A Scandinavian shag rug. Rya rugs are popular in the United States as area rugs because of their dramatic color combinations. The highest quality rya rugs, also quite expensive, are hand-knotted.

R

sculptured carpet (*skulp*-cherd kar-pit)   Carpet (or rugs) in which the pile is cut in different lengths to form a pattern or design.

shag rug or carpet   A rug or carpet with an extremely long pile.

tufted rug (*tuf*-tid rug)   The most common type of rug construction. Tufted rugs are formed by needles rapidly punching yarn into the rug backing to form a pile that can be looped, cut, or sheared. *See* pile, cut pile fabric, and shearing.

twist rug   A rug or carpet made of twist, a strong, long-wearing yarn that has been tightly twisted in its manufacture. Twist rugs and carpets are recommended for high traffic areas. They have a corkscrew-like cut pile that forms a pebbled look. *See* cut pile fabrics.

Wilton rug (*wil*-ten rug)   A woven, cut-pile rug with a velvety texture. The designs in Wilton rugs often show an Oriental influence. Wilton rugs are quite expensive. *See* cut pile fabric and pile.

runless   A type of seamless nylon hosiery in a lock-stitch mesh.

run-resistant   Knitted fabric constructed to make runs difficult. *See* interlock knitting.

Russian leather (*rush*-uhn *leth*-er)   A common name in leather for the hide of an animal with the fur removed.

rustle (*russ*-uhl)   Another word for scroop, the rustle that certain fabrics such as silk taffeta have. Scroop is considered a desirable characteristic in luxury fabrics.

rya (*ry*-ah)   A Scandinavian shag rug. Rya rugs are popular in the United States as area rugs because of their dramatic color combinations. The highest quality rya rugs, also quite expensive, are hand-knotted.

R

Defect	Explanation	Severity
Reed Mark (also Open Reed)	An actual streak, line, or mark observed in the warp direction of the goods. They are found in all woven fabric as it comes from the loom in the loom state or gray state. Rather prominent in lightweight cottons, some silks, certain rayon fabrics, and particularly in woolen and worsted fabrics. Causes include a worn out reed, loose reed wires, bent wires in the reed, wrong-draws, incorrect reeding, too much tension on the warp, and so forth. In the great majority of cases reed marks are obliterated altogether in the finishing of the goods.	Major or Minor
Reed Misdraw	Where one or more ends are drawn through the reed contrary to design.	Major or Minor
Reed Streak	A warp-wise defect attributed to a bad reed. It may appear as light and heavy streaks because of uneven placement of the yarn, varying its affinity for dye.	Major
Reedy	A condition characterized by open streaks following the pattern of the reed wires. This can be the result of a too-coarse reed, wrong reed-draw arrangement, or improper setting of the loom.	Major
Rolling Streak	Curled, buckled, or rolled-up, the fabric might be easily cut in the shearing. This blemish creates a great deal of trouble throughout finishing unless remedied prior to entering the finishing department of the mill. One of the most annoying blemishes for the weaver and the finisher.	Major
Rope Marks	Long, irregular, and indistinct lines or markings on dyed or finished fabrics.	Major
Rough	A term used to describe a rough or crinkled appearance resulting from over-sanforization.	Major

Defect	Explanation	Severity
Runner (also Dropped Stitch)	In knits, a vertical line of unformed stitches resulting from a broken needle or jack. Most machines have a devise to stop the machine when needles break.	Major

saddlebag   A pouch-like purse with a flap that folds over the top opening.

saddle shoe   An oxford-style shoe with a contrasting piece of leather (somewhat in the shape of a saddle) across the instep.

safari bag   A soft leather purse with a curved rectangular shape, a buckled center strap, two outside pockets with buckled flaps, and two strap handles.

sailcloth (*sayl*-kloth)   Originally, a firmly woven cotton canvas used for making sails. Today, sailcloth is a very heavy, strong, plain-weave fabric made of cotton, linen, jute, nylon, or polyester. It comes in many qualities and weights. In common usage, the terms duck, sailcloth, and canvas often are used interchangeably. Sailcloth can be used for sportswear, slipcovers and upholstery, and curtains and draperies. *See* canvas and duck.

sailor collar   A collar that is "V"-shaped in front with a deep square or rectangle in back; may be trimmed, appliquéd, or plain.

salt and pepper   A fabric made of a combination of white and black yarns. The term usually is used to describe tweed fabrics. *See* tweed.

sandal   A shoe with bands and straps attached to a sole. It fastens with a buckle or tie.

Sanforize (*san*-for-eyez)   Trademark of Cluett Peabody and Company Incorporated for a process of preshrinking fabric to leave a residual shrinkage of less than 1%, a desirable characteristic. *See* residual shrinkage.

saran (seh-*ran*)   The generic name for a man-made fiber derived from vinylidene chloride. Saran is strong, resists common chemicals, sunlight, and weather. It is used primarily in the fabric field for upholstery on public transportation vehicles and for garden furniture.

sari (*sah*-ree)   A piece of fabric twelve to sixteen feet long used by Hindu women to drape and cover the body. The fabric is often silk with silver or gold threads forming a border design; other fabrics are also used. A sari is wrapped around the waist and then over the torso. Fabrics used for this type of dress are referred to as sari cloth.

sash (sash)   Soft fabric or a ribbon tied at the waist as a belt.

satchel (*sach*-ehl)   A large rectangular purse with a buckled, snapped, or clasped flap and a wide shoulder strap.

sateen (sa-*teen*)   A strong, lustrous, mercerized, satin-weave fabric made of cotton, blends of cotton with polyester, or spun-yarn fabric characterized by floats running in the filling direction. Sateen is also used to distinguish between cotton satin-weave fabrics and satin-weave fabrics made of silk or man-made fibers. It is used for linings, draperies, and comforters. *See* weaving and satin weave.

sateen weave   Characterized by floats running filling-wise. *See* float.

satin (*sat*-uhn)   One of the basic weaves. A shiny, smooth silk, acetate, rayon, or other man-made fiber combination woven in satin weave made with a cotton filling. It has a smooth, lustrous surface because the warp floats. It is used for linings of coats, jackets, facings, and ties. It is also used for draperies, upholstery, bedspreads, and sheets. Satin weave has proved so popular that various types of satin-weave fabrics have developed. Following is a listing of many of the types of satin fabrics. *See* weaving and sateen.

> **antique satin** (an-*teek sat*-uhn)   A satin-weave fabric primarily used for draperies. It can be used on either side. The face is a classic lustrous satin; the reverse has a slubbed look similar to shantung. *See* shantung.

> **crepe-backed satin**   (*crayp*-bakt *sat*-uhn) A satin that can be used on either side. The face is satin, the back is crepe. It is often used as a jacket or coat lining. *See* crepe and satin crepe.

> **double-faced satin** (*duhb*-buhl-fayst *sat*-uhn)   A satin fabric with a satin appearance on both sides unlike ordinary satin, which has a definite right and wrong side.

> **duchesse satin** (doo-*shess sat*-uhn)   One of the heaviest and richest looking satins. It is important for such formal clothing as wedding gowns.

S

slipper satin (*slip*-ehr *sat*-uhn)   A tightly woven satin fabric, usually lighter in weight than duchesse satin, and used for many purposes including evening shoes or slippers.

satin brocade   A satin with a raised woven-in design. It resembles a fine embroidered pattern.

satin crepe   A heavy reversible fabric with satin on one side and crepe on the other. It is used in fall and winter dresses and linings.

satin weave   Characterized by a smooth surface caused by floats running warp-wise.

saturation regain   The moisture in a material at 95% or 100% relative humidity.

savonnierie   A French rug made to imitate Oriental knotted rugs with rococo patterns.

Saxony (*saks*-seh-nee)   Saxony is a heavyweight, napped coating fabric, traditionally made from merino wool. Saxony originated in Saxony, Germany. *See* merino.

scales   Protective covering of the wool fiber.

scallops (*skal*-uhps)   Decorative semicircular curves usually used as edge trimming. They are popular clothing accents and often are used on café curtains. *See* curtains and draperies and café curtains.

Schiffli (*shif*-lee)   An embroidery machine that can imitate many different hand embroidery stitches. *See* embroidery.

scoop neck   A neckline in the shape of the letter "U."

Scotchgard (*skahch*-gawrd)   Trademark of the 3M Company for an oil- and water-repellent finish. *See* finishing.

Scottish tweed (*skaht*-ish tweed)   Originally made in Scotland, Scottish tweed is a term often used today for tweed woven with very nubby yarns with white warp and colored filling. *See* Irish tweed.

scouring   A finishing process for removing oil, sizing, dirt, grease, and swint from wool and other fabrics.

S

screen printing (skreen *print*-ing)   In screen printing, a sheer fabric, such as silk or nylon gauze, is stretched over a wood or metal frame to form a screen. The entire screen, except for the design area to be printed, is coated with a substance that closes the pores of the fabric screen. The dye is poured onto the screen and forced through the uncoated design areas onto the fabric below. A different screen must be used for each color in the print.

scrim (skrihm)   An open, plain-weave, mesh fabric used for curtains, bunting, and as a supporting fabric for some laminated fabrics. Scrim was traditionally made of cotton, but today usually is made of nylon or other man-made fibers. *See* bunting.

scroop (skroop)   A characteristic rustling or crunching sound acquired by silk that has been immersed in solutions of acetic or tartaric acid and dried without rinsing. It is probably caused by acid microcrystals in the fibers rubbing against each other. It is also the rustle that certain fabrics such as silk taffeta have. Scroop is considered a desirable characteristic in luxury fabrics.

scrubbed (skrubd)   *See* scrubbing.

scrubbing (*skrub*-ing)   Another name for the brushing method of raising a nap. Scrubbed denim, for example, means napped denim. *See* napping.

sculptured rug (*skulp*-cherd rug)   A floor covering in which the pile is cut in different lengths to form a Jacquard design made with different heights.

scutching   The separation of the outer covering of the flax stalk from the usable fibers.

Sea Island cotton (see *eye*-lehnd *kaht*-uhn)   A species of American cotton once produced off the coast of the Carolinas. It has a long, lustrous, staple fiber, averaging about 2". It is now produced on the Lesser Antilles, Montserrat, St. Kitts, Nevis, and St. Vincent.

seal (seel)   A common name in leather for the hide of an animal with the fur removed.

seam binding (seem *bynd*-ing)   Usually a narrow strip of twill weave fabric finished at each edge. It is stitched to a raw edge of fabric to cover it and prevent it from raveling. Strips of bias fabric can be used in the same way, and when they are, they are also called seam binding. *See* trimming.

seamless (*seem*-lihs)   A self-explanatory term. A seamless garment has no seams or fewer seams than the ordinary cut-and-sewn garment of its type. The word seamless is used primarily for garments that are given their final shape by heat-setting (called boarding in the case of hosiery) or molding. *See* cut-and-sewn, heat-setting, boarding, and molding.

seam-line pockets   Pockets set into a seam and hidden behind the garment fabric.

seconds   Factory rejects with defects that could affect the wear of the item.

seed yarn   A very small nub often made of dyed man-made fibers applied to a dyed or natural-base yarn.

seersucker (*seer*-suhk-ehr)   A puckered, lightweight, cotton, cotton blend, silk, or man-made fibered fabric made by alternating plain and crinkled stripes. A puckered look appears in the alternating stripes and is achieved in the actual weaving process. Groups of tight warp yarns alternate with groups of slack or loose warp yarns so that when the filling thread is woven in, the loose yarns pucker. Seersucker is used incorrectly as a synonym for plissé. Seersucker is available in plain colors and stripes and is also popular in plaids and prints. It is used for summer dresses, boys shirts, shorts, men's summer suits, and bedspreads. Seersucker effects can be imitated in knits. *See* woven seersucker, crinkle crepe, and plissé.

self-belt   A belt made of the same fabric as the clothing with which it is worn. It may simply be a sash or a stiff belt with a buckle.

selvage (*sehl*-vij)   The long, outer, finished edge of both sides of a woven fabric that does not ravel because the filling yarns wrap around the warp yarns. It may also be called self-edge or selvedge.

semi-fashioned (*sehm*-ee *fash*-und)   A hosiery term for seamless hosiery that has had a fake seam added so it will resemble full-fashioned hosiery. *See* full-fashioned.

senna knot   Type of knot used to make pile in Persian hand-tied rugs.

sequin (*see*-kwin)   A shiny, usually metallic, decoration or spangle. Sequins are sewn to clothing, especially evening dresses because they shimmer and sparkle in the light. Sequins usually have a single, central hole for fastening to the garment or fabric. Sequins are also known as paillettes (pie-*yets*). Fabric covered with sequins is available by the yard.

serge (surj)   A smooth, even, twill weave worsted fabric with the diagonal wale showing on both sides of the cloth. Traditionally, a basic, hard-wearing woolen suiting, it is used for men's and women's suits, coats, and dresses. It is piece-dyed to a solid color. In cotton, silk, or rayon, it is used for linings. *See* weaving and twill weave.

S

sericulture (*sehr*-ee-kuhl-chuhr)   The raising of silkworms and production of silk.

set-in (or slash) pockets   Pockets made by cutting an opening in the garment and stitching the pocket to the inside of the garment so only the opening is visible.

sewing-knitting machine (*soh*-ing-*nit*-ing meh-*sheen*)   The latest machine for making fabrics. In the best known of these, the malimo machine, the warp thread is placed on top of the filling thread and the two are stitched together with a third thread.

shade cloth   The name for any fabric used to make window shades.

shades   A window covering that plays a double role. Shades provide both light control and privacy and can also lend a decorative accent. Shades range from the traditional roller blinds, available in versions that exclude light completely to those that permit some light to come in, to some with a more decorative purpose such as Austrian shades. Following is a listing of some of the popular types of shades. The term blind is a synonym for shade.

accordion shades (uh-*kor*-dee-un shaydz)   Shades made of accordion pleats sharply creased at regular intervals horizontally across their width. Accordion shades take up relatively little room when drawn up to uncover the window. *See* pleats and accordion pleats.

Austrian shades (*aws*-tree-uhn shaydz)   Shades made of fabric shirred across the width of the shade. When drawn up, Austrian shades hang in graceful loops of fabric. *See* shirring.

roller blinds   Roller blinds are shades wound around a roller or dowel when the window is exposed. Originally made only in neutral colors, today these shades often are made in colors or matched and coordinated with the draperies in a room.

roller shades   A synonym for roller blinds.

Roman shades (*roh*-men shaydz)   Shades similar to Austrian shades. When the window is exposed, the fabric of Roman shades hangs in graceful folds at the top of the window. Austrian shades are shirred throughout when they cover the window, but Roman shades hang straight and only form folds when drawn up to uncover the window.

sky line shades   Another name for Roman shades.

S

Venetian blinds (veh-*nee*-shen blyndz)   One of the most popular window coverings to control light and privacy. Venetian blinds are made of strips of fabric, metal, or plastic. These strips can be tipped to shut out light completely or opened to varying degrees to filter light to the desired intensity. They can also be raised to the top of the window to bare it completely. Conventional Venetians hang with the slats or strips horizontal to the windowsill, but vertical Venetians are also available and often are used as room dividers as well as window coverings. Venetians are available in various colors and widths.

shading   Crushing of the pile of a rug so that it seems to have light and dark spots in it.

shadow printing (*shad*-oh *print*-ing)   A printing method in which only the warp yarns are printed with a design before the fabric is woven. The resulting fabric has a wavy, shadowy effect. It is also called warp printing.

shadow stripes (*shad*-oh strypes)   Faint impressions of stripes achieved by using yarns of the same color but different twists in weaving a fabric. The shadow effect comes from the way in which the light strikes the yarns of varying twists. *See* twist.

shag (shayg)   A floor covering with relatively long, loose wool or man-made fibered pile.

shantung (*shan*-tung)   A silk fabric with a nubby surface similar to but heavier than pongee. It was originally a rough, hand-loomed, plain-weave fabric woven of wild silk in Shantung, China. Slubs in the yarn provided a textural effect with an irregular surface. Today the term shantung is applied to a plain-weave fabric with heavier, rougher yarns running in the crosswise direction of the fabric. These are single complex yarns of the slub type. The fabric can be made of cotton, silk, wool, rayon, or other man-made fibers. It is used for dresses, suits, and draperies. *See* slub and silk.

shape retention   A fabric's ability to retain the original shape of a garment after being used or cleaned.

S

sharkskin   (1) A heavy weight, fairly lustrous cotton, linen, silk, or man-made fiber fabric with a sleek, hard-finished, crisp, and pebbly surface and a chalky luster. Today, it is almost always made of acetate or triacetate. Filament yarns, when used, are twisted and woven tightly in a plain-weave or basket-weave construction, depending on the effect desired. Staple fiber yarns are handled in the same manner, except for wool. Sharkskin is best known in its stark white color especially popular for tennis outfits and for permanently pleated white skirts when they are in fashion. (2) A wool fabric in twill weave, originally made of yarns of two colors; it is so called because it resembles leather sharkskin in durability. The yarns in both warp and filling alternate white with a color such as black, brown, or blue. The diagonal lines of the twill weave run from left to right; the colored yarns from right to left. Used for men's and women's suits and slacks, it comes in a clear or semifinished worsted. Patterns include plaids, stripes, nailheads, and bird's-eye. It is also made in man-made fibers and blends.

shawl   A triangular or oblong piece of cloth worn around the shoulders; it is often fringed.

shawl collar   A collar formed by cutting the lapel and collar in one continuous piece.

shearing (*sheer*-ing)   A method of removing the hair from an animal (the wool from sheep, for example) without injuring the animal. Shearing also refers to trimming the pile on a fabric to a desired height.

sheath-core yarn   A bulky yarn of synthetic fibers consisting of a core of fine denier fibers with considerable shrinkage and a cover or wrapping of coarse denier relaxed fibers.

shed   The opening between warp yarns through which filling yarns are passed.

shedding   The raising and lowering of the warp ends by means of the harness and heddles to form the shed (passage) for the filling yarn to pass through from one side of the loom to the other.

sheer   The opposite of opaque. Sheer fabrics are usually made in an open weave to create fabrics with varying degrees of transparency. Batiste, organdy, and voile are examples of sheer fabrics. *See* batiste, organdy, and voile.

sheer curtains   Thin fabrics of polyester, cotton, and blends that hang next to the window glass.

sheet   A rectangular piece of fabric used to cover and protect the top and sides of a mattress. This is usually referred to as a bottom sheet. A top sheet is placed on top of a bottom sheet to protect the skin from a sometimes scratchy blanket and to protect the blanket from soil.

Traditionally, sheets were made of linen or cotton; today they are more likely to be made of cotton and polyester blends for easy care. At one time, sheets were white; today they are available in many colors and patterns.

Shetland yarn (*sheht*-lehnd yarn)   Officially, only yarn from sheep raised on the Shetland Islands off the coast of Scotland. However, the term often is used to describe soft, fluffy, two-ply woolen yarns popular in hand knitting. It is also used to describe fabrics that look as if they were made from such yarns.

shiki (shiki rep) (shih-*kee* [shih-*kee* rehp])   Heavy rayon, acetate, and cotton, or other mixtures identified by wavy filling-wise cords. It is used for draperies.

shirring (*sher*-ing)   A method of gathering fabric to create decorative fullness. Shirring consists of three or more parallel rows of stitching, placed about 1/2" to 1" apart, and drawn up (gathered) together to form bands of controlled gathers. Shirring is used in clothing and in items of home furnishings.

shirting (*shurt*-ing)   Any lightweight fabric appropriate for shirts or blouses. The term top-weight (its opposite is bottom-weight) is often used for this type of fabric instead of the word shirting. Some crepes and satins, as well as voile and Oxford cloth, are examples of shirting fabrics although there are many others.

shoddy (*shahd*-ee)   Originally, a fabric made from reprocessed wool. Today, the word is used for a fabric—or anything else, for that matter—that is poorly made or made of inferior materials. *See* reprocessed fibers and reused wool.

shoot   Another term for filling, weft, woof, and shute. The crosswise thread that interlaces with the warp threads on a woven fabric.

shortie glove   A wrist-length glove with a side or center palm opening that can be snapped or buttoned.

short-staple cotton   Fibers 1/4" to 15/16" long.

shot   Another name for iridescent and changeable fabric. Fabric woven with yarns of one color in the warp and another color in the filling so that the fabric seems to change color as the light strikes it.

shoulder bag   Any type of purse with shoulder straps.

shoulder pad (*shohl*-dehr pad)   A support placed in the shoulder area of a garment to give a wider look to the shoulder when this look is in

S

style. A thinner version known as a shoulder shape is used in coats and suits to maintain shape and give support in the shoulder area. Shoulder pads and shoulder shapes are available in notions departments and in fabric stores. *See* findings.

shower curtain   A shower curtain is a length of fabric hung around a bathroom shower or shower-tub combination to keep water from splashing out onto the floor. Shower curtains should be waterproof. When decorative, nonwaterproof shower curtains are used, a waterproof liner, usually made of plastic, should be placed inside.

showerproof (*shou*-er-proof)   One of the many terms used to describe varying degrees of imperviousness to water. A showerproof fabric will repel water to a limited extent, but is not waterproof. *See* waterproof.

shrinkage-controlled fabric (*shringk*-ihj-*kuhn*-trohld *fab*-rik)   Fabric treated in some way to prevent it from shrinking more than a specified amount. Unfortunately, the term shrinkage-controlled is an arbitrary standard and varies from manufacturer to manufacturer and gives the consumer no true measure of quality. Shrinkage-control is usually achieved by shrinking the fabric in the finishing steps or by the addition of finishing agents to the fabric.

shute (shoot)   Another term for weft, woof, shoot, and filling. The crosswise thread that interlaces with the warp threads on a woven fabric.

shuttle (*shuht*-uhl)   The part of the weaving machine (loom) that carries the filling yarn over and under the warp yarns.

shuttleless loom   A machine that carries the filling yarns through the shed by the use of air or water jets and grippers.

silence cloth (*sy*-lehns kloth)   A cloth or padding put on a dining table to protect it and (as the name suggests) to prevent the clatter of dishes against the table. A silence cloth is usually a napped, fairly heavy fabric. Silence cloths are placed beneath tablecloths and are called silencers.

silencer (*sy*-lehns-ehr)   *See* silence cloth and table pad.

S

silhouette (sihl-oo-*eht*)   Literally, shadow or outline. Silhouette refers to the shape of a garment. When the silhouette is soft, soft drapeable fabrics are popular; when the silhouette is stiff, crisper fabrics with body are in demand. *See* crisp fabric and soft fabric.

silicone (*sil*-eh-kohn)   Generic name for certain compounds obtained from silicon, a component of sand. Silicones are used in fabric finishing to impart stain and wrinkle resistance. *See* finishing.

silk   The product of the silk worm and the only natural filament fiber (it is produced in a long thread). Silk was the leading luxury fiber for thousands of years. There were many types of silk and many ways of making it into cloth. Today, man-made fibers have to a very large extent replaced silk, but the traditional names for certain silk fabrics are still used and include the following:

China silk (*chy*-nuh silk)   A lightweight, inexpensive silk fabric used primarily for linings. It is available today, but often difficult to find. It is also referred to as Jap silk.

Honan silk (hoh-*nan* silk)   Silk similar to pongee. *See* pongee.

Macclesfield silk (*mak*-les-feeld silk)   Macclesfield silk was originally woven in Macclesfield, England. The name has come to apply to small, yarn dyed, dobby designs used in men's neckties.

pongee (pon-*jee*)   A plain-weave, fairly lightweight silk fabric with a slight slub to the yarns. Today, the terms Honan and pongee are used interchangeably for fabrics with this texture, but made from man-made fabrics.

raw silk   A term used incorrectly for wild silk. Raw silk is the silk fiber before it has been processed in any way. Raw silk is coated with a glue-like substance called sericin. The sericin is removed in later processing and is not silk.

shantung (*shan*-tung)   A silk similar to pongee in that it, too, is made with slubbed yarns, but in shantung the unevenness of the yarns is even greater. Shantung is one of the fabrics that originated in silk and has been imitated extensively in the man-made fibers.

surah (*soor*-ah)   A silk recognized by its sheen and its fine twill weave. Surah is popular for dresses and neckties and is also imitated in man-made fibers.

Thai silk (ty silk)   Silk made in Thailand. Most Thai silk is fairly heavy weight, often slubbed, and made in vivid colors that are usually iridescent or changeable. *See* changeable.

tie silk (ty silk)   Any silk used for men's neckties. Surah is one of these silks. Small, colorful patterns are often featured in this type of silk. *See* surah.

S

tussah (*tuss*-ah)   Silk fabric woven from silk made by wild, uncultivated silkworms. Tussah is naturally tan in color, cannot be bleached, and has a rougher texture than cultivated silk. Wild silkworms eat leaves other than mulberry leaves which cultivated silkworms eat exclusively. The difference in diet accounts for the different fiber and fabric characteristics. Tussah is also used to describe fabrics designed to imitate this kind of silk. *See* wild silk.

tussore (*too*-sorh)   Another name for tussah.

wild silk (wyld silk)   The silk from uncultivated silkworms that eat leaves other than mulberry leaves. Wild silk is coarser and is more uneven than cultivated silk. The resulting fabric is usually duller in finish and rougher in texture than other types of silk. Tussah is a silk fabric made from wild silk.

silk broadcloth   A soft spun-silk fabric in plain weave, used for shirts, blouses, and sports dresses.

silk culture   The care of the worm that produces silk fiber, from the egg to the moth.

silk illusion   A net similar to tulle but even finer in mesh, used primarily for bridal veils.

silk noil (silk noyl)   Short ends of silk fibers used in making rough, textured, spun yarns or in blends with cotton or wool; sometimes called waste silk.

singeing (*sihnj*-ing)   Removing surface fibers and lint from a cloth with hot copper plates or gas flames.

single knit (*sihng*-guhl nit)   Fabric made on a rotary machine with one set of needles around the cylinder. Single knit, made on a weft knitting machine, is another term for plain knit. *See* knitting and plain knit.

single yarn   One strand of fibers or filaments grouped or twisted together. *See* singles.

single-breasted   A garment that closes down the center front with only one row of buttons or other type of closure.

singles   A strand of several filaments held together by twist.

sisal straw (*sy*-suhl straw)   A type of straw used for rugs and ropes.

sizing (*syz*-ing)   Starch, gelatin, glue, wax, casein, or clay added to fabrics in the finishing stages to give fabric additional body, a smoother appearance, and more weight. Cotton fabrics are those most commonly treated in this manner. At one time, sizing had to be replaced after each cleaning. Today, with more advanced finishing techniques, sizing is rarely used and fabrics usually retain their initial appearance through cleaning. A few fabrics such as needlepoint canvas are still sized so that they can be handled more easily. This in no way affects their final performance. Sizing also refers to the starch that is applied to the warp yarns to help prevent abrasion during the weaving process. This sizing is usually removed from the fabric in one of the finishing steps.

skein (skayn)   A coil of yarn, which, unlike a spool of thread, has no center supporting object. The term skein and hank are sometimes considered synonyms. *See* hank.

ski wear   Clothing suitable to wear while skiing, such as warm, waterproof pants, jackets, and so forth.

skiver (*skyv*-ehr)   A common name in leather for the hide of an animal with the fur removed.

sky line shades   Another name for Roman shades. These shades hang straight when they cover a window and only form folds when drawn up to uncover the window. When the window is exposed, the fabric hangs in graceful folds at the top of the window. *See* shades, Roman shades, and Austrian shades.

sleeve cap   The top part of the sleeve at the shoulder that may be set flat (smooth), pleated, or shirred (gathered).

slide   An ornament that slides up and down a chain; it enables one to adjust the size of the neck opening. Typically used on a bola (a man's western style "necktie").

sling-back shoe   A pump having an open back with a strap across the back of the heel.

slipcover (slip-*kuv*-ehr)   An unattached covering for a sofa or chair. Slipcovers are made with openings so they can be removed for cleaning. They are also called loose covers.

S

slipper satin (*slip*-ehr *sat*-uhn)   A heavy, tightly woven rayon, acetate, or silk satin fabric, usually with a cotton back and lighter in weight than duchesse satin. It is used for many purposes, including evening shoes or slippers.

sliver   A filmy sheet of fibers resulting from carding.

slouch hat   A soft hat with a deep crown and a wide flexible brim.

slub (sluhb)   An elongated nub. Slub yarn is identified by its elongated nubs. A slub is an uneven area in a yarn that gives the fabric made from it a degree of texture. Slubs can be produced naturally (as in hand spinning which often has slubs) or artificially, by deliberately making them in spinning. Slubs in man-made fibers are usually produced by making parts of the fiber thicker than others. Short, staple fibers mixed with other fibers in the yarn will produce slubs. Nub is another word for slub.

slub dyed   Silver dyed or printed.

small wares (smawl wayrz)   *See* findings.

smocking (*smahk*-ing)   Rows of shirring done in a pattern to add some give (stretch) to a garment and for decoration. A common pattern of smocking is to gather the fabric with stitches that cross each other diagonally, forming a honeycomb-like pattern. It is often done with colored embroidery thread and gives an effect similar to shirring. *See* shirring.

snakeskin (*snayk*-skin)   A common name in leather for the skin of a snake.

snood (snood)   A net or fabric pouch worn on the back of a woman's head to hold hair; it can be worn with or without a hat.

soft fabrics (soft *fab*-riks)   Fabrics that tend to drape in soft folds and to cling instead of standing away from the figure or item being covered. Soft fabrics is usually used as the opposite of crisp fabrics. Single knits usually are considered soft fabrics.

soil release (soyl ree-*leess*)   A special finish applied to some man-made fiber fabrics in an attempt to overcome one of their disadvantages: the tendency to retain dirt, especially water-borne and/or oil-based stains, once it has penetrated the fibers. Polyester is one of the fibers that retains oil-based stains.

solution dyeing (suh-*loo*-shuhn *dy*-ing)   The solution for man-made fiber is colored before making it into fiber. Dyestuff is put into the spinning solution and the color is locked in as the fiber is coagulated. Synonymous with spun dyeing and dope dyeing. *See* dyeing, spun dyeing, and dope dyeing.

sorting   Separating wool fibers by touch according to fineness of fibers.

Southwestern wools   From Texas, New Mexico, Arizona, and southern California.

soybean (*soy*-been)   A small herb of the bean family of India and China; source of protein for certain man-made fibers.

space dyeing (spayss *dy*-ing)   A method of dyeing yarn by dipping in dye or spotting in various places along the yarn. This causes different sections of the yarn to appear in different colors. The resulting fabric often has unusual, rainbow-like effects.

spaghetti straps   Very narrow, tubular cloth straps.

spandex (*span*-deks)   The generic name of man-made fibers derived from a chemical substance called segmented polyurethane (resin). This man-made elastic fiber has a good deal of stretch and recovery for its weight. Spandex is used extensively in foundation garments and is much more comfortable than rubber because it is lighter in weight. Spandex is also found in some fabrics where stretch is considered desirable, such as in ski clothes. *See* polyurethane.

specialty fibers   Hair fibers from various breeds of goats and camels. Also included are cow- and horsehair, fur from rabbits, and feathers of the duck, goose, and ostrich.

specific gravity   The density of a fiber relative to that of water at 4° centigrade.

spectator shoe   A pump with a contrasting toe and back, and a stacked (or built up) heel.

spinneret (spin-er-*et*)   A spinneret, which looks very much like a showerhead (a jet or nozzle containing very fine holes), is used in the manufacture of man-made fibers. The material from which the fibers are formed is forced through holes in the spinneret (extruded) while it is in a syrupy or melted state. The resulting long strands harden into filament fibers. *See* filament and fiber.

spinning (*spin*-ing)   A method of drawing out and twisting together fibers to make a continuous thread or yarn. Spinning also refers to the manufacture of man-made fibers as they are formed by forcing the material from which they are made through a spinneret. In conventional spinning, the tighter the twist, the stronger the yarn, but too tight a twist can weaken the final yarn. Crepe yarns have such an extremely high twist that the yarn actually turns back on itself (kinks), producing the characteristic crepe or corkscrew look. Fabrics can be given shadow effects by the use of two yarns which have been twisted in opposite directions during spinning. The light will

S

strike each of these yarns in a different way producing this effect. *See* spinneret.

spinning quality   The ease with which fibers lend themselves to yarn-manufacturing processes; cohesiveness.

Spitalfields (*spiht*-uhl-feeldz)   An English town and the home of Huguenot weavers, it is now a lace-making center. In this town, the hand-woven Jacquard silk Spitalfields tie originated.

splash yarn   An elongated nub yarn that has been tightly twisted around a base yarn.

sponging (*spunj*-ing)   A method of shrinking wool fabrics involving the application of water to the fabric followed by drying it, usually with some heat, in order to shrink it. Some wool fabrics sold by the yard are labeled sponge shrunk, ready for the needle, and they should not shrink again when cleaned.

sportswear   Clothing worn for active or spectator sports or recreational activities.

spread (spred)   Any kind of covering. A bedspread is usually a decorative covering that covers the blanket and pillows on a bed during the day. Bedspreads are available in many styles from simple throws arranged casually over the bed to tailored box spreads. A box spread is a shaped and fitted bedspread with a tailored appearance. The corners are square, giving the spread its name. *See* throw.

spun dyeing   *See* solution dyeing, dyeing, and dope dyeing.

spun fiber yarn (spuhn *fy*-ber yarn)   (1) A yarn twisted by spinning. (2) Yarn made from staple lengths of man-made fibers instead of the long filaments in which man-made fibers are formed. To accomplish this, long filament fibers are chopped into staple lengths and spun to imitate natural fiber yarns. *See* filament and staple.

spun polyester (spuhn powl-ee-*es*-tehr)   *See* spun fiber yarn.

spun rayon (spuhn *ray*-on)   *See* spun fiber yarn.

spun silk   Yarn or fabric made from short fibers of pierced cocoons or from short ends at the outside and inside edges of the cocoons that cannot be reeled.

stabilizing   Treating a fabric so that it will not shrink or stretch more than a certain percentage, perhaps 2%.

stable knit (*stay*-buhl nit)   Any knit unlikely to stretch excessively. Double knits are usually stable knits.

stand-up collar   A collar that rises from the neckline to form a narrow, circular strip or band around the neck.

staple (*stay*-puhl)   Short lengths of fiber, measured in inches or fractions of inches, like those naturally found in cotton and wool. These short lengths must be spun to obtain a length sufficient for weaving or knitting. Silk is the only natural fiber that does not come in staple lengths, but instead in filament lengths. Man-made fibers often are cut into staple lengths for spinning to imitate natural fibers. *See* spinning, filament, and spun fiber yarn.

staple fabrics   Those cloths which, over a period of years, have a steady sale or demand. Such cloths as muslins, flannels, broadcloth, shantung, and taffeta are staples that have to be kept in stock.

static electricity   Stationary electric charges caused by rubbing an article or exposing it to abrasion. Static electricity attracts small particles to the object.

stencil printing (*sten*-sil *print*-ing)   A type of resist printing where portions of the design are covered with metal or wood so the covered parts do not take the dye. *See* printing and resist printing.

stitch (stich)   A single passage of a threaded needle through fabric and back again, as in sewing or embroidery. Stitches may be made by hand or done on a sewing machine to hold layers of fabric together or to decorate fabric such as embroidery, stitchery, and needlepoint. The most commonly used hand stitches follow. *See* embroidery, needlepoint, and stitchery.

>   **back stitch** (bak stich)   One stitch taken backwards on top of another to lock the stitch in place or for extra strength. The back stitch is often used to end a row of running stitches, but can also be used in a continuous row in the same way as a running stitch. *See* running stitch.

>   **hemming stitch** (*hem*-ing stich)   A stitch used to finish the raw edge of a fabric, usually by turning up and catching the edge to another point on the fabric. The needle is inserted in a slanted direction into the edge being hemmed, then into the fabric which is to be caught. Many other types of stitches can also be used for hemming. *See* hem.

S

running stitch (*run*-ing stich)   The basic hand stitch. The needle is inserted into the fabric and then moved in and out, joining two sections of fabric together. The stitches formed are ideally of the same length on both the top and the bottom layer of the fabric.

stitchery (*stich*-er-ee)   The contemporary approach to traditional embroidery in which the same basic stitches are used, but in a freer, less restricted manner to create their own form and shapes. The yarns used in stitchery go beyond traditional wool and silk embroidery floss. Anything can be used to make the stitches from ribbon and cord to narrow strips of fabric or even fishline. Stitchery may be used to decorate clothing, home furnishings items, and for wall hangings. *See* embroidery.

stock tie   A long, wide piece of fabric wrapped around the neck several times and looped over itself in front.

stockinette stitch (stahk-ih-*neht* stich)   In hand weft knitting, characterized by vertical wales on the face and horizontal courses on the back of the fabric. *See* plain stitch.

stole (stohl)   A long rectangle or triangle of fabric or fur worn as a wrap around the shoulders.

straight sleeve   A narrow, tube-like short or long set-in sleeve; sometimes turned back at the bottom edge.

straw   A fairly stiff material made from the stems, leaves, bark, or stalks of various plants. It is usually braided or woven to form a fabric. Straw is used in large quantities for hats when they are in style. Most straw today is used for baskets and handbags of various kinds. Chip straw is used almost exclusively for baskets. It is a by-product of the lumber industry and is made from chips and other pieces of wood, including shavings. Leghorn straw is a braided straw popular for hats and is made from wheat grown in Italy. Panama, another braided hat straw, is made from the screw pine. Other types of straw include Bangkok, linen (straw made to resemble woven linen), Milan, ramie, sisal (used for rugs and ropes), toyo, and Tuscan.

stretch fibers (strech *fy*-berz)   Rubber or man-made elastic fibers (such as spandex and anidex) that are naturally elastic or man-made fibers, highly twisted, heat-set, and untwisted to leave a strong crimp. Polyester has a certain degree of natural stretch and more can be given to the yarn in the processing or in the finishing of the fabric. Occasionally, polyester woven fabrics are described as stretch fabrics. Usually, stretch implies a degree of visible give in a fiber or fabric that stretches and then returns quickly to its original shape. Stretch fabrics are sometimes described as elastic. *See* elastic, crimp, and recovery. *See also* spandex and anidex.

stretch yarn A textured yarn that has good stretch and recovery. It can also refer to yarns made of fibers that have elastic properties or to those yarns whose elastic properties are obtained by alterations of the basic fiber.

stretchable knit (*strech*-eh-buhl nit) Any knit that has a good deal of give or stretch. Most single knits are considered stretchable knits.

striations (stry-*ay*-shuhnz) The many fine microscopic lines extending lengthwise on the viscose rayon fiber; a mark of identification.

string tie A narrow necktie tied in a bow or simply knotted.

stripe (stryp) A band of color, usually on a plain ground. Stripes are usually used in multiples. They can be narrow or wide, in all one color, in patterns of alternating colors, or in multicolored patterns. Common types of stripes include:

awning stripes (*awn*-ing strypz) Stripes seen on awnings designed to protect windows from sun. Awning stripes are sometimes used on fabric for apparel and are usually brightly colored and at least 1^1/$_2$″ wide. Awning stripe patterns may also have a narrow stripe about ^{1}/$_4$″ wide on each side of the main stripe.

balanced stripes (*bal*-uhnst strypz) A pattern of stripes in which the same colors and widths are used on both sides of the center. A blue stripe on a white ground with a narrow red stripe on each side is an example of a balanced stripe; a blue stripe on a white ground with a narrow red stripe on the right side and a narrow yellow stripe on the left side is an example of an unbalanced stripe.

blazer stripes (*blay*-zer strypz) Types of stripes originally used on jackets, ultimately called blazers, because of the bright blazing colors used in the stripes. Blazer stripes are usually at least 1^1/$_2$″ wide and are vividly colored.

chalk stripes (chawk strypz) Narrow white stripes usually on a dark colored ground fabric. *See* pin stripes.

pin stripes (pin strypz) Narrow stripes in any color. When pin stripes are white, they are often called chalk stripes.

S

Roman stripes (*roh*-men strypz)   Narrow, multicolored stripes that cover an entire fabric. The colors may be as vivid as those of blazer stripes or as subtle as soft ombré shadings. *See* blazer stripes and ombré.

unbalanced stripes (uhn-*bal*-uhnst strypz)   *See* balanced stripes.

stripper   A mechanical device that pulls the bolls off when they enter the rollers of the machine.

stroller   A three-quarter length fur coat.

structural design   A woven-in pattern as opposed to one printed on a fabric.

structured apparel   Clothing designs that give a garment shape even when not being worn. For example, a jacket that has padding, lining, binding, and a fitted waist.

studs (studz)   Small, decorative objects added to fabric. They are usually round and metallic and are occasionally jewelled. Studs have teeth on the bottom that are pushed through the fabric by hand or with a tool called a stud setter. The teeth are then bent against the fabric to hold the stud in place.

stuff   Another name for fabric. Any braided, felted, woven, knitted, or nonwoven material, including cloth, hosiery, and lace. Stuff is also referred to as cloth, material, and goods.

stuffer warp   A warp that passes straight through the carpet to form a stuffing.

style   The combination of design features that give a garment its distinctive appearance. Also used in a more general way to express personal awareness of how to combine apparel and design elements for distinctive effect, as in a "sense of style."

sublistatic printing (suhb-lih-*stat*-ihk *print*-ing)   A technique in which the design, printed on rolls of paper, is pressed against the fabric. When heat is applied, the design is transferred to the fabric.

substrate (*suhb*-strayt)   An underlying support or foundation. An example is a fiber substrate prepared with a mordant before dyeing.

suede (swayd)   A common name in leather for the hide of a cow with the fur removed. Soft, tanned leather with the flesh side buffed into a nap.

suede fabric   A woven or knitted fabric of cotton, man-made fibers, wool, or blends, finished to resemble suede leather. It is used in sport coats, gloves, linings, and cleaning cloths.

suiting (*soot*-ing)   (1) A heavy, fairly coarse linen fabric in plain, twill, or herringbone weaves, used for women's and men's suitings. It is also made in cotton, spun rayon, or acetate. (2) Fabric heavy enough to tailor well and take a sharp crease. Suiting fabrics should be durable and wrinkle resistant. Custom and climate determine what is considered a suiting weight in different places. Typical suiting fabrics include tropical suiting, panama, flannel, butcher rayon, tweed, and crash. *See* separate listings for these fabrics.

sulfur dye (*suhl*-fuhr dy)   A dye derived from chemicals containing sulfur. It is used mostly for vegetable fibers. It has fair resistance to washing and poor resistance to sunlight.

summer-weight suiting (*sum*-er-wayt *soot*-ing)   Another name for tropical suiting. A general term for many fabrics that have the characteristics of suiting fabrics: they are crisp, take sharp creases well, and are lightweight for wear in hot weather. A typical summer-weight suiting is linen.

sunburst (or fan) pleats (*suhn*-buhrst [ahr fan] pleetz)   Narrow pleats that begin at a central point and fan out to the edge of a fabric. They are often narrow at the top of the fabric and wider at the edge and are especially popular for skirts.

supported vinyl (suh-*por*-tid *vy*-nel)   Vinyl backed with fabric. Supported vinyl wears better than unsupported vinyl when used in upholstery. *See* vinyl.

surah (*soor*-ah)   A soft, usually twilled fabric, made of silk, rayon, acetate, or other man-made fibers. Since the diagonal of the wale has a flat top, it may be described as a satin-faced twill recognized by its sheen and its fine twill weave. It is woven in plaids, stripes, solid colors, or prints. It is used for neckties, mufflers, dresses, blouses, and trimmings. Foulard is often sold as surah. *See* foulard and silk.

surplice neck (*suhr*-plihs nehk)   A V-shaped neckline formed by diagonally overlapping fabric.

swag (swag)   A decorative, draped fabric section placed over a window. Swags usually are used in conjunction with draperies or curtains.

S

swatch (swahch)   A small piece of fabric, usually large enough to show color and pattern. It is given to a potential buyer as a sample.

sweatshirt   A loose, collarless, heavy cotton jersey pullover. It also is found in a jacket style with a hood.

sweatshirt fabric (*sweht* shuhrt *fab*-rik)   A knitted fabric with a smooth face and a fleecy, pile back. Sweatshirts were originally designed for exercise during which perspiration was encouraged, but they are also worn for warmth in cold weather and are available in several styles. They were made of cotton for its absorbency, but acrylic versions are also available.

sweetheart neckline   A low-cut neckline with the bottom edge cut in a shape resembling the top of a heart.

swint (swihnt)   Perspiration on the wool fiber.

Swiss (swis)   A fine, sheer, lightweight, crisp fabric of almost any fiber whose name has been almost forgotten except in the form of dotted (or figured) Swiss. It is used for curtains. *See* dotted Swiss.

Swiss dot   Another term for dotted Swiss. *See* dotted Swiss.

synthetic fiber (sin-*thet*-ik *fy*-ber)   A man-made textile fiber derived from natural bases or produced by chemical synthesis. These chemicals were never fibrous in form; more frequently referred to as man-made synthesized fiber.

S

Defect	Explanation	Severity
Sand Roller Marks	These run in the filling direction and may be caused by uneven tension and pull on the cloth as it winds around the sand roller on the loom. Irregular tension between the sand roller and the cloth roller also causes these marks.	Major or Minor
Sanforize Corrugation	A washboard effect resulting from a malfunctioning sanforizer blanket.	Major
Sanforize Pucker (also Pucker)	A warp-wise distortion resulting from uneven wetting-out during sanforization, generally due to faulty spray heads. It may appear as a wavy selvage or affect other areas of the fabric. The fabric will appear wavy or puckering when spread on the cutting table. Confined to one spray head, the pucker generally is 8" to 10" wide. It is difficult to detect while inspecting on an inspection machine with fabric under roller tension.	Major or Minor
Sanforize Roughness	A term used to describe a rough or crinkled appearance resulting from over-sanforization.	Major or Minor
Scrimp	A defect resulting from a fabric being printed in a folded or creased condition when passing through the print machine. There will be areas not printed and the pattern will be destroyed when the fold or crease is opened or stretched out.	Major
Seam Impression	The imprint of a seam made under pressure. In printing, the back-greige or cushion-fabric seam imprints on the fabric.	Major
Section Marks	Caused by uneven tension of the warp or a section of the warp has slipped during the dressing or slashing operations. Seen in the fabric by the way the warp yarn of the section leaving is loose, and the filling shows a cockled or corduroy effect. In many cases the affected areas are a total loss because the material often cannot be saved.	Major

Defect	Explanation	Severity
Selvage (Beaded)	A term used to describe a selvage that has a concentration of ends drawn together forming a cord or bead.	Minor
Selvage (End Breaks)	These are caused by improper shed because the shuttle cannot function properly, there is poor temple setting, shuttles have not been sandpapered to make them smooth, weak selvage threads were used, a crowded reeding of the selvage ends, too tight a weave construction, damaged or bent reed wires, and poorly plied yarn with one of the plies being loose or out altogether.	Major
Selvage (Scalloped)	An unevenness characterized by a regularity of ins and outs. This can be the result of a tenter frame pulling too tight, leaving indentations between the clips or from tension buildup in the shuttle during weaving, resulting in an indentation at each bobbin change.	Minor
Selvage (Slack or Wavy)	The condition where the edge of a fabric is longer than the center, causing it to wave or pucker when laid on the cutting table.	Major or Minor
Selvage (Tight)	A condition where the selvages of a fabric are shorter than the center, causing the center to lie in waves on the cutting table.	Major
Selvage (Torn)	Generally descriptive of the condition where a selvage is torn repeatedly by a tenter frame while attempting to attain an excessive width. Also, any place where a selvage is torn.	Major
Selvage (Turn-down)	A place where a selvage folds on itself and runs through squeeze rolls setting the fold. Also, where a selvage is folded under or over during any roll-up operation.	Minor

Defect	Explanation	Severity
Shade Bar	A distinct shade change of short duration across the width of the fabric. It may be attributable to a change in the character of the filling or a machine stop somewhere in the preparation, dyeing, or finishing processes.	Major
Shade Change	A term used to describe a general change in shade, either abrupt or gradual, that is not confined to, or cannot be described as, shade bars.	Major
Shaded (Cross)	Where there is a noticeable shade difference from one side of the fabric to the other.	Major or Minor
Shaded (Side to Center)	Where there is a noticeable shade difference from the side of the fabric to the center.	Major or Minor
Shady Filling	Bright or dim areas across the fabric, usually for the full length of one bobbin. There are other reasons for shady filling in cloth, such as some defect or irregularity in any process, treatment, or operation in processing from yarn to fabric.	Major or Minor
Shear Marks	An unevenly marked or cut nap on the cloth. Slubs, knots, and kinks often tend to make for unevenness in shearing. Burlers, speckers, and menders are ever on the alert for places that may have been nipped or caught by the razor-sharp blades on the shear. Shear marks easily show to poor advantage when light strikes the fabric.	Major
Shed-splitting	A term used to describe multiple yarn floats resulting from improper harness setting. If the harness was not properly set, the shuttle can split the shed, and pass over and/or under ends contrary to the design of the weave.	Major

Defect	Explanation	Severity
Shiners	Often caused by faulty weaving that gives a flat effect to the yarn, and is easily noted when rays of light strike the fabric. They appear in fabrics of filament acetate or rayon and silk because of poor winding of the yarn. Improper friction in the mouth of the shuttle also gives the effect to many fabrics.	Major or Minor
Shives	Vegetable matter found in woolen fabrics such as neps, straw, leaf particles, motes, shives, and so forth.	Major
Shuttle Mark	A fine line parallel to the filling, resulting from abrasion of the warp ends by the shuttle or from a shuttle taking on oil stains of some sort prior to performing its work of going through the shed of the loom. These marks often cause trouble in finishing fabrics.	Major
Shuttle Smash	This occurs when a few or many warp ends are broken because an imperfect shuttle is being used, or when two shuttles meet or "kiss" in the shed of the loom. This is one of the worst defects that can occur, and it often causes great loss of time in repairing the damage and impedes loom production. Other reasons for smashes include a trapped shuttle in the shed of the loom or a harness strap loosening or breaking altogether, thereby allowing the frame to drop altogether and hindering the smooth action of the loom in its three basic motions: shedding, picking, and beating-up.	Major
Singling	A single yarn appearing in a plied-yarn fabric.	Major
Skew (also Bias)	In wovens, where the filling yarns are off-square to the warp ends; in knits, where the courses are off-square to the wales.	Major or Minor

Defect	Explanation	Severity
Skip Stitch	In knits, the wrong formation of the knit design, characterized by a yarn floating intermittently for short distances over yarns with which it should have been interlooped. This results from a malfunctioning needle or jack.	Major
Skipping	An irregular, uneven height of the harnesses in the shedding motion of the loom will cause skipping or skip marks. The result is that the warp ends affected will not weave in regular formation with the filling at all times. Small float areas result and must be fixed when the fabric goes to the dry-finishing department in the textile plant.	Major or Minor
Slack End	The result of a loose or broken end puckering as it is gradually woven into a fabric.	Major
Slack Filling Pick	One which shows loops throughout the yarn; usually caused by improper shuttle tensions.	Major
Slack Selvages	These result from too much of a spread, or cramming of selvage ends in the reed, thereby creating slackness in the selvage areas. Other causes include too loose a weave construction, use of improper yarns as to count, twist or ply, and the edge threads wound too hard or too high as to number on the warp beam.	Major or Minor
Slack Warp	A term used to describe a fabric woven with less than required tension. Extremes result in an overall crimped or cockled appearance and a stretchy unstable fabric.	Major or Minor
Sloughed Filling	A defect caused by extra winds of filling slipping from the bobbin and being woven into the fabric. This is usually the result of soft bobbins wound with insufficient tension or too much power on the picker stick of the loom.	Major

Defect	Explanation	Severity
Slub	A term used to describe a short, thick place in a yarn, usually symmetrical. It is usually caused by a thick or heavy place in yarn, by lint getting onto yarn feeds, by an extra piece of yarn that is woven into fabric, and by fly waste being spun in yarn in the spinning process.	Major or Minor (depending on size)
Slubby Filling	A bobbin of filling containing numerous slubs. Thick, uneven places in filling yarn caused by uneven yarn winding, and poor carding, combing, and/or spinning of the fibers in the manufacture of the yarn are also causes. Soft, slubby yarn results from some irregularity in one of the manipulating machines or frames.	Major or Minor (depending on size)
Slubby Warp	Occurs when some warp yarns become uneven because of short fibers or certain wastes working out of place, usually as the result of improper settings for the number of twists per inch in the yarn. Often referred to as soft slub or tight slub yarn.	Minor
Sluff-offs	Small masses of yarn that come off the nose of the bobbin and sets in the shuttle. Caused by poor or inferior winding of the yarn and is one of the banes of the weaver.	Major
Sluggy Filling	A bobbin of filling containing numerous gouts or slugs of waste fiber.	Major
Slugs	Uneven yarn, or light or heavy places in fabric because of faulty yarn or weaving, over-carding, over-drafting the stock, or spinning the yarn counts to higher than necessary.	Major
Smash (see Shuttle Smash)	A term used to describe a place in a fabric where a large number of warp ends have been ruptured and repaired.	Major

Defect	Explanation	Severity
Snap	In printing, the result of a hard particle becoming lodged under a doctor blade, holding the blade from the engraved roll, or allowing color to escape on either side of the particle.	Major
Snare	Fabric that shows tangled masses or clumps of roving or yarn in a cloth; can be removed in burling and specking operations.	Major
Soft Warp	Usually implies a warp that has not been sized correctly, causing chafing and weakening of the ends as they go through the successive operations from yarn to fabric.	Major
Soiled End	A dirty, oily looking spot on the warp yarn or on a package-dyed yarn.	Major
Soiled Filling	A dirty, oily looking spot on the filling yarn or on a package-dyed yarn.	Major
Specky Goods	Small particles or specks of vegetable matter that come to the face of the material. Difficult to remove altogether, it is sometimes necessary to speck dye the goods or to carbonize the stock before manipulation from raw material to finished fabric.	Major
Spot	A discolored place or stain on a fabric resulting from any number of causes and having any number of sources. Terms applied include color spots, resist spots, drip spots, water spots, and oil spots.	Major

Defect	Explanation	Severity
Start-up Marks	Blemishes in fabric caused by the "starter-up man" turning the warp over to the weaver without fixing all the places where these marks occur. A second meaning is that the cloth may show bright or dim mark lines in the filling direction. Caused by the weaver not starting his loom at the correct warp tension, often because of failure to check the pick wheel on the loom which will even the tension if checked by the careful weaver. These marks are very irksome, as well as detrimental, and experienced weavers are constantly watching for them.	Major
Stop Mark	In wovens, a defect resulting from the warp yarn elongating under tension while a loom is stopped; when it is started again the slackness is taken up by the weave, leaving a distortion across the width of the fabric. In knits, a similar distortion results from the relaxation of the yarns during a machine stop.	Major or Minor
Straying End	In warp knits, the result of a broken end straying out of position and being knitted in an irregular manner into the fabric as the machine continues to run.	Major

GARMENT
AND
TEXTILES

tab   A small flap that often has a buttonhole at its end.

table linen   Any fabric, regardless of fiber content, suitable for a table covering.

table pad   A table covering used to protect the table and prevent clatter. Table pads usually are heavier and stiffer than silence cloths and usually are made with a felt back and a plastic top. *See* silence cloth.

taffeta (*taf*-eh-tah)   A fine, yarn-dyed, closely woven, plain-weave, smooth on both sides, stiffened fabric with a crisp feel and a sheen on its surface. Taffeta was originally made of silk, but is also made of rayon, cotton, acetate, or other man-made fibers. It is named for the Persian fabric "taftan." The rustle of silk taffeta is called scroop, and it may be a solid color, printed or woven so that the colors appear iridescent. A list of the most common types of taffeta follows. It is used for dresses, blouses, ribbons, draperies, bedspreads, and curtains. *See* scroop.

antique taffeta (ann-*teek taf*-eh-tah)   A stiff taffeta designed to resemble fabrics from the eighteenth century. It is often made with iridescent or changeable effects. *See* changeable fabric.

changeable taffeta (*chayn*-juh-buhl *taf*-eh-tah)   *See* changeable fabric.

faille taffeta (fyle *taf*-eh-tah)   Taffeta made with a prominent crosswise rib as in faille. *See* faille.

moiré taffeta (mwa-*ray taf*-eh-tah)   The most common moiré fabric. A moiré is a watermark design produced by passing fabric through heated rollers engraved with the designs.

paper taffeta (*pay*-per *taf*-eh-tah)   A lightweight, crisp taffeta used for evening clothes.

taking up   Winding up finished cloth on the merchandise beam as weaving proceeds.

tambour curtains (*tam*-boor *kur*-tenz)   Imported Swiss, heavily embroidered batiste, lawn, or polyester curtains.

tam-o'-shanter (*tam*-uh-*shan*-tehr)   A flat, round, fabric cap with a tassel or pompon on top; the style originated in Scotland.

tanguis (*tahn*-goo-ees)   A species of cotton averaging $1^1/_4$" in length. It is grown in Peru, which grows other types of cotton including pima and Egyptian.

tank top   A snug-fitting, knitted garment, styled like a man's T-shirt; named for tank suit or swim suit. It may be worn as a top with pants.

tapa cloth (*ta*-pah kloth)   A papery cloth made by pounding and flattening the inner bark of certain trees found in the Pacific Islands. It is often used in America for decorative wall hangings. *See* bark cloth.

tapestry (*tap*-es-tree)   A Jaquard woven fabric in cotton, wool, or man-made fibers. Traditionally, a decorative wall hanging woven to depict a scene. The filling threads are changed in color to fit the design. On the back, shaded stripes identify this fabric. It is used extensively for wall hangings, table covers, draperies, and upholstery. Some rugs are made in tapestry weaves. The word is also used for needlepoint, but this use is generally considered incorrect. Machine-made fabrics, also called tapestry, have regular designs on the surface and a slightly looped pile. They are used for such things as coats and handbags.

tarlatan (*tar*-le-ten)   A thin, open fabric used extensively for theatrical costumes and hangings. It is transparent, but layers are usually used to provide a degree of opacity. Tarlatan usually has a stiff glazed finish. *See* opacity.

tarnish-resistant fabric (*tar*-nish-ree-*ziss*-tent *fab*-rik)   A fabric used for wrapping silver to keep it from becoming darkened by atmospheric pollution. The cloth itself is made to absorb sulfur from the atmosphere, a major cause of tarnish.

tartan (*tart*-uhn)   A pattern made of intersecting stripes. Each tartan pattern is associated with a certain specific family called a clan. Plaid, a term used for tartan, is actually the name of a shawl made of tartan fabric. The use of plaid has become so general that tartan is almost always limited to authentic clan designs. Some of the most common tartans follow, but there are many others.

T

Barclay (*bar*-klee)   Wide stripes of black on a yellow ground crossed at intervals by narrower white stripes.

Black Watch (blak wahch)   A regimental tartan of the 42nd Royal Highland Regiment. It consists of green stripes on a light blue ground.

Campbell (*kam*-bell)   A tartan made of green stripes on a blue ground, crossed with darker blue, narrower stripes. The blue ground is also crossed with darker blue, narrow stripes.

Cumming (*kum*-ing)   Stripes of dark and light green combined with red and blue stripes to form the plaid. In faded or antique colors, this tartan is especially attractive.

Linsay (*lin*-zee)   A pattern of crossed stripes of green and bright pink.

Mackay (meh-*kay*)   A checked pattern of stripes of blue on light green.

Ogilvie (*oh*-gel-vee)   One of the more complicated tartans. It combines stripes of red, yellow, greenish blue, and dark blue in an intricate pattern.

Rob Roy   A classic hunting jacket pattern of red and black checks.

Stewart (*stoo*-ert)   The tartan of the royal family of Great Britain. Stewart tartan has narrow stripes of yellow, blue, and white widely spaced on a red or white ground.

tassel (*tass*-el)   Several strands of yarn loops joined together below the top and cut at the end. Tassels are used in rows as home furnishings trimmings and singly for such uses as zipper pulls or on the corners of pillows.

Tattersall check (*tat*-er-sol chek)   Tattersall checks are an overcheck pattern in two colors, usually on a white or other colored ground. An example is a pattern of brown lines going in one direction, crossed by green lines in the opposite direction, forming the checks on a yellow background. These checks were named for Richard Tattersall who used the pattern on horse blankets. *See* overcheck.

tatting (*tat*-ing)   A method of lace-making worked with the fingers and a shuttle that holds the thread. Tatting forms a narrow, knotted lace, often used for edging.

T

teasel (*tee*-zel) A plant with a prickly flower head. It is used for raising a nap on fabrics. *See* napping.

tenacity The tensile strength of a fiber, expressed as force per unit of linear density of an unstrained specimen. It is usually expressed in grams per denier or grams per tex. *See* tex.

tensile strength (*ten*-suhl strengkth) The maximum tensile stress required to rupture a fiber, expressed as pounds per square inch or grams per square centimeter.

tentering (*ten*-ter-ing) A fabric finishing step in which the fabric is stretched on a frame to its finished width and final shape, then dried to maintain these dimensions.

territory wools From the Rocky Mountain plateau states.

terry cloth (*tayr*-ee kloth) A heavy-weight absorbent cotton pile fabric made of extra heavy warp threads (cotton or blends of cotton and other fibers) with uncut loops on one or both sides. It is noted for its ability to absorb moisture. It may have linen pile in a "friction" towel. Terry cloth is used primarily for bath and face towels, face cloths, bath rugs, beach wear, and robes, but it is also used for wearing apparel such as sportswear. It is also called Turkish toweling. *See* velour, towels, and knit terry cloth.

tex A system of yarn numbering that measures the weight in grams of one kilometer of yarn.

textiles (*teks*-tylz) An extremely broad term referring to any materials that can be made into fabric by any method. It also refers to the resulting fibers themselves. *See* fabric.

textiles converter A business that buys unfinished fabrics, has them bleached, printed, and finished by another business specializing in particular types of finishes, then sells the end product.

Texturalized (*teks*-trah-lyzd) Trademark of Bancroft Licensing for a method of adding texture to otherwise smooth yarns. *See* textured yarn.

texture (*teks*-chur) One of the elements that determines the way in which a finished fabric looks. It is the surface effect of a fabric; that is, stiffness, roughness, smoothness, softness, fineness, dullness, and luster. Texture can be altered by the processing of yarn, by blending the yarn, or in the finishing of the fabric. Texture also influences the hand of a fabric. *See* hand.

textured A surface woven with a nubby yarn construction. It may be made in any fiber.

textured yarn (*teks*-churd yarn) A man-made filament yarn geometrically modified or otherwise altered or treated in some way to change its basic characteristics, such as crimping, coiling, or curling, so that the naturally smooth nature of the man-made filament is changed. Texturing may also alter certain undesirable characteristics of these fibers, such as their tendency to be transparent and to pill.

Thai silk (ty silk) Silk made in Thailand. Most Thai silk is fairly heavyweight, often slubbed, and made in vivid colors usually iridescent or changeable. *See* changeable.

thermal (*thur*-mal) An adjective used to describe fabrics which are warmer for their weight than other fabrics. It is usually limited to those fabrics woven in a honeycomb pattern leaving small spaces in which air can be trapped. Thermal fabrics are popular for underwear and blankets. *See* honeycomb.

thermal woven A porous cloth so constructed that air warmed by the body is trapped between the yarns. First used in underwear, it is now used for blankets and the reverse sides of comforters.

thermoplastic (thurm-oh-*plas*-tik) A word used to describe fibers that are heat-sensitive. Most man-made fibers are thermoplastic. A thermoplastic fiber has the property of softening or fusing when heated and of hardening again when cooled. With the application of heat and pressure, it can be molded and remolded. This can be both an advantage and a disadvantage. It is advantageous because in fabrics made of thermoplastic fibers, certain features like pleats can be made permanent through heat-setting. However, care must be taken in drying and ironing fabrics made of thermoplastic fibers because of their sensitivity to heat. *See* man-made fibers and heat-setting.

thermosetting (thurm-oh-*set*-ing) A process for giving thermoplastic fibers or fabrics certain characteristics, such as crimp or permanent pleats through the application of heat. Thermosetting is also used to develop certain finishes in a fabric to produce desirable characteristics such as durable press. *See* heat setting, thermoplastic, and durable press.

thick and thin yarn Produced by varying the diameters of man-made fibers.

T

thread A special type of a thin, continuous length of tightly twisted ply yarn used primarily for sewing. Thread occasionally is used instead of yarn, as in the terms "warp thread" and "filling thread." The most common types of thread follow:

buttonhole twist (*but*-uhn-hohl twist) A thick, twisted silk cord. Buttonhole twist is lustrous and is used for topstitching (decorative, straight stitching, usually along seams of garment edges). It is also used for sewing buttons onto a garment as well as for making buttonholes. It may be used for embroidery.

carpet thread (*kar*-pit thred) A heavy thread used for repairing carpets and for sewing on buttons. Carpet thread was originally made of cotton, but usually is made of polyester today.

cotton thread (*kot*-uhn thred) Formerly the most common thread, but difficult to find today. It is usually made in two types. A plain thread with a dull surface is called basting thread. Mercerized cotton thread has a shiny surface that enables it to slide smoothly through fabric and is suggested for general purpose sewing. Polyester thread has replaced cotton thread to a large extent. *See* mercerization.

cotton-wrapped polyester (core) thread (*kot*-uhn-rapt powl-ee-*es*-ter [kohr] thred) A type of polyester thread made with a polyester core wrapped with cotton, theoretically giving the thread characteristics of both fibers.

nylon thread (*ny*-lon thred) The thread introduced as an alternative to silk thread that has more "give" than most natural fiber threads. It is used extensively for sewing man-made fiber fabrics, especially knits.

polyester thread (powl-ee-*es*-ter thred) Thread made of 100% polyester. Polyester thread has more "give" than most natural fiber threads and is used extensively for sewing man-made fiber fabrics, especially knits. It can be used on almost any fabric. Polyester thread is strong, but tends to knot easily.

silk thread (silk thred) A classic sewing thread for fine work and for sewing silks and woolens. It has more "give" than other natural fiber threads, but less than polyester or nylon. It is used primarily for sewing on silk fabrics.

three-dimensional polymer A polymer formed when molecules unite in both length and width, producing a relatively rigid structure. This is typical of polymers used in processing.

throw   Any piece of fabric—such as an afghan or bedspread—that does not fit closely to the item it is covering, but instead is arranged on or over it casually. *See* afghan and spread.

throwing   The combining and twisting of strands of reeled silk into tightly twisted yarn.

ticking (*tik*-ing)   A broad term for extremely strong woven fabrics which are used as a covering for pillows, mattresses, and box springs, home-furnishings, and for work clothes and sports clothes. It is a heavy, tightly woven carded cotton fabric usually in a pattern of alternately woven stripes in the warp, Jacquard or dobby designs, or printed patterns. It is usually twill but may be sateen weave. When ticking is used in clothing, striped ticking with narrow woven stripes is usually most popular. Red and white, black and white, and navy and white are the most popular ticking color combinations.

tie dyeing   A form of resist dyeing. Items to be dyed are tied or knotted so that the folds of the fabric form barriers to the dye to create patterns or designs on the fabric. *See* dyeing and resist dyeing.

tie silk   Any silk used for men's neckties. Surah is one of these silks. Small, colorful patterns are often featured in this type of silk. *See* silk and surah.

tie-back   A full length (either to the windowsill or to the floor) curtain or drapery looped back at the side of the window with a band of trimming or self-fabric. The curtain or drapery is closed at the top of the window, and almost entirely open at the point of the tie-back. The look is popular in informal houses in such fabrics as organdy and batiste and in formal houses in luxurious fabrics.

tier (teer)   One of a series of bands, ruffles, or flounces arranged one above the other.

tights   An opaque, skin-tight, fabric pantyhose-type garment closely fitting the figure and extending from the neck down, or from the waist down. Originally worn by dancers, tights are now adapted for women's and children's fashions.

tissue taffeta   A crisp, lightweight taffeta. *See* paper taffeta.

toggle   A bar-shaped button fastened to a garment with a loop.

toile (twahl)   The French word for cloth. Toile is also a woven fabric that has been printed, usually in one color only, with a scenic design. This is occasionally called toile de Jouy. It is most commonly found in home furnishings fabrics. Toile is also used in the field of expensive designer clothing where the word is used to describe a fabric pattern for a garment.

toile de Jouy (twahl deh *joo*-ee)   Cotton fabric printed in pictorial designs. The original toile was printed by Oberkampf in 1759 at Jouy, France. It is used for draperies and bedspreads. *See* toile.

top hat   A silk hat with a high cylindrical crown and a short, rolled up brim.

tops   Long wool fibers in the combed sliver.

topstitching   A decorative stitch that reinforces seams, pocket edges, or collars. It is often done in a color that contrasts with the background fabric.

tote   A sturdy rectangular bag with an open top and two strap handles.

tow   Short flax fibers, separated by hackling (combing) from the longer fibers. Also, the poorly hackled, uneven linen yarn made from these short fibers. It may also refer to a continuous loose rope of man-made filaments drawn together without twist to be cut in lengths for spun yarn.

tow linen   Fabric made of uneven, irregular yarns composed of the very short fibers.

towel   A rectangular piece of fabric used for drying (people, glasses, dishes). Following is a list of common types of towels:

dish towel   One of the few textile products which is still made of linen (occasionally they are made of cotton or even paper). Dish towels are used for hand-drying dishes after washing. Many linen dish towels are made in Ireland and printed with colorful pictures. Dish towels can also be made of terry cloth and huck toweling. *See* terry cloth and huck.

face cloth   A piece of terry toweling, usually square in shape. It is used for washing the face and body and may also be called a wash cloth.

glass cloth   A towel used to dry drinking glasses, glass plates, and silver. It is made from linen. Glass towels are often checked red and white and may have the word "Glass" woven into the fabric.

terry cloth   A cotton or cotton and man-made fiber fabric with a looped pile on one or both sides. It is made into towels for drying

T

after a bath. It may also be used for dish towels. *See* pile. *See also* knit terry cloth.

Turkish toweling (*turk*-ish *tahl*-ing)   Another name for terry cloth. *See* towel and terry cloth.

velour (veh-*loor*)   A knit or woven fabric with a thick, short pile. Terry velour cloth has cut loops to produce the velour effect. It also has a rich look, but is not as effective in drying as conventional terry cloth. It may also be spelled velours.

toweling (*tahl*-ling)   The name given to any fabric which is meant for use as a towel; that is, for drying purposes. *See* towel.

toyo straw (*toy*-oh straw)   *See* straw.

tracing cloth (*trays*-ing kloth)   A nonwoven, transparent fabric used for tracing designs and especially patterns. Since tracing cloth is fabric, it can be marked and altered more easily than paper used for the same purpose.

trademark (*trayd*-mark)   A word, letter, device, or symbol that has been legally registered and serves to distinguish the merchandise of one manufacturer from another. It alludes distinctly to the origin or ownership of the product to which it is applied. For example, Dacron is a trademark of DuPont for their polyester fiber.

traditional (truh-*dish*-uhn-el)   A word used for fabrics or methods of making fabrics that have been in use for a number of years.

tram silk (tram silk)   A low-twist, ply silk yarn formed by combining two or three single strands.

transparent velvet   A sheer-cut pile velvet usually all rayon or with rayon pile, suitable for evening dresses, wraps, and millinery.

trapunto (trah-*pun*-toh)   A form of quilting in which fabric is quilted only in certain areas. The design to be quilted, a monogram for example, is first worked through two layers of fabric. Then, the backing fabric is slit so that the quilted areas can be padded with yarn, cord, or a filling such as fiberfill. *See* fiberfill.

trash   Bits of fiber, dirt, and plants left in a fabric. During certain fashion periods, when a natural look is important, trash is considered desirable. It shows as tiny specks of darker coloring in a lighter fabric and is usually found in cotton and wool fabrics.

trench coat   The officers' coat worn during World War I. It is double-breasted and belted. It has a high-closing collar and shoulder flaps.

Trevira (trah-*veer*-ah)   The trademark of Hoechst Fibers Incorporated for their polyester fiber.

triacetate (try-*ass*-eh-tayt)   A thermoplastic fiber classified under the generic name of acetate, although it is a modification of acetate. Triacetate fabrics resist shrinkage, wrinkles, and fading. They do not dissolve in acetone, can be washed at higher temperatures than those made of acetate, and can be ironed with the heat set for linen. *See* acetate.

tricot (*tree*-koh)   A term originating from the French tricoter, meaning to knit. It is a fabric made by a warp-knitting (tricot) machine, a machine in which parallel yarns run lengthwise and are locked into a series of loops. Warp knits have a good deal of crosswise stretch. *See* two-bar tricot.

trilobal (try-*loh*-buhl)   A fiber with a modified cross section having three lobes.

trimming (*trim*-ing)   Anything used to decorate clothing or home furnishings. Following is a list of some of the more common types of trimmings:

ball fringe (bawl frinj)   A trimming that consists of round fluffy balls (pompons) attached by threads to a band of fabric by which it is sewn to fabric. It is often used on curtains and upholstery.

banding   A narrow, flat fabric that is woven, knitted, or braided, and is used as is to trim an edge or folded over to bind an edge.

bias tape (*by*-us tayp)   A strip of fabric cut on the diagonal between the lengthwise and crosswise grain of the fabric. Because bias tape has considerable stretch, it is used to bind edges where a certain degree of stretch is necessary for a smooth finish. Curved areas are often finished with bias tape. Bias tape can also be used for purely decorative trimming. It is available precut and packaged in a wide range of colors.

binding (*bynd*-ing)   Any narrow fabric used to enclose (bind) edges, usually raw edges. It also can be used for purely decorative purposes. Bias tape often is used as binding. *See* bias tape.

braid (brayd)   A term used to describe narrow trimmings with multicolored designs woven into them. Various types of braid, such as peasant braid, are popular during certain fashion periods.

bullion (*bool*-yun)   A twisted, shiny, cord-like fringe used primarily in upholstery.

chainette fringe (*chayn*-et frinj)   A yarn fringe designed to resemble chain. It is used as a trimming for window shades.

cord (kord)   A heavy, round string consisting of several strands of thread or yarn twisted or braided together. *See* cording.

cord gimp (or guimp) (kord gimp [ahr gimp])   Cord gimp combines cord with gimp. *See* cording and gimp.

cording (*kord*-ing)   A round decorative edging. The term is also used to describe white cord covered with bias strips of fabric to form welting or piping. *See* welting.

festoon (fes-*toon*)   A decorative cord accented by tassels. It forms a decoration for the edge of such items as table cloths.

fringe (frinj)   A trimming made of hanging yarns, cords, or tassels. It may be made in loop form or with the loops cut.

frog   A decorative fastening for clothing consisting of twisted cord wound into a design that looks like three petals joined to a similar design on the opposite edge of an opening with a loop of the cord.

galloon (ga-*loon*)   A closely woven, flat braid used for accenting draperies and furniture. Also called braid. The term galloon is also used for any narrow fabric with decorative edges, such as scallops finished the same on each side. Lace made in this way is called galloon lace.

gimp (or guimp)   An edging often with small scallops of fine cord along its edges. Gimp was originally designed to hide upholstery tacks on chairs and sofas, but now is used for other decorative purposes.

knotted fringe (*not*-id frinj)   Fringe in which the hanging sections are knotted to form a pattern, and the ends are allowed to hang like regular fringe. *See* fringe.

military braid (*mil*-eh-tair-ee brayd)   A flat, ribbed braid used for decorating military and other uniforms. It is also used as a trimming on clothing when the military look is popular.

moss fringe (mawss frinj)   A short, thick fringe made of fluffy yarns of wool or acrylic.

picot trimming (*pee*-koh *trim*-ing)   A narrow band edged with a series of delicate loops.

T

piping (*pyp*-ing)   Another name for welting. *See* welting.

pompon (*pahm*-pahn)   A fluffy ball, usually made from yarn and used as a decorative accent.

rattail (*rat*-tayl)   A narrow, round cord used for trimming and for macramé. *See* macramé.

rattail fringe (*rat*-tayl frinj)   A decorative edging made of rattail in which the rattail forms loops across the edging. *See* rattail.

ribbon (*rib*-ehn)   A narrow, woven fabric with two finished edges. Both natural and man-made fibers are used in making ribbon. It is available in many patterns and colors and in such fabric constructions as velvet, satin, and grosgrain. *See* velvet, satin, and grosgrain.

rick-rack (rik-rak)   A flat braid woven in a zigzag, serpentine shape. It is available in several widths and is an extremely popular and inexpensive trimming.

ruche (roosh)   A ruffle. *See* ruffle.

ruffle (*ruhf*-fuhl)   A piece of fabric gathered along one edge. Ruffles are narrow and are used to trim necklines, sleeves, hems, and the edges of home furnishings items such as pillows and slipcovers.

seam binding (seem *bynd*-ing)   A flat, narrow twilled ribbon, used to cover raw edges of seams to protect them from ravelling.

tassel (*tass*-el)   Several strands of yarn loops joined together shortly below the top and cut at the end. Tassels are used in rows as home furnishing trimmings and singly for uses such as zipper pulls or on the corners of pillows.

twill tape (twil taype)   A narrow, twill-weave ribbon, fairly heavy in weight. It is stitched into garment areas such as collar lapels, shoulders, and facing edges for strength and to prevent stretching. It is also used in the seams of slip covers and other home furnishing items for added strength. Twill tape is usually available only in white and black. *See* weaving and twill.

welting (*welt*-ing)   A decorative edging that lends a certain degree of strength to the area in which it is sewn. Welting is made by covering cord with bias strips of matching or contrasting fabric. It is a popular finish for seams on upholstery and slipcovers and occasionally is used on clothing. Welting and piping are synonyms. When used on clothing, it is usually called piping. *See* cord and bias.

T

tropical suiting (*trahp*-ih-kel *soot*-ing)   A general term for many plain-weave fabrics that have the characteristics of suiting fabrics (they are crisp, take sharp creases well, and are lightweight for wear in hot weather). If called tropical worsted, it is an all-wool worsted fabric. A typical tropical suiting is linen.

tropical worsted   A lightweight, plain weave suiting for men's and women's summer wear. To be labeled "tropical worsted," it must be all-wool worsted. It is made in a variety of fiber blends and mixtures.

t-shirt   A knitted cotton undershirt with short sleeves that may be worn for sports or work without an outer garment.

t-strap shoe   A shoe with a strap across the instep which intersects with a strap coming up the throat (center) of the shoe, forming a "T."

tuck (tuk)   A small, narrow section of fabric folded and then stitched, either down the fold of the tuck or across each end. Pin tucks are the narrowest of tucks. Tucks usually have a decorative function and are narrow, whereas pleats made in much the same way, are usually used to control fullness as well. However, horizontal tucks are taken in children's clothing for a functional purpose so that the garment can be lengthened when the child grows. *See* pleats.

tuck stitch   A variation of a basic stitch in weft knitting to make a knobby, bumpy, knitted texture. Unknitted loops are slipped from one needle to another. On the following row, the unknitted loops are knitted as regular stitches.

tuft (tuhft)   A bunch of yarns or threads forced through a quilt, mattress, or upholstery to secure the stuffing. *See* quilt.

tufted carpet   Made by needling pile yarns into a previously woven backing of jute or cotton.

tufted fabric   A fabric ornamented with soft, fluffy, slackly twisted ply yarns (usually cotton). Most tufts are inserted by needles into a woven fabric, such as unbleached muslin, textured cotton, and rayon plain-weave cloth. When tufts are spaced (as coin dots), a bedspread is called candlewick; when placed in close rows, the fabric is called chenile. "Loom tufted" means tufts woven in as the cloth is woven. Tufted fabrics are used for bedspreads, mats, and robes. *See* rugs.

tufting   A brush-like button of clipped cotton yarn that appears at regular intervals on mattresses. Also, the most common method for

T

making rugs. Groups of yarns are forced through a backing fabric. The yarns are held in place permanently when the underside of the rug is coated, often with liquid latex.

tulle (tool)   A soft, fine, transparent silk net. Formerly made only of silk, tulle is now made of nylon or rayon, and is a favorite for evening dresses and bridal veils. *See* net.

tunic   A blouse-like garment that falls to the hips or below and often is gathered at the waist or belted.

turban   Fabric that is twisted and draped around the head to form a hat. It is an adaptation of an oriental headdress.

Turkish rug   A hand-tied oriental rug made in Turkey. Names of Turkish rugs include Bergama, Ladik, Ghiordes, Kulah, and Oushak.

Turkish towel (*turk*-ish tahl)   A bath towel, face towel, or washcloth made of terry cloth. *See* terry cloth and towel.

Turkoman rug (*tehr*-kuh-muhn rug)   A hand-tied oriental rug from Turkestan. Names include Bokhara, Beshir, Tekke Turkoman, and Samarkand.

turtleneck collar   A high, close-fitting collar rolled or turned down on itself.

tuscan straw (*tuss*-kan straw)   *See* straw.

tussah silk (*tuss*-ah silk)   Silk fabric woven from silk made by wild, uncultivated silkworms. Tussah is strong, but coarse and uneven. It is naturally tan in color, cannot be bleached, and has a rougher texture than cultivated silk. It is used in shantung and pongee. Wild silkworms eat leaves other than mulberry leaves eaten exclusively by silkworms. The difference in diet accounts for the different fiber and fabric characteristics. Tussah is also used to describe fabrics designed to imitate this kind of silk. *See* wild silk.

tussore (too-*sohr*)   A synonym for tussah silk. *See* tussah and wild silk.

tuxedo collar   A shawl collar cut in one width and which extends the full length of the front edge of a jacket.

tweed (tweed)   A term derived from the river Tweed in Scotland, where the fabrics were first woven. It is now used to describe a wide range of light to heavy, rough-textured, sturdy fabrics characterized by their mixed color effect. Tweeds can be made of plain, twill, or herringbone weave, usually yarn-dyed, and often are made in two or more colors, all wool unless otherwise indicated. Now cotton, linen,

T

rayon, synthetics, or blends may be made to resemble wool tweed. Knots are sometimes used to resemble tweed slubs. In women's wear, a tweed may look rough, but feels soft or even spongy. It may be nubbed or slubbed. Tweed is used for coats, suits, jackets, slacks, draperies, and upholstery. Following is a listing of the common types of tweeds. *See* slub.

Donegal (*don*-eh-gahl)   Originally, a fabric woven by hand in County Donegal, Ireland. Today, the word is used to refer to any tweed with thick, usually colored slubs as part of the fabric.

Harris (*hair*-iss)   Tweed hand-woven from yarns spun by hand or machine on the islands of the Outer Hebrides off the coast of Scotland. Harris is one of these islands.

Irish (*eye*-rish)   Tweed made in Ireland, Northern Ireland, or Eire. These tweeds generally can be distinguished by a white warp and colored filling threads. Donegal is a type of Irish tweed.

Linton (*lin*-ton)   The trademark of Linton Tweed, Ltd., Carlisle, England. These tweeds are noted for their softness and subtle or vivid colorings.

Scottish (*skot*-ish)   Originally made in Scotland, Scottish tweed is a term often used today for tweed woven with very nubby yarns, often with white warp and colored filling. *See* Irish tweed.

tweed-textured   An exaggerated chevron or tweed-like structural design with accentuated nubs.

twill (twill)   (1) A weave with a diagonal rib (twill line) that runs from the upper left to the lower right, or from upper right to lower left. In a twill weave, each filling thread passes over or under at least two warp threads, to a point where the filling thread goes under moving up and over by at least one thread in each row. Herringbone weave is a broken twill weave and forms "V"s in the weave pattern. (2) A narrow ribbon, fairly heavy in weight. It is stitched into garment areas such as collar lapels, shoulders, and facing edges for strength and to prevent stretching. It is also used in the seams of slipcovers and other home furnishings items for added strength. Twill tape usually is available only in white or black.

twist   A technical term referring to the way in which yarn is turned during the course of its manufacture. It is the number of times (turns) one inch of yarn is twisted. In carpeting, twist is a corkscrew-like, uncut pile. Yarns of different colors may be twisted together to form pile loops causing a pebbly appearance. It resists footmarks and is good for high traffic areas.

two-bar (double-bar) tricot   A warp knit in which two sets of yarns are required, one knitted in one direction and the other in the opposite direction. A ribbed surface results. It is synonymous with double-warp tricot knit.

Tyrolean (or alpine) hat (tuh-*roh*-lee-uhn [ahr *al*-pyn] hat)   A soft felt hat with a narrow brim turned up on one side and a cord band with a feather, wrapped around a rather pointed crown.

T

Defect	Explanation	Severity
Tear Drop	Small or short distortions noted when one or more picks are affected because of some irregularity in the weaving. Usually caused by improper tension on the filling yarn, filling stop motion, or beating-in action in the loom. Faille, taffeta, repp, and comparable fabrics often show this defect.	Major or Minor
Temple Bruise	A streak along the edge of a fabric that has been scuffed and/or distorted by a damaged, malfunctioning, or poorly set temple.	Major
Temple Marks	Woven fabric which shows a series of pin holes or faint warp streaks along the selvage edges of the cloth. Caused by faulty temples.	Major
Tender Goods	Cloth that is weak because of the use of dried-out yarn, too strong a scouring liquor, by redyeing after stripping or not stripping the cloth to remove the coloring on the goods, poor singeing, excessive napping or shearing, or uneven tensions or poor settings on one or more of the several machines used to finish fabric, such as incorrect settings on the shear, press, or other machines.	Major
Thick Bar or Thick Place	A place across the width containing more picks or heavier filling than is normal to the fabric. Two or more filling picks give a thick or bloated effect to the goods. Caused by improper setting of the cloth in the loom after a "start-up," uneven tension and weights on the warp beam, not setting the pick-wheel correctly after stopping the loom, poor functioning of the takeup pawl because of possible improper setting or tension, or skipping.	Major or Minor
Thick Stripes	Those too thick in diameter. They tend to throw off the general appearance of the fabric. Caused by uneven yarn, incorrect drawing-in or reeding-in of the warp threads, and incorrect yarn sizes.	Major or Minor

Defect	Explanation	Severity
Thin Bar or Thin Place	A place across the width containing less picks or lighter filling than that which is normal to the fabric. It occurs in the loom when two or more warp ends do not interlace with the filling yarn. It is often caused by the filling yarn breaking or snapping, the loom failing to stop or knock-off, or by an irregular action of a harness frame. Thin bars may be interspersed throughout the width of the goods if a harness strap on a harness frame breaks or skips. It gives a "flat" in the warp direction of the cloth. It may also be caused by a warp end being broken and causing the two ends on each side to weave side-by-side to produce a "flat" in the vertical direction of the material.	Major
Thin Stripes	Linked with thick stripes, these come from poor setup of the pattern, faulty weaving, and improper drawing-in or reeding-in of the warp yarns.	Major or Minor
Tight Ends	In wovens, one or more ends running taut because of abnormal tension in the cloth, and usually run for considerable length unless observed by the weaver. It tends to force the filling to the surface of the fabric and, in yarn dyes where a contrasting filling is used, is evident, and characterized by a fine-lined streak of filling show-through similar to that of an open reed. Tight warp ends are sometimes difficult to detect as cloth is woven. In warp knits, a tight end will cause a fine-lined, length- or warp-wise distortion in the fabric.	Major
Torn Selvages	Fabrics not presentable because of selvage ends missing, uneven tying-in of broken ends, knots and slubs. Often, it is caused by generally poor work on the part of the weaver. Selvages serve as a binding point for the filling when weaving, and as guides to maintain the proper width when dyeing, printing, and finishing fabric. A good selvage, found on any material at the full width,	Major

Defect	Explanation	Severity
	produces the effect of a frame around a picture and is usually a cloth of proper quality and construction. A well-woven selvage assures a well-woven cloth.	
Trapped Shuttle	A defect resulting from a loom stopped abruptly, trapping the shuttle in the shed. The effect is that of distorting the fabric and stretching the yarn; the resulting slackness is woven into the fabric on startup of the loom.	Major
Tucking Defect	In knits, when the tuck stitch is unintentional and contrary to the design of the fabric. This may occur intermittently or continuously and is the result of a malfunctioning needle or jack.	Major
Turned Selvages	There are many reasons for these turned selvages, such as filling yarn with too much twist in it, an improperly set warp beam (or one that is not set at proper tension under weights), an uneven warp tension, a faulty or uneven weave repeat, poor selvage matching as to yarn, selvage weave used, and so forth. Turned selvages also come from improperly rolled cloth cuts in yardage, whereby the cloth is "off-angle," expander bars not working correctly, and poor tension.	Major

Ulster (*uhl*-ster)   Originally, the name for a frieze overcoating fabric made in Ulster, Ireland. Today, the word is usually used as a synonym for overcoat. *See* frieze.

Ultra Suede   Registered trademark for a Skinner brand fabric of Spring Mills, Inc. This extremely soft, suede-like fabric has been one of the major successes in developing new fabrics from man-made materials.

unbalanced plaid (un-*bal*-uhnst plad)   An unbalanced plaid is one in which the arrangement of the stripes is different on the crosswise and lengthwise grain of the fabric. In constructing a garment of this type special care must be taken in matching the plaid design.

unbalanced stripe (un-*bal*-uhnst stryp)   A pattern of stripes in which different colors and widths are used on each side of the center. A blue stripe on a white ground with a narrow red stripe on the right side and a narrow yellow stripe on the left side is an example of an unbalanced stripe.

unbalanced yarns   Yarns in which there is sufficient twist to set up a torque effect, so that the yarn will untwist and retwist in the opposite direction.

unbleached muslin   A cotton plain-weave printcloth fabric in grey goods and lightweight sheetings, used for ironing board covers, dust covers, and dust cloths.

uncut velvet (un-*kut vel*-vit)   A velvet in which the pile is left in loop form. It is made by the wire method and also occasionally is called terry velvet. *See* velvet.

underlay (*un*-der-lay)   A synonym for padding or rug cushion. It usually describes the layer of fabric of sponge rubber or hair placed underneath a carpet or rug to provide it with longer life, to give it a more luxurious appearance and feeling, to prevent the rug from slipping, and to make the rug softer and more cushiony. Carpet padding is made of cattle hair, rubberized hair, rubber, and combinations of jute and cattle hair, as well as some man-made fibers. *See* rugs and carpets, padding, and rug cushion.

uneven plaid   A synonym for unbalanced plaid. *See* unbalanced plaid.

uneven twill weave   The filling passes under more yarns than ones it passes over.

unfinished worsted   A suiting fabric in twill weave, finished with a nap longer than those of other worsteds.

union cloth   A traditional name for fabric made from two or more different fibers, such as a fabric woven with a wool worsted warp and a cotton filling. The term "union cloth" was used primarily when this fabric was used for underwear, perhaps because a union suit was another name for shoulder-to-ankle, one-piece underwear. *See* union suit.

union dyeing (*yoon*-yen *dy*-ing)   Dyeing different fibers in the same cloth in one shade. *See* dyeing.

union suit   A one-piece knitted undergarment extending from the neck to the knee or longer.

unisex   A clothing or hairstyle intended to be equally suitable for either sex.

unpressed pleat (*un*-prest pleet)   A pleat (folds) the edges of which have not been set by pressing. The rounded edges create a look that is softer than pressed pleats. The term unpressed pleats is usually used for wide unpressed pleats, whereas cartridge pleats, also unpressed, describe narrower, decorative pleats.

unravel (un-*ra*-vel)   The term unravel means the same as ravel. It is the tendency of fabric to come unwoven or unknitted at unfinished edges. Loosely woven fabrics tend to unravel more than those made of tight weaves. Occasionally, the tendency to unravel is desirable in order to create a fringed edge.

unstructured apparel   Apparel with little, if any, detail in tailoring. It takes its shape from the person wearing it. For example, a jacket that does not have padding, lining, or insets.

U

unwashable fabric   A fabric that should not be washed by hand or by machine. Such fabrics are usually labeled "dry clean only."

upland   Cottons of the species *Gossypium hirsutum* (goh-*syp*-ih-oom hir-*soo*-toom). They usually produce staples from $3/4''$ to $1^1/2''$.

Defect	Explanation	Severity
Undershot	A pick of filling deflected from its normal path through the shed and extending unbound under warp ends with which it should have been interlaced. This condition is most common within 12" to 15" of the selvage and results from an improper loom setting.	Major
Uneven Cloth	Fabric that shows a faulty surface effect or texture caused by uneven places, such as light or heavy texture, shaded effects, slippage of a section of the warp on the warp beam, uneven or poor loom tensions, improper weights on the warp beam, and so forth.	Major
Uneven Double and Twist	Results from uneven twisting on the doubler and twister frames. Poor winding also causes this undesirable streaked effect. Should be sought for in fabric weaving because this defect is sometimes not observed until the cloth is ready for the trade.	Major
Uneven Filling or Chopped Filling	A filling with variations of diameter noticeable enough to detract from the appearance of a fabric. Shaded or barred areas observed in cloth are often caused by one shuttle not properly timed or having unevenly-wound filling in it. The feeler or filling-stop motion in the raceplate of the loom, if not functioning properly, also causes these uneven marks. Other causes are choke on a drafting roll, poor distribution of fiber length, less than optimum draft distribution, incorrect roll settings, and eccentric behavior of drafting rolls.	Major
Uneven Napping, Uneven Shearing	Fabric not been uniformly napped or sheared. Caused by poor setting of the shearing blades or improper height of the fabric so that it could be napped evenly. If settings are too close to the cloth, the latter may be tendered, or ripped, or an off-angle effect may result.	Major

Defect	Explanation	Severity
Uneven Printing	Shade variations in the motif that run from side-to-side or from end-to-end in the goods. Usually caused by improper action of the doctor blade or knife on the printing machine or by incorrect roller settings.	Major or Minor
Uneven Shrinking	A bowed, ballooned, or waved effect on the surface of fabric. Fabric of this type will not lay smooth and flat on a horizontal surface. Caused by some error in the finishing of the goods.	Major
Uneven Warp Ends	Streaked warp lines resulting from yarns that vary in diameter or from irregularity in the yarn plies.	Major

valance (*val*-enss)   A decorative fabric or board installed across the top of a window or a top for curtains or draperies. It is usually hung from a rod and made of fabric or fabric over a stiffening material, such as buckram. A valance differs from a ruffle in that it is absolutely flat. *See* buckram, trimming, and ruffle.

valenciennes lace (vel-en-see-*enz* layss)   A flat bobbin lace worked with one thread forming both the background and the design for lace.

vat dyeing (vat *dy*-ing)   Vat dyeing refers to the type of dye rather than to the way in which the dyeing is done. This process uses an insoluble dye made soluble in its application. It is put on the fiber and oxidized to its original insoluble form. Excellent colorfastness to washing and sunlight.

Velcro (*vel*-kroh)   The trademark for a patented, burr-like fastening device with one side made of a velvet-like material and the other of small stiff hooks. This fastening can be used for clothing and home furnishing items; it also has many industrial applications. Velcro is available to the consumer for use in home sewing and decorating.

velour (veh-*loor*)   A knit or woven fabric with a thick, short, cut pile. The term is applied to cloths with a fine raised finish, a cotton cut pile fabric with thicker pile than cotton velvet, a woolen, and knitted goods with the feeling of woven velour. Cotton cut-pile velour is heavier than velvet and is used for draperies, upholstery, and bedspreads. Terry velour cloth has cut loops to produce the velour effect and is often used for bath towels. Terry velour has a rich look similar to velvet or velveteen, but is not as effective in drying as conventional terry cloth. *See* pile, velvet, velveteen, and terry cloth.

velvet (*vel*-vit)   A fabric with a short, closely woven pile. There are two methods of making velvet. One method uses double-cloth construction in which two layers of fabric are woven with long threads joining them together. After the double fabric is woven, the center threads are cut, producing two pieces of velvet. The other method of making velvet utilizes wires. In the weaving process, the yarn is lifted over the wires to form the pile. When the wires are removed, the yarn is cut to form the velvet surface. Velvet was originally made of silk, but today it is made of many other fibers, such as rayon, nylon, and acrylic cut-pile fabrics. Nylon is one of the most popular. When used for draperies and upholstery, it is somewhat heavier than dress velvet. Some knit fabrics with a pile are called velvets, but this is incorrect. Following is a listing of some important types of velvet:

beaded velvet Another name for cut velvet. *See* cut velvet.

cisele velvet (*sis*-eh-lay *vel*-vit) A satin weave fabric with a velvet pattern woven in. Similar fabrics are made by flocking. *See* flock.

cut velvet A fabric with a pattern of velvet on a sheer ground. It is occasionally imitated by the burn-out method of printing. *See* Jacquard, printing, and burn-out printing.

faconne velvet (*fass*-oh-nay *vel*-vit) A cut velvet made by the burn-out method of printing. *See* cut velvet, printing, and burn-out printing.

Lyons velvet (*lee*-ohn *vel*-vit [correct pronunciation]; *lye*-onz *vel*-vit [common pronunciation]) Velvet originally made of silk in Lyons, France. Lyons is a thick, stiff velvet with a very short pile. Today, this type of velvet (often called Lyons-type) is made of man-made fibers. It is used for home furnishings as well as for evening wear.

mirror velvet Velvet with the pile pressed flat in one of several directions to impart a shimmering appearance.

nacré velvet (na-*kray vel*-vit) A velvet with a changeable appearance created by using one color for the pile and another for the backing.

panne velvet (pan *vel*-vit [correct pronunciation]; pan-*ay* [incorrect but common pronunciation]) Velvet with the pile flattened in one direction. *See* mirror velvet.

uncut velvet (un-*kut vel*-vit) A velvet in which the pile is left in loop form. It is made by the wire method and also occasionally is called terry velvet. *See* velvet for description of wire method.

V

velvet rug   A floor covering woven on a plain harness loom with cut pile. It has solid color or printed pile.

velveteen (vel-veh-*teen*)   A cotton pile-weave fabric in filling pile construction, characterized by a plain weave or twill back. It is made to look like velvet and is used for dresses, coats, jackets, millinery, and suits. When used for draperies and upholstery, it is somewhat heavier than dress velveteen. It differs from corduroy in that the pile on velveteen covers the surface and is thicker than the pile on corduroy. It differs from velvet in that the pile in velvet is made with the warp threads whereas the pile in velveteen is made with the filling threads. The distinction between velvet and velveteen originated when velvet was made only from silk. Today, man-made fibers are being used for both velvet and velveteen. *See* velvet.

Venetian blinds (veh-*nee*-shun blyndz)   One of the most popular window coverings for controlling light and privacy. Venetian blinds are made of strips of fabric, metal, or plastic. These strips can be tipped to shut out light completely or opened to varying degrees to filter light to the desired intensity. They can also be raised to the top of the window to uncover it completely. Conventional Venetian blinds hang with the slats or strips horizontal to the windowsill, but vertical Venetian blinds are also available for use as room dividers as well as window coverings. Venetian blinds are available in various colors and widths.

Venetian lace (veh-*nee*-shun layss)   *See* Venise lace.

Venice lace (*veh*-niss layss)   *See* Venise lace.

Venise lace (veh-*neess* layss)   A needlepoint lace usually having a floral pattern connected by picot edgings. It is also called Venice lace and Venetian lace. *See* picot.

vent   An opening in the lower part of a seam. It is typically found in the back or sides of a jacket or skirt.

Verel (veh-*rel*)   Trademark of Eastman Kodak for their modacrylic fiber.

vicuna (vy-*koon*-ah)   A wild member of the llama family found in Latin America. It produces the world's most valuable specialty fiber which, in turn, produces one of the most expensive wools. The wool is used to make vicuna cloth. *See* llama.

vignette (vihn-*yeht*)   An advertising display that shows one or more products actually in use.

V

vinal (*vy*-nel)   The generic name for a man-made fiber derived from polyvinal alcohol. Vinal fibers soften at low temperatures, but resist chemicals. Although vinal is no longer made in the United States, it is made in Japan and is found in tires, some home furnishings, and industrial products.

vinal-vinyon (*vy*-nel *vin*-yon)   A recent combination of two molecules resulting in a new fiber similar to acrylic with excellent flame retardancy. This fabric is found primarily in garments such as children's sleepwear which must meet high flammability standards. It is soft to the touch. *See* flame-retardant fabric.

vinyl (*vy*-nuhl)   Any fabric made with a base of vinyl, including those listed as vinal and vinyon. The term usually is used to refer to thick fabrics coated with a vinyl-based coating used for such purposes as upholstery and raincoats.

vinyon (vin-*yon*)   The generic name for a man-made fiber derived from polyvinyl chloride, a derivative of natural salt, water, and petroleum. Vinyon fibers soften at low temperatures and resist chemicals. Vinyon is often referred to as polyvinyl chloride. Its primary use is in commercial products.

virgin fibers (*vur*-jun *fy*-berz)   By Federal Trade Commission standards, fibers never made into fabric before. The term is used primarily for wool fibers to differentiate between these and reclaimed, reprocessed, and reused fibers. *See* reprocessed fibers, reclaimed fibers, and reused fibers.

virgin wool   A term applicable to fabrics or products that do not use wastes from preliminary processing of new wool. It is new wool made into yarns and fabrics for the first time.

viscose process (*viss*-kohs *prahs*-ess)   A method of making rayon fibers from purified cellulose.

viscose rayon (*viss*-kohs *ray*-on)   Rayon made by the viscose process used to make the majority of rayon on the market today. True viscose rayon is not strong, especially when wet. This has led to modifications of the viscose process to produce high wet modulus rayon. *See* high wet modulus rayon.

visor   An eyeshade with a deep front brim attached to an elastic or buckled head strap.

visual design   When the design shows up in an effect in the weave.

V

v-neck A neckline cut in the shape of the letter V.

voile (vwal [correct pronunciation, used very rarely]; voyl [common pronunciation]) A sheer, transparent, low-count, crisp or soft, lightweight, plain-weave muslin with a thready feel, made of highly twisted yarns. It can be comprised of wool, cotton, silk, rayon, polyester, or other man-made fibers. Voile is especially popular when made of cotton or blends for summer wear and is often printed to match heavier fabrics. Voile is used for clothing, especially for blouses and summer dresses, and for curtains and similar items.

V

waffle cloth   A fabric with a characteristic honeycomb weave. When made in cotton it is called waffle piqué. It is used for coatings, draperies, dresses, and toweling.

waffle weave (*wahf*-uhl weev)   Identical to honeycomb and thermal weaves. A weave resulting in fabrics with diamonds or other geometric shapes resembling a waffle. *See* thermal.

wales (waylz)   In knitted fabrics, a column of loops parallel to the loop axis and lying lengthwise on the fabric. In woven fabrics, a series of ribs or ridges usually running lengthwise on the fabric. Wales are diagonal ridges characteristic of the twill weave. Wale describes the pile ribs found on corduroy fabrics. The terms narrow wale, pin wale, and wide wale describe different types of ribs in corduroy. No-wale corduroy has an allover pile shorter than the pile on velveteen. *See* corduroy, velveteen, and pile.

wall-to-wall carpeting   A carpet of any fiber or fibers and in any construction that covers the entire floor.

warp (wawrp)   The group of yarns placed first on a loom in weaving. Warp runs parallel to the selvage, forming the length of the fabric. The filling threads are interlaced over and under the warp threads in a pattern or weave. *See* weaving and selvage.

warp beam (wawrp beem)   A cylindrical spool at the back of the loom on which warp yarns are wound.

warp knit (wawrp nit)   A warp knit is made on a machine in which parallel yarns run lengthwise and are locked into the series of loops. It is a process that makes a more dimensionally stable fabric than weft knitting. Warp knits have a good deal of crosswise stretch. It is frequently run-resistant. Examples are tricot and Raschel.

warp printing (wawrp *print*-ing)   A printing method in which only the warp yarns are printed with a design before the fabric is woven. A hazy, grayed effect is produced. The resulting fabric has a wavy, shadowy effect. It is also called shadow printing.

warp yarns (wawrp yarnz)   Yarns that run parallel to the selvage or long dimension of a fabric.

wash and wear   A term used to describe fabrics and garments that can be washed and then worn with little or no ironing. Originally, the fabrics were chemically treated and cured (baked). There are no standards governing its use. *See* easy care and durable press.

wash test   A trial washing of an inconspicuous part of a garment to determine if the color is fast to washing.

washable   A very inexact term, meaning only that an item can be washed and does not have to be dry cleaned. The term is unsatisfactory, however, since it does not say how the item should or can be washed—by machine or by hand or with hot or cold water.

washable fabric   A fabric that can be washed. The method of washing (by hand or machine) may not be designated.

wash-fast fabric   One that will not fade or shrink excessively during laundering.

waste silk   Another name for silk noil. Short ends of silk fibers used in making rough, textured, spun yarns or in blends with cotton or wool.

water repellent fabric (*waw*-ter ree-*pell*-ent *fab*-rik)   The chemical treatment of a fabric to reduce its affinity for water. Pores of the fabric are open, and the degree of repellency varies. A water repellent fabric will give protection in a shower, but not in heavy rain. Water repellency is often created with wax or silicone resin finishes that enable the pores of the fabric to stay open so that it is more comfortable to wear than waterproof fabrics. Another name for water repellent is water resistant. *See* waterproof fabric.

water softener   A chemical compound added to the rinse water or to the soap and the rinse water if the water is very hard. Its purpose is to prevent the formation of soap film that tends to gray the fabric.

waterproof fabric (*waw*-ter-proof *fab*-rik)   A fabric that will not permit water to penetrate it. Among methods of waterproofing are coating the fabric with rubber or plastic. True waterproof fabrics are warm and clammy to wear because their waterproof nature also prevents the evaporation of perspiration and blocks the circulation of air.

weather-ometer   A devise that simulates weather conditions, such as sunlight, heavy dew, rain, and thermal shock. The deteriorating effects of these conditions on fabrics are the objectives of tests in this devise. These effects can be determined in a few days.

weaving (*weev*-ing)   Weaving is a method of making fabric in which threads called filling threads pass over and under other threads called warp threads, at right angles to the filling threads. Different weaves are determined by the number of warp threads over which the filling threads pass. Following is a listing of the most common weaves:

basket weave (*bas*-kit weev)   Basket weave is made with two or more filling threads passing over and under an equal number of warp threads on alternate rows.

plain weave (playn weev)   Plain weave, the best known and most basic form of weaving, is made by passing the filling thread over and under one warp thread in alternating rows.

satin weave (*sat*-uhn weev)   A weave that produces a very smooth surfaced fabric. It is made by passing the filling threads under several warp threads before passing over one warp thread. Satin weave is used to make sateens in which cotton filling thread goes over several cotton warps, then under one warp.

twill weave (twill weev)   A weave with a diagonal rib (twill line) that runs from the upper left to the lower right, or from upper right to lower left. In a twill weave, each filling thread passes over or under at least two warp threads, with the point where the filling thread goes under moving up and over at least one thread in each row. Herringbone weave is a broken twill weave which forms Vs in the weave pattern.

webbing (*web*-ing)   A strong, narrow fabric made from jute or man-made fibers. It is used for belts and straps that must resist strain. Webbing is usually woven and is used on the underside of upholstered chairs and sofas.

wedgie (*wehj*-ee)   A woman's shoe with a wedge-shaped heel, the highest part of which is at the back of the shoe.

weft (wehft) Another name for filling, the crosswise thread that interlaces with the warp threads on a woven fabric. Other names are woof, shoot, and shute.

weft knitting (wehft *nit*-ing) A process in which the thread runs back and forth crosswise in a fabric. *See* warp knitting.

weighted silk Fabric in which metallic salts have been added in the dyeing and finishing to increase its weight and to give a heavier hand. An FTC ruling requires weighted silk to be marked and the amount of weighting indicated.

weighting Finishing materials applied to a fabric to give increased weight.

welt The final edge on certain knitted items, such as women's stockings. The welt on stockings is usually thicker than the rest of the stocking and is usually made of a different, stronger stitch so that garters can be fastened to it.

welt pockets Typical set-in pockets with one or two strips of fabric (varying from 1/4" to 1" deep) attached to the opening.

welting (*welt*-ing) A decorative edging that lends a certain degree of strength to the area in which it is sewn. Welting is made by covering cord with bias strips of matching or contrasting fabric. It is a popular finish for seams on upholstery and slipcovers and is occasionally used on clothing. Welting and piping are synonyms. When used on clothing, it is usually called piping. *See* cord and bias.

wet decating A finishing process to add luster to wool fabrics.

wet look A descriptive term for extremely shiny fabrics. Fabrics such as vinyl and ciré are often described as wet-look fabrics.

whipcord (*whip*-kord) An extremely strong, twill-weave worsted fabric made in fairly heavy weights of cotton, wool worsted, and fabrics of man-made fibers and blends. It is similar to gabardine, but heavier and with a more pronounced diagonal rib on the right side. It is so named because it simulates the lash of a whip. Cotton whipcords are often four-harness warp-twill weaves. It is used for draperies and upholstery, uniforms, riding clothes, and other wearing apparel where a strong fabric is required. *See* twill under entry for weaving.

white-on-white A fabric in any fiber mixture or blend that has a white woven-in design on a white background. Usually, it is a fabric with a white dobby or Jacquard design on a white ground, common in madras, broadcloth, or nylon. *See* madras.

wickability (wihk-uh-*bihl*-eh-tee)   The property of a fiber that allows moisture to move rapidly along the fiber surface and pass quickly through the fabric.

wide wale (wyd wayl)   In knitted fabrics, the wale is a row of loops lying lengthwise on the fabric. In woven fabrics, wale is a series of ribs or ridges usually running lengthwise on the fabric. Wale describes the pile ribs found on corduroy fabrics. Wide wale describes one of the different types of ribs in corduroy. *See* corduroy, velveteen, and pile.

wild silk (wyld silk)   Silk produced by moths of species other than *Bombyx mori*. Uncultivated silkworms eat leaves other than mulberry leaves. Wild silk is tan to brown in color, less smooth, and more uneven than cultivated silk. The resulting fabric is usually duller in finish and rougher in texture than other types of silk. *See* silk and tussah.

Wilton (*wil*-ten)   A floor covering (usually woolen or worsted) with buried pile, cut or uncut, and a velvety texture. It is often made with carved designs in plain color or multicolored. The designs in Wilton rugs often show an Oriental influence and are quite expensive. *See* cut pile, fabric pile, and rugs and carpets.

windbreaker (*wind*-bray-ker)   A jacket made of a closely woven fabric or a fabric treated with a finish designed to prevent the passage of air. The fabric used in windbreakers often has a degree of water repellency because of its tight construction.

Windsor knot (*wihn*-zehr naht)   A fairly loose, bulky necktie knot originated by the Duke of Windsor.

wire   Each row of pile or tufts on the surface of a rug.

woof   Another name for filling, the crosswise thread that interlaces with the warp threads on a woven fabric. Other names are weft, shoot, and shute. *See* filling.

wool (wuhl)   The term used for the fleece of lambs and sheep, but also applies to similar fibers from such animals as the angora and cashmere goats, the llama, and other animals used for clothing. It is unlike carpet wool, which is much coarser and unsuitable for clothing. Wool refers to fleece wool used for the first time in the complete manufacture of a wool product. Wool differs from hair and fur in that it has a natural felting ability. *See* felt, woolen, and worsted.

wool broadcloth   A smooth, silky napped woolen in twill weave. Nap obliterates the weave. It is used for men's dinner jackets and formal evening wear, and for women's coat and suits.

wool crepe   Made of either woolen or worsted yarns. The crepe texture is produced by keeping the warp yarns slack.

Wool Products Labeling Act   A law requiring that all wool products moving in "commerce" must be labeled. Carpets, rugs, and upholstery fabrics containing wool come under the Textile Fiber Products Identification Act (TFPIA). The Act, effective May 3, 1960, lists generic names and definitions of man-made fibers (in sixteen categories) as decreed by the FTC.

wool rug   A wool floor covering made of carded yarn.

woolen (*wuhl*-en)   A class of wool fabrics made of short-staple carded yarns. Woolens usually have a fuzzy surface, do not shine from wear, and may hold a crease well. Woolens may have a nap. *See* worsted.

woolen yarn   carded yarn made of relatively short fibers of varying lengths.

worsted (*woos*-tid [correct pronunciation]; *wur*-stid [common pronunciation])   A type of wool yarn or fabric made from a long-staple combed yarn. Worsted fabrics are made from yarns combed as well as carded (woolen yarns have only been carded). Combing eliminates short fibers and impurities so the resulting yarn is compact and sturdy. Worsted yarns are smoother than woolen yarns and when woven into fabric, result in a fabric with a clean, smooth surface as opposed to the fuzzy, soft surface of woolens. Worsted fabrics wear better than woolen fabrics, resist felting at points of wear, and have a harder surface than woolens. *See* carding and combing.

worsted yarn   A combed yarn made of long-staple wool fibers.

woven seersucker   A crinkled, striped cotton fabric made by weaving some of the yarns in tighter tension than others. *See* seersucker.

wrap belt   A belt wrapped around the waist several times and buckled or tied.

Defect	Explanation	Severity
Warp Float	A warp end extending unbound over or under picks with which it should have interlaced.	Major
Water Spots	Usually caused by wet fabric allowed to remain too long before drying; color migrates, leaving blotchy spots.	Major
Wavy Cloth	A term used to describe cloth woven under conditions of varying tension and preventing the even placement of filling picks. The result is a fabric with randomly alternating thick and thin places. Generally, this is traceable to a faulty let-off or take-up motion on the loom.	Major
Wavy Selvage	The condition where the edge of a fabric is longer than the center, causing it to wave or pucker when laid on the cutting table.	Major
Weaving Slack	Caused by uneven tension weights on the warp beam. Usually presents a sleazy appearance to the goods. Weavers have to check constantly to prevent this effect from occurring because it is one of the most difficult to eradicate in the finishing of the goods. It is one of the main reasons for rating the cloth as a second.	Major
Weaving-over, Weaving-under	Caused by irregular timing of the box motion on the loom, and often noted in certain fabrics such as checks, ginghams, plaids, overplaids, and multicolored warp and filling fabrics. Cloth with this defect presents a distorted effect on the eye.	Major
Wild Filling	A piece of loose or stray yarn jerked into the shed along with a regular pick of filling.	Major

yard goods (yard goodz) *See* yardage, piece goods, and fashion fabrics.

yardage (*yard*-ihj) Fabrics sold to the consumer by the yard. Yardage is also called piece goods, yard goods, and fashion fabrics.

yarn A generic term for a continuous strand spun from a group of natural or synthetic staple fibers (short lengths of fibers), filaments (long lengths), or other materials twisted or laid together for use in weaving, knitting, or some other method of intertwining to form textile fabrics.

yarn dyed In yarn dyeing, fiber already made into yarn that will be used for the manufacture of fabric, dyed, usually on a spool, under heat and pressure. Yarn dyed fabrics are considered more colorfast than piece dyed fabrics or printed fabrics.

yoke (yohk) A fitted or shaped piece of fabric fullness principally designed to control fullness from gathers, pleats, or darts. Sometimes a yoke is used strictly as a decorative design element. Yokes are generally found in the shoulder area of shirts, blouses, and dresses, but are also used in the waist and hip areas of skirts and slacks.

GARMENT
AND
TEXTILES

Z

Zantrel (zan-*trel*)   Trademark of American Enka for their high wet modulus rayon fiber. *See* high wet modulus under entry for rayon.

Zefran (*zef*-ran)   Trademark of Dow Badische for their acrylic, nylon, and polyester fibers.

zein (zyn)   Cornmeal from which protein is derived for synthetic fibers.

zephyr yarn (*zef*-er yarn)   A fine, soft yarn with a low twist popular for hand knitting. Originally made from wool, zephyr is usually made of acrylic and often has other fibers such as silk added to it.

zibeline (*zib*-eh-leen)   A heavily napped coating fabric with the long sleek nap brushed, steamed, and pressed in one direction, thus hiding the underlying satin weave. Zibeline is usually made of a combination of such fibers as camel hair or mohair with wool, cotton, or a man-made fiber as the largest percentage.

zipper (*zip*-er)   A garment closure made of interlocking teeth attached to strips of fabric known as the zipper tape. Zippers were originally made of metal, but are now available with polyester or nylon molded teeth on a woven or knit polyester tape. Most zippers are attached to garments by stitching the zipper tape to the garment seam. Invisible zippers do not show once they are attached to the garment because the teeth of an invisible zipper are covered by the zipper tape and hidden in the seam of the garment. Zippers come in every size and color and can be used functionally or decoratively.

z-twist   A right-hand twisted yarn.

Bibliography

American Fabrics, *American Fabrics Encyclopedia of Textiles*, 3rd ed. Englewood Cliffs, N.J.: Prentice-Hall, Inc., 1980.

Blackmon, A. G. *Manual of Standard Fabric Defects in the Textile Industry*, Graniteville, S.C.: Graniteville Co., 1975.

ICS Learning Systems, Inc. *Speaking of Fashion*, 1st ed. Scranton, Pa.: Intext, Inc. & ICS Intangibles Holding Co., 1982 & 1994.

Joseph, Marjory L. *Essentials of Textiles*, 3rd ed. New York: Holt, Reinhart & Winston, Inc., 1984.

Kleeberg, Irene C. *The Butterick Fabric Book*, New York: Butterick Publishing, 1975.

Penney, J. C. *Quality Control Guidelines*, Dallas, Tex.: Unpublished, 1992.

Wingate, Isabel Barnum. *Textile Fabrics and Their Selection*, 8th ed. Englewood Cliffs, N.J.: Prentice-Hall, Inc., 1984.

SELECTED INTERNET RESOURCES

American Fiber Manufacturers Association, Inc.
http://www.apparel.net/afma/
A trade organization representing United States producers of manufactured fibers, filaments, and yarns.

American Society for Testing and Materials
http://www.astm.org/
Developer and publisher of 10,000 technical standards including those for textiles.

The American Textile Partnership
http://apc.pnl.gov:2080/AMTEXWWW/amtex.html
A collaborative research and development partnership among industry, government, and universities with the purpose of strengthening the United States textile industry. Features include AMTEX policies, technology briefs, project descriptions, and AMTEX slide shows.

The Apparel and Textile Network
http://www.at-net.com/
Features include the Marketplace ("the largest apparel and textile marketplace on the Internet"), selected manufacturers' showroom (the Private Showroom is accessible by password only), Fashion Bytes (weekly on-line news), DuPont Corner (current events, trends, brands, and DuPont contacts), trade show information, trade associations, internet links, and classified advertisements.

Apparel Exchange
http://www.apparelex.com/
Links to over 26,000 companies in the textile and apparel industry. The site includes a link to the *Davison's Textile Blue Book*, directories, industry news, and associations.

Apparelmart
http://www.apparelmart.com
Lists 13,000 manufacturers and labels. Link to *The National Register of Apparel Manufacturers* published by Marche Publishing, Los Angeles, California.

Apparel Manufacturer's Sourcing Web
http://www.halper.com/SourcingWeb/sweb.html
Organized into seven major source categories: fabrics, construction materials, trimmings, buttons-fasteners-closures, labels-tags-tickets, equipment, and services, notions and supplies.

Apparel Net
http://www.apparel.net/
An on-line guide to the apparel industry with links to manufacturers, organizations, and clothing.

Bobbin Blenheim On-Line
http://www.bobbin.com/
The on-line version of the industry's first sewn products manufacturing magazine. Includes links to the various Bobbin expositions.

Cotton Incorporated
http://www.cottonincorp.com/
The primary source of information regarding United States Upland cotton. Features include news, technical-fashion-information, and importer services.

Fabric Link
http://www.FabricLink.com/
An educational resource for consumers and retailers. Divided into three parts: Consumer Guide, Fabric University, and the Retailer's Forum. Some of the features are tradename fibers, clothing and fabric care, consumer safety issues, internet links to key associations, and government agencies.

Fashion Net
http://www.fashion.net/
Fashion related. Features include designers, fashion shows, newsgroups, directories, and job listings.

Federal Trade Commission
http://www.ftc.gov/
One of the federal agencies responsible for consumer safety.

International Textiles and Apparel Association
http://netserver.huec.lsu.edu/itaahome.html
A global organization of textile and apparel scholars.

National Textile Center
http://ntc.tx.edu/
A research consortium of four universities with the stated goals of creating new materials, improving manufacturing processes, training personnel, and strengthening textile research and educational efforts.

Office of Textiles and Apparel
http://www.ita.doc.gov/industry/textiles/otexa.html
The Office of Textiles and Apparel is part of the United States Department of Commerce. Features include OTEXA functions, trade statistics, trade agreements, and exports and imports.

Textile Information Center
http://www.texinfo.com/
An extensive directory of manufacturers.

The Textile Institute
http://www.texi.org/
From fiber engineering to fashion retailing, there are 9,000 Textile Institute global members. Features of this site include events, publications, issues forum, and virtual library.

World Textile Publications Limited
http://www.vitalo.com/worldtextile/
The company, based in West Yorkshire, England, publishes numerous journals (e.g., Textile Month, International Dyer, and Wool Record), directories (e.g., International Carpet Yearbook, Wool Trade Directory of the World, and Chinese Textile Industry Directory), and newsletters (e.g., Textiles Eastern Europe, UK Textile News, and International Carpet Bulletin) for the textile industry.

SELECTED TEXTILE-RELATED ASSOCIATIONS

American Association for Textile Technology, Gastonia, NC

American Association of Textile Chemists & Colorists,
Research Triangle Park, NC

American Fiber Manufacturers Association, Washington, DC

American Fiber, Textile, Apparel Coalition, Washington, DC

American Flock Association, Boston, MA

American Textile Manufacturers Institute, Washington, DC

American Yarn Spinners Association, Gastonia, NC

Association of Knitted Fabrics Manufacturers, New York, NY

Association of the Nonwoven Fabrics Industry, Cary, NC

Embroidery Council of America, North Bergen, NJ

Felt Manufacturers Council, Boston, MA

Industrial Fabrics Association International, St. Paul, MN

Institute of Textile Technology, Charlottesville, VA

International Linen Promotion Commission, New York, NY

International Society of Industrial Fabric Manufacturers,
Newberry, SC

International Textile and Apparel Association, Monument, CO

Knitted Textile Association, New York, NY

National Association of Textile Supervisors, Millbury, MA

National Needlework Association, Ridgefield, CT

Northern Textile Association, Boston, MA

Southern Textile Association, Cary, NC

Textile Association of Los Angeles, Los Angeles, CA

Textile Research Institute, Princeton, NJ

Textured Yarn Association of America, Gastonia, NC

United Textile Workers of America, Voorhees, NJ

Wool Bureau, New York, NY

ALSO AVAILABLE FROM DELMAR PUBLISHERS

Textiles: Concepts and Principles
Virginia Hencken Elsasser
© 1997

This book is designed to be an introduction to textiles for those planning to enter careers requiring a basic knowledge of textiles. These careers include interior design, fashion design or merchandising, costuming, textile marketing, product development, buying, and retailing. Information relevant to both furnishing and apparel is included.

TABLE OF CONTENTS